W9-BCX-653

INSTRUMENTS OF THE ORCHESTRA

THE FRENCH HORN

THE
FRENCH HORN

Some Notes on the Evolution of the Instrument
and of its Technique

R. MORLEY-PEGGE

SECOND EDITION

LONDON/ERNEST BENN LIMITED

NEW YORK/W. W. NORTON & COMPANY INC.

First published by Ernest Benn Limited
Sovereign Way, Tonbridge, Kent &
25 New Street Square, Fleet Street, London, EC4A 3JA
and W. W. Norton & Company
55 Fifth Avenue, New York, 10003

First published 1960

Second edition 1973

Distributed in Canada by
The General Publishing Company Limited, Toronto

© *The Trustees of the Morley-Pegge Estate 1973*

Printed in Great Britain

ISBN 0 510-36601-5

ISBN 0 393-02171-8 (USA)

TO THE MEMORY OF

W. F. H. B.

Preface to the Second Edition

IT IS VERY gratifying to the author that enough interest has been shown in the history of the horn to warrant a second edition of this book. Since its original publication a lot of research has been undertaken into what, for lack of a better word, I must call artistic horn playing. The fruit of this research, the work of Dr Horace Fitzpatrick, is recorded in his book *The Horn and Horn-playing and the Austro-Bohemian Tradition: 1680–1830*. Much new light has been shed on an aspect of the horn's history hitherto shrouded in fog. I am thus able in this edition to correct a few dates and include in the biographical section one or two early players and teachers about whom I previously had insufficient information.

June 1971   R. M.-P.

Preface to the First Edition

A YEAR OR TWO before the war, that unrivalled authority, the late W. F. H. Blandford, was invited to write a book on the horn. He refused, on the ground that to do it properly would entail much fresh research on the continent which he felt he could not undertake. During the thirty years or so during which I was privileged to enjoy his friendship he was at all times ready to share with me his wide knowledge, backed as it was by considerable practical experience, for he was an excellent amateur horn player. It is therefore not without diffidence that I have ventured to attempt what he, *le grand maître*, was reluctant to do, more especially as the fresh research in Central Europe has yet to be undertaken.

Since Blandford's day, however, interest in the evolution of wind instruments has become far more widespread, and specialist books in the English language have been appearing in increasing numbers during the last few years. But so far no specialist book readily accessible on the horn has appeared, and so, in spite of its incompleteness, the present modest work is offered in the hope that it will in some measure make good the deficiency.

I have thought it worth while to include a chapter on the development of the valve, which has so completely revolutionized the method of writing for the horn; it is perhaps not out of place here, since the valve was originally conceived with the object of doing away with loose crooks for the horn. I have also included a chapter on the evolution of playing technique which has, I believe, passed through more distinct phases in the case of the horn than in that of any other instrument.

Sources of information are necessarily similar for all instruments. The active collecting and handling of old specimens, public and private collections, catalogues—few in number and all too often insufficiently detailed in the case of wind instruments—old tutors, dictionary articles, press reports, accounts of international exhibitions, and, especially in the case of valves, patent specifications. Much of the information gleaned from such sources needs interpretation, a case in point being the problem of whether 'stopping' raises or lowers the pitch, but there are others. Practical experience is therefore necessary, and is here backed by half a century of professional horn playing in old and new music, often on period instruments. There will no doubt be disagreement with some of my views, but I have tried to find a logical solution to a few of the problems with which the would-be historian is faced. A number of musical examples have been added to show how technique developed between the mid-17th and mid-19th centuries. I have said nothing about acoustics, now become a highly specialized subject, but have, on the other hand, included a certain amount of technical matter that chiefly concerns the performer.

In a work such as this the writer is necessarily much beholden to many friends, without whose good offices it could never have been written. To them I am much indebted, and in particular to Messrs A. C. Baines, W. Bergmann, Raymond Bryant, Jacques Chailley, former Secrétaire général of the Paris Conservatoire, Farquharson Cousins, Alan Hyde, Bernard Izen, Kurt Janetzky, expert on the horn music of Bach and Handel, R. Jenkins, Edgar Knopf, for information about the Prager horns, Lyndesay Langwill, Ch. Levasseur, O. McConathy, Eric Mc-Gavin, Ch. Mackerras, H. Meek, Georges Migot, Curator of the Paris Conservatoire Museum, the late F. G. Rendall, Lorenzo Sansone, and Dr Winternitz, Curator of the musical instruments, Metropolitan Museum of Art, New York.

There are still many gaps to be filled in the history of the horn, but if this book has proved of some interest and encouraged further research, I shall be more than satisfied.

R. M.-P.

July 1960

Contents

List of Illustrations

An Eighteenth-century Parisian Horn and Trumpet
Maker's Workshop   *Frontispiece*

[*These plates are inserted immediately preceding Chapter 1*]

In the text

xiii

[*The numerous music examples are not listed*]

Le Cor, même avec ses imperfections, n'en est pas moins le plus beau des instruments à vent, par le timbre, par la qualité de ses sons; et l'émotion qu'il fait naître a un charme auquel on convient que personne ne peut résister.

DAUPRAT

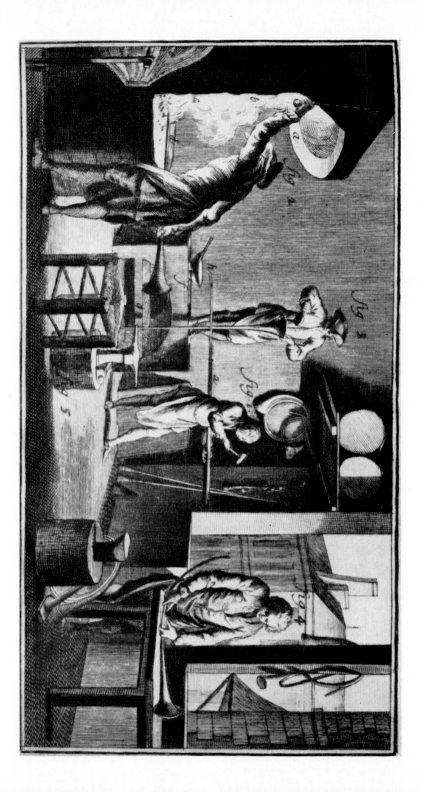

PLATE I

1. One of a number of woodcuts made by Sebastian Brandt (1457–1521) to illustrate an edition of Virgil's works published in Strasbourg by Grüninger in 1502. The same series of woodcuts was used again for another edition of Virgil published in 1517 by Jacobus Sacon in Lyons. Attention was first drawn to the Grüninger edition by Julius Rühlmann (*Neue Zeitschr. f. Musik*, 1870, p. 303), and to the Sacon edition by G. de Marolles (*Monographie abrégée de la Trompe de Chasse*, p. 6). (See pp. 9 *et seq.*)

2. One of two etched plates by Wenzel Hollar (1607–77). These plates are mentioned in Parthey's catalogue of Hollar's works (*Berlin*, 1853, p. 443). An almost identical helical horn figures in the foreground of the picture 'Allegoria dell' udito' by Jan Breughel (1568–1625) in the Prado in Madrid. (See p. 11.)

3. Two helical horns in the hunting equipment gallery of the Staatliches Historisches Museum in Dresden. The mouthpiece of the smaller horn has an inscription that reads 'zv DRESEN'. Estimated date *c.* 1572. The larger horn appears to date from the very early years of the 17th century. (See pp. 11 *et seq.*)

I, 1

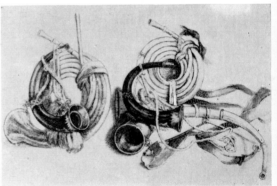

I, 2

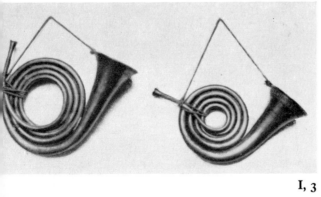

I, 3

PLATE II

1. Brass single-coil horn in C alto or D-flat (doubtless D of the period) with ornamental embossed bell rim and a mouthpiece that fits into a short detachable shank. No inscription of any kind, but the instrument is almost certainly French and dates from the closing years of the 17th century: it might well have served as the model for the horns in two pictures by J.-B. Martin painted in 1688 and now in the Versailles museum. Diameter of hoop 44 cm., and of bell 14 cm. Approximate length 2·40 m. (In private ownership, Paris.)

2. Copper triple-coil French horn with ornamental bell rim and stay of brass. Ivory mouthpiece of unusual shape and probably coeval. Diameter of hoop 37·5 cm., and of bell 17·3 cm. By present-day standards its pitch is E-natural (presumably F of the period). Signed: WILLIAM BVLL LONDINI FECIT 1699. (Formerly in the Galpin collection: now Carse No. 307.)

3. Brass helical horn with twelve coils, measuring only 16 cm. across the coils with a bell diameter of 17·3 cm. The bell is detachable and the horn is shown in its original case. It dates traditionally from the reign of Queen Anne (1702–14), and this, as far as the case is concerned, has been confirmed by experts of the Victoria and Albert Museum. Pitched in E-flat by present standards. No mark or inscription of any kind. Could this be one of those 'English cors de chasse' mentioned by Mattheson? (See p. 13.) (Carse No. 254.)

4. Brass two-coil *trompe de chasse* in D (pitch approximately that of the present-day *trompe de chasse*). The mouthpiece fits into a short detachable shank. Diameter of hoop 54 cm., and of bell 27·5 cm. Approximate length 4·545 m. This is the model known as the *trompe Dauphine*. Marked: FAIT A PARIS EN 1729 PAR LE BRVN ORDINAIRE DU ROY. (In private ownership, Paris.)

5. Brass triple-coil French horn in F, partly strapped with leather. The mouthpiece may be coeval but looks like the work of Thos. Key, the London maker of the first half of last century. Marked: NICOLAS WINKINGS MAKER REDLYON SQUARE NR HOL-BORNE. *c.* 1750. Winkings figures in Mortimer's London Directory 1763 as 'Nicholas Winkings, French-horn maker to His Majesty's Hunt, Red-Lion-Street, Holborn'. Diameter of hoop 33 cm., and of bell 22·8 cm. This is no doubt the type of horn used at Ranelagh and other London pleasure haunts in the 18th century. (Castle Museum, Norwich.)

6. Brass triple-coil *cor de chasse* in D. Diameter of hoop 36 cm., and of bell 26 cm. Marked: FAIT A PARIS PAR CARLIN ORDINAIRE DU ROY RUE CROIX DES PETITS CHAMPS. *c.* 1755–60. May have been intended for orchestral use since the horns normally used at that time in the hunting field were of the two-coil pattern. (Author's collection.)

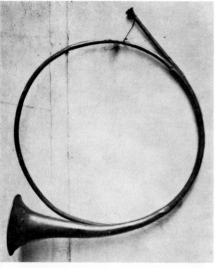

II, 2

II, 1

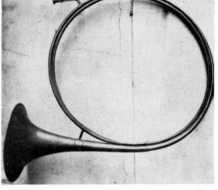

II, 4

II, 3

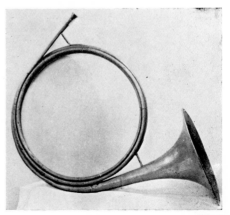

II, 5

II, 6

PLATE III

1. French horn with the earliest known type of crook. No inscription of any kind, but possibly English. 18th century. (Carse No. 296.)

2. French horn, the so-called *cor à l'anglaise* (i.e., with a tuning slide). Built for a player using the left hand in the bell. Crooks of a similar pattern to those shown in 1 above would be used with this horn. Marked: SMITH & SONS FECIT and, in smaller letters, SOLD BY KEY 2 PALL MALL LONDON. Probably made in the late 18th century by John Smith, of Wolverhampton, who had three sons.

3. French horn after the German model. Marked: CLEMENTI. Made, probably, in Germany about 1800 and sold by Clementi. This well-known firm's name is found on many early 19th-century instruments, both woodwind and brass, but it is more than doubtful if they actually made any other than the Nicholson flutes of which there are so many in collections. (Royal Military School of Music, Kneller Hall Museum.)

4. French horn of similar pattern to No. 2 above but built the more usual way round. Marked: W. SANDBACH, LONDON. Formerly the property of Cornelius Bryant, or O'Brien, who was a member of the Covent Garden orchestra *c.* 1815. (In private ownership.)

5. Orchestral horn with F crook, originally the property of M. Corret of the Théâtre des Arts, Rouen. The elaborate decoration in the bell embodies the names of six famous horn players: Lebrun, Punto, Duvernoy, Domnich, Kenn, and Dauprat. Marked: RAOUX A PARIS in very small letters, with a fleur-de-lis at either end. *c.* 1824. (Paris No. 1410.)

6. Orchestral horn with E crook. Handsomely decorated bell. Marked: COURTOIS NEVEU AINE RUE DES VIEUX AUGUSTINS A PARIS. *c.* 1820. (Author's collection.)

III, 1

III, 2

III, 3

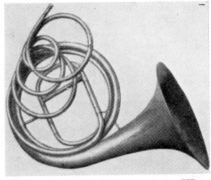

III, 4

III, 5

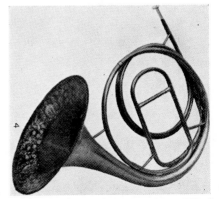

III, 6

PLATE IV

1. *Inventionshorn* crooked in F. The higher crooks, from F upward, have only one 'working leg' to the slide and each has its own mouthpipe. One circle of the hoop is thus cut out of the circuit. Crooks for E and below have the normal type of slide, and the fixed mouthpipe with which the instrument is provided is used. The actual tuning slide is graduated. Marked: MACHT IOHANN GOTTFRIED HALTENHOF IN HANAU AM MAYN 1776. (Paris No. 1183.)

2. *Cor-solo* presented to Louis-François Dauprat on the occasion of winning, in 1798, the first *premier prix* ever given for the horn at the Paris Conservatoire. It is shown here with the D crook. Marked, on the inner turn-over of the secondary bell-rim: FAIT PAR RAOUX RUE SERPENTE NO. 8 A PARIS. There is also the small round monogram *poinçon* L.J.R. (Lucien-Joseph Raoux). The secondary bell-rim and the mouthpipe are of silver. (Paris No. 585.)

3. *Cor-solo* crooked in E, with silver secondary bell-rim and mouthpipe. Marked: COURTOIS NEVEU RUE DES PROUVAIRE (*sic*) ST. EUSTACHE A PARIS. *c.* 1800. (Royal Military School of Music, Kneller Hall.)

4. *Cor-solo*, with F, E, E-flat, and D crooks, and case bearing the name of the owner, Baron d'Ivry. A beautifully made instrument, dated 1816. Marked: COURTOIS FRERE RUE DU CAIRE A PARIS. (In private ownership, France.)

5. *Cor-solo* with F crook used by the celebrated virtuoso Jacques-François Gallay. Marked, in very small letters, with a fleur-de-lis at each end: RAOUX A PARIS. *c.* 1822. (Paris No. 1412.)

6. *Cor-solo* with F crook, made for a player using the left hand in the bell. This horn is fitted with the water-key embodied in the Stuckens patent of 1826 (see p. 57). Marked: J. GOODISON, MAKER, 7 SHERRARD STREET, GOLDEN SQUARE, LONDON. Probably made about 1835. The presence of the water-key and of the continental type of decoration in the bell—much damaged—as well as the general appearance of the instrument lead to the belief that it was, in fact, made by Charles Sax, of Brussels, and that Goodison did little more than put his name on it. This is the only example of a *cor-solo* model with an English maker's name on it known to the writer. (Bate Collection, Oxford.)

IV, 2

IV, 1

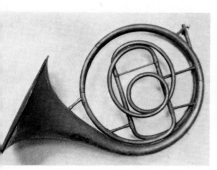

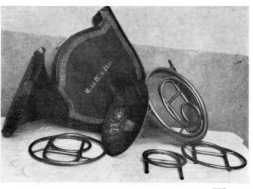

IV, 3

IV, 4

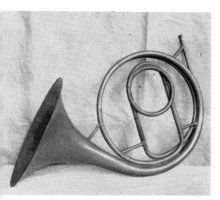

IV, 5

IV, 6

PLATE V

Omnitonic Horns

1. The earliest known omnitonic horn, made by J.-B. Dupont, of Paris, about 1815. Not in playing order. (See p. 57.) (Paris No. 1184.)
2. Dupont's 1818 patent, made and marketed by J.-C. Labbaye. Marked: FAIT PAR LABBAYE FILS FACTEUR D'INSTRU-MENS BREVETE DU ROI RUE DE GRENELLE No. 39 A PARIS. (See p. 57.) (Paris No. 1185.)
3. Charles Sax's patent of 1824. The most successful, commercially and otherwise, of all omnitonic horns. The water-key on this horn is the prototype of that fitted to most present-day brass instruments. Marked: C. SAX A BRUXELLES. The instrument is put into the desired key by setting the projecting graduated plunger at the appropriate mark. (See p. 57.) (Paris No. 586.)
4. Radius French horn, the only known English omnitonic model. Marked: J. CALLCOTT'S RADIUS FRENCH HORN. Prize Medal. These instruments appear to have been made by Thos. Key, of Charing Cross, c. 1851. (See p. 61.) (Bate Collection, Oxford.)
5. Key-changing mechanism of the Gautrot omnitonic horn described on p. 60. c. 1875. (Messrs Couesnon, Paris.)
6. Prager system. One of the last models made. Maker Aug. Knopf, of Markneukirchen. c. 1938.

V, 1

V, 2

V, 3

V, 4

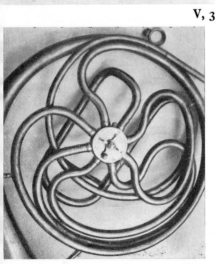

V, 5

V, 6

PLATE VI

Horns with detachable valves

1. Horn with two rotary valves of very early design. The valve mechanism may be a subsequent addition to the horn, which looks earlier than about 1835 which would be the approximate date of the valves. There are eight conical crooks for A, As, G, F, E, Es, D, and C, a shank for B-flat alto, and two cylindrical couplers marked B for use with the C crook (B-flat basso) and Des for use with the C crook. There is no tuning slide, either for the instrument itself or for the valve loops, but there are two short tuning bits. When first examined the first valve (semi-tone) was found to be 'ascending', but further examination showed this to be due to an incorrect setting of the rotor. Marked: VERFERTIGT JOHANN GOTTFRIED KERSTEN IN DRESDEN. (Reid Museum, Edinburgh University.)

2. Two-valve horn with what appears to be an experimental valve arrangement, the first (whole tone) valve being an ordinary Stölzel valve, and the second an early type of double-piston valve. Marked: KEY 20 CHARING CROSS LONDON. Probably made about 1838. (Messrs J. & R. Glen, Edinburgh.)

3. Horn with two Stölzel valves. Here, as on 1 above, the first valve gives the semitone. The instrument has two conical 'master' crooks, one a single- and the other a double-coil, and seven cylindrical couplers, an original mouthpiece, and its original box. It is possible to crook this horn in every key from C alto to G basso. Marked: KEY 20 CHARING CROSS LONDON. c. 1840. (Bate Collection, Oxford.)

4. Cor-solo to which has been added subsequently a set of two early Périnet-type valves. The original F crook has been retained. Stays and bell-rim of silver. Dated 1814. Marked, in very small letters: RAOUX A PARIS. Engraved on the instrument are the initials G. P. (Giovanni Puzzi?) and 'Barham Livius'. (Carse No. 166.)

5. Horn with a set of two Stölzel valves of the kind called in France sauterelle. The sauterelle was only put on the instrument when the work being played called for the cor à pistons. Handsomely painted bell. By E.-J.-M. Dujariez, a former apprentice of L.-J. Raoux. c. 1840. (Private ownership in France.)

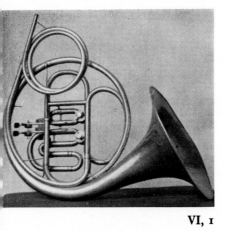

VI, 1

VI, 2

VI, 3

VI, 4

VI, 5

PLATE VII

1. Horn of nickel-silver with three rotary valves and F crook. Marked, in Cyrillic characters: WILHELM GLIJER IN WARSAW IN 1835 (date in Arabic numerals). The valves, similar to many in use today, are far in advance of any other valve of that time. (Author's collection.)

2. Horn with two Stölzel valves the springs of which are housed in two narrow cylinders soldered to the valve casings. The bell is beautifully painted and perfectly preserved. Marked: GOUDOT JNE. À PARIS. Goudot appears to have been associated with the firm of Husson et Duchêne, of Mirecourt, but had his own premises in 1845 and 1846 at 18 rue Grenetat, Hôtel du Mouton Couronné (probably an office only). The segment of the hoop nearest the bell is a dummy, put in solely for the sake of appearance, an arrangement not uncommon on two-valve horns of this period. (Bate Collection, Oxford.)

3. Horn with three Vienna valves and F crook. This instrument, an early example of that still used by the horn players of the Vienna Philharmonic Orchestra, is by the original patentee of the double-piston valve. Marked: LEOPOLD UHLMANN K. K.: HOF INSTRUMENTEN FABRIK IN WIEN. *c.* 1850. (Messrs Boosey & Hawkes.)

4. Horn with the ascending third valve imagined by Jules Halary about 1847. Marked: HALARI FOURNISSEUR DE L'EMPEREUR A PARIS. *c.* 1860. (Paris Conservatoire, but not catalogued.)

5. Horn with three rotary valves identical with the system patented in 1857 by Higham, of Manchester. Marked: COR D'APRÈS LE NOUVEAU SYSTÈME DE CYLINDRES À ROTATION À COL-ONNE D'AIR PLEINE ET PROGRESSIVEMENT CONIQUE, INVENTÉ PAR ALPHONSE SAX JUNIOR, RUE D'ABBEVILLE, 5BIS, PARIS. Made between 1860 and 1867. (Paris No. 673.)

6. Three-valve horn with B-flat alto crook. Military model. Marked: F. BESSON 7 RUE DES TROIS-COURONNES-DU-TEMPLE A PARIS. *c.* 1865. (Author's collection.)

VII, 1

VII, 2

VII, 3

VII, 4

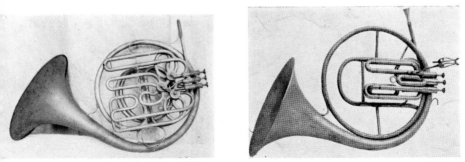

VII, 5

VII, 6

VIII, 1

VIII, 2

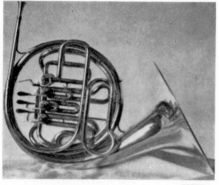

VIII, 3

VIII, 4

VIII, 5

VIII, 6

PLATE VIII

Modern Horns

1. Single B-flat horn with a long variable slide to the thumb valve. This valve can be tuned to lower the pitch to any extent from a semitone to a fourth. String-action valves. Marked: C. F. SCHMIDT. Grossherzogl Sächs: Hof-Instrumentenmacher BERLIN S.W.19. früher WEIMAR.

2. Five-valve Sansone model single horn in B-flat, by Sansone, New York. This system, devised by the horn player Lorenzo Sansone, was originally made to his specification by Wunderlich in Chicago, in 1914. After 1922 horns of this model were also made by Kruspe (Erfurt) and Alexander (Mainz). Subsequently Sansone set up his own factory in New York. The thumb valve can be used to put the horn into A, or can be tuned to three-quarters of a tone to facilitate good intonation for stopped notes. The little-finger valve puts the horn in F, so that with special fingering the downward compass of the instrument can be extended to equal that of the F horn. Crank-action valves.

3. Compensating F/B-flat horn marked: ED KRUSPE ERFURT Modell Prof. Wendler Made in Germany. String-action valves. A very fine instrument.

4. Compensating F/B-flat horn, Prof. Allegri system. By Cazzani, Milan. The compensating effect is obtained by means of a twin set of valves to each valve loop. Crank-action valves.

5. Compensating F/B-flat horn with piston valves, the third valve being *ascending* on both sections. System originally devised by the late Louis Vuillermoz. By Selmer, Paris. This is the type of instrument used by nearly all the horn players in the major French orchestras.

6. Double horn in F/B-flat, Horner model, by Kruspe, Erfurt. This is the model originally made by Kruspe about 1902 for Anton Horner, late of the Philadelphia Symphony Orchestra, and used by him throughout his career until his retirement. It is still one of the most popular models of double horn and one that has been widely copied. String-action valves.

CHAPTER I

Preliminary

THE NAME 'French horn' has given rise to much speculation as to whether the term is just one more of those puzzles, like 'cor anglais' and 'basset horn', whose terminology has intrigued so many writers of the past hundred years, or whether it really does mean what it says and the instrument did in fact hail from France. It is the present writer's firm conviction that the second alternative is the correct one, in spite of the absence of any cast-iron proof: his reasons for this belief are set out at some length in the next chapter. Though it may be only circumstantial, what evidence there is points very definitely to a French origin, and there are good reasons for believing the instrument was known and used in England under the name 'French horn' well before 1680, the date so often quoted as that of its 'invention'.

This horn, on which complex musical fanfares could be sounded, was a fined-down version in hoop-like form of the 16th-century multicoil helical horn, known in France as the *cor à plusieurs tours*. This *cor à plusieurs tours* was a clumsy, large-bore affair never extensively used in the hunting field, and not at all in England. But as will be shown later, it was almost certainly the instrument for which the 17th-century composers wrote when they required horns to illustrate scenes of the chase in their theatrical works. These horns were made in various sizes.

Essentially the French horn is a long, slender, conoidal tube, the bore of which increases very gradually over the first two-thirds or so of its length and then expands rapidly to end in a large everted bell. It is coiled in the form of a hoop in one or more complete circles, the bore at the outset being about 9 to 10 millimetres and the diameter of the bell varying from about 16 cm. in the case of 17th-century examples to 30 cm. or a little more for modern horns of the German model. The narrow end is provided with a mouthpiece that is more or less funnel-shaped, the inner profile of which has a marked influence on the quality of the tone emitted.

The length of the earliest types, hunting horns pure and simple, appears to have been the same as that of the contemporary trumpet in D, that is to say about 2·275 m. The simple, completely unmechanized horn, in all essentials exactly the same as it was in the early years of the 18th century, is still used in France in the form of the *trompe* or *cor de chasse*. This horn is in D (length about 4·50 m.), and very effective a quartet of them playing their harmonized hunting fanfares can be—in the open air and at some distance away. A similar horn, but in E-flat, is used in the band of the *Chasseurs alpins*.

For musical purposes horns have been made in every sort of length between about 2·50 m. (horn in C alto) and 5·65 m. (horn in B-flat basso); parts have been written—very occasionally—for horn in A basso, which implies a tube length of nearly 6 m. For a brass instrument to be satisfactory, however, it is essential that the proportions of its tube be kept within certain limits, since the human lips cannot properly control an air-column that is too long, too short, too wide, or too narrow. The horn is at its best when its overall length lies between 3·75 m. and 4·50 m., which covers the tonalities of F, E, E-flat, and D: the classical composers seldom wrote important solo passages for it in any other key. Apart from the physical strain involved when very high or very low horns are used, the tone is apt to be harsh with the former and woolly with the latter. Such a horn will, naturally, emit only those sounds that comprise the harmonic series germane to its tube length, and what these sounds will represent in terms of actual pitch for horns of different lengths will be found set out fully in the chart in Appendix 1.

Once the horn, still in its hunting form, was admitted to the orchestra, instruments in various keys—that is of various overall lengths—became essential. In order to overcome the inconvenience of having to have several instruments, horns were made incomplete in themselves, to be completed by the addition of the requisite amount of tubing to put them into the desired key. This extra tubing was made up with rings of assorted lengths called *crooks*, the crook being placed between the mouthpiece and the instrument itself. Thus the composer had only to select the horn key most suitable for his purpose, write the part out in C, and mark it 'Horns in F', 'Horns in D', or whatever the chosen key might be, and the player would simply put on the appropriate crook and play the part as written in the key of C.

About the middle of the 18th century it was discovered that by closing the bell with the hand to a greater or lesser extent it was possible to obtain a number of notes outside the harmonic series to which the instrument had up to then been strictly confined. Great inequality of tonal value between the natural and some of the closed notes was absolutely unavoidable even in the most skilful hands, but within the restricted range of about an octave and a half between the fourth and twelfth harmonics—the best part of the horn's compass for solo work—a chromatic scale could be played with almost even tone quality. At the same time the new technique enormously improved the quality of the tone as a whole, and definitely assured the horn of a permanent and important place in the symphony orchestra.

THE MODERN HORN

Even with the extra scope afforded by hand technique, which for many years remained more or less a vested interest jealously guarded by a few virtuosi, the horn was still hog-tied to the single harmonic series of its tube length. From this thraldom it was freed once and for all in the second decade of the 19th century by the invention of the valve. The horn now became fully chromatic without any hand stopping and the use of crooks was no longer necessary, though both, especially hand stopping, still have their uses in these days of extreme mechanization.

In spite of these and other advantages, and although a brass instrument able to give an even chromatic scale over its entire compass had long been desired, the valve had an uphill struggle to gain general acceptance, and this was especially true in the case of the horn. Early valves had serious mechanical defects which adversely affected both tone and certainty of attack, but even when by mid-century these had been overcome, prejudice against the valve horn still remained very strong, especially in some countries. How strong it was in France may be gathered from a letter to the writer from his erstwhile teacher, François Brémond, professor of the horn at the Paris Conservatoire from 1891 to 1922:

> Mazet dou Bartas,
> 27 avenue Schoelcher,
> Houilles (S-et-O).
> jeudi 10 août 1922

Mon cher Pegge,[1]

En attendant que nous puissions causer, un dimanche vers 3 h., par exemple le 20 août prochain, je vous écris ces quelques lignes à la hâte pour répondre à ce qui vous intéresse le plus. La classe de Cor à Pistons n'a pas été reprise depuis 1863,[2] et c'est moi qui ai demandé à Monsieur Ambroise Thomas[3] de vouloir bien me permettre de faire une classe de Cor à Pistons chaque semaine.[4]

J'ai ensuite obtenu de faire jouer le morceau à déchiffrer au Concours avec le Cor à Pistons (à cet effet il y avait une mécanique mobile que l'élève ajoutait en public), puis enfin j'ai fait jouer solo et morceau à vue avec le Cor à Pistons, mais en maintenant les phrases de cor simple: et dès cette époque (1897) la classe de Cor à Pistons était, non officiellement mais virtuellement reprise par moi. Cor simple jusqu'en 1896—Cor simple et à Pistons de 1897 à 1902—Cor à Pistons depuis 1903. C'est le système ascendant que je conseillais.

. . . et en attendant d'avoir le plaisir de vous voir je vous serre cordialement la main.

(*signed*) BRÉMOND.

For many years two valves were considered sufficient for the horn; players were still proficient enough in their knowledge of hand horn technique to be able to do without the third valve which added weight, and weight was an important consideration with the hand horn. Two-valve horns were still being made in the early years of the present century, but by then they had become virtually obsolete. Piston valves were always used in England, France, and Belgium, while the Germans, Italians, and the Central European countries in general preferred the rotary action.

The type of horn in almost universal use today is the double horn in F and B-flat alto, which combines in a single instrument the equivalent of a three-valve horn in F and a three-valve horn in B-flat, each with its properly tuned valve slides. The valves have double windways and two sets of tuning slides, and an extra valve actuated by the thumb which serves to direct the air-stream at will through either section. This ingenious device was first brought out by the well-known horn maker Kruspe, of Erfurt, about 1898. Such an arrangement is a tremendous help to the player since high notes can be attacked with infinitely less risk of accident on the B-flat than on the F horn. Thus the performer, relieved of the apprehension of a possible cracked note, plays with far more confidence and less fatigue. The disadvantage of the double horn is that its tone is apt to be coarser than that of the older type, to which must be added the instrument's not inconsiderable weight. For a long time past the Germans have made their horns with a larger bore and bell than the French, but it is only within recent years that it has been accepted in England where, before World War I, no orchestra would admit it. Many years ago the writer asked that well-known player of the day, Thomas R. Busby, what he thought of German and Austrian horns: 'Cow's horns, we call 'em' was his answer. Those great players Paersch and Borsdorf when they came to England in the 1880s were obliged to discard their German instruments and adopt the French type. Modern

music, with its ever increasing demands for slick technique and more
and more power, is assuredly better served by the German horn than by
any other: conductors today would look with a very jaundiced eye at any
player who had the temerity to bring into the orchestra an instrument of
the French type.

There are, of course, a few exceptions to this, as to all general rules.
The Viennese still remain faithful—but for how much longer?—to their
own special model of single F horn with three double-piston valves,
which has remained virtually unchanged for a century.[5] It is very difficult to play, but in spite—or perhaps because?—of this there is no finer
horn section to be found anywhere than that of the Vienna Philharmonic
Orchestra. Another exception is the instrument used in France. This is a
double horn in F, with an 'ascending' third valve: the instrument is fully
described in Chapter 3. Its bore lies midway between that of the old
French horn and the present-day German model, but piston valves are
still preferred to the German rotary action.

Some players, generally to be found among those who occupy the
first or third chair, prefer a single B-flat horn with an extra valve, controlled by the thumb, which may either carry a semitone slide or a slide
long enough to give the instrument a downward range equal to that of
the F horn. The single horn has the advantage of less weight, but the
fingering and the intonation are apt to be rather tricky, while unless in
the hands of a sensitive player its tone can be very harsh.

Both single and double horns are sometimes provided with a fifth
valve which, in the case of the last, is usually reserved for muting with
the hand to avoid the necessity of the otherwise unavoidable semitone
transposition. On the single B-flat horn the fifth valve is normally tuned
to put the instrument in F so that, although the valves are not tuned for
that key, it is possible to produce the lowest notes of the F horn: in such
cases the thumb valve will in principle be tuned to put the horn in A,
which greatly facilitates the fingering for certain passages in sharp keys.
It is, however, a moot point whether the advantages gained by the fifth
valve are worth the considerable extra weight involved.

NOTES

[1] *Translation.*

Thursday, 10 August 1922

My dear Pegge,

    Until such time as we can have a talk together one Sunday about
3 o'clock—I suggest next Sunday week 20 August—here are a few
hasty lines on the subject that specially interests you. The valve-horn

class had not been held since 1863,[2] and it was I who asked M. Ambroise Thomas[3] to allow me to hold one valve-horn class every week.[4]

I then got permission for the sight-reading test at the annual public examination to be played on the valve horn (for this the student fitted a detachable set of valves to his instrument in public), and finally for both the set piece and the sight-reading test to be played on the valve horn, hand technique being retained for specifically hand-horn phrases. From then on (1897) the valve-horn class was virtually, if not officially, reinstated by me. Hand horn until 1896—hand and valve horn from 1897 to 1902—valve horn since 1903.

[2] A valve-horn class with Meifred, a pioneer French valve-horn player and improver, as professor had been instituted in 1833. It was discontinued in 1863 on Meifred's retirement.

[3] Ambroise Thomas was Principal of the Paris Conservatoire from 1871 to 1896.

[4] Three horn classes were held weekly. Individual tuition, as practised in English music schools, did not form part of the Conservatoire curriculum.

[5] Though he has no details of the actual instrument or of the extent to which it is superseding the classic Vienna horn, the writer has heard that the Viennese have recently evolved a double horn with the characteristic bore and bell of their single F horn.

CHAPTER 2

The Evolution of the Instrument

HISTORICAL NOTICES ON the French horn in tutors and elsewhere have a way of beginning with some such words as: 'The horn is one of the oldest wind instruments . . .'. Whether such a statement arises from a sort of paternal pride on the part of the author—a case of the wish being father to the thought—or from sheer lack of reflection, it inevitably induces in the uninformed reader a wholly false impression that the French horn, as such, is an instrument of great antiquity, which, of course, it is not. It is, in fact, an offshoot of the craftsmanship of the late Middle Ages, whereas the 'horn . . . one of the oldest instruments' is simply the primitive conch or animal's horn that is among the earliest ancestors of all instruments sounded by means of a cup- or cone-shaped mouthpiece. It is quite unmusical, but uses are still found for it in various parts of the world. Two instances of its inclusion—for graphic reasons— in a modern score that come to mind are the *Stierhorn* blown by the night watchman in Wagner's *Die Meistersinger*, and Benjamin Britten's use of a cow-horn in his *Spring Symphony*.

The undiscriminating word 'horn' is chiefly responsible for the confusion. This overworked monosyllable has been used to mean practically anything, musical or otherwise, that was ever made out of or in the likeness of animal horn, as well as much that is not. Specific words like 'trumpet' or 'trombone' leave us in no doubt as to their precise meaning, whereas 'horn', unless qualified by an explanatory epithet, is completely vague: the indiscriminate use of the word in the United States to mean more or less any wind instrument does not help to clarify matters.

With the remote ancestry of the French horn, common to all brass instruments, it is not proposed to deal. The subject is one that calls for highly specialized scholarship that the writer does not possess, for it is of direct interest only to the ethnologist. It matters little to the musician whether the First Trump was a conch, an animal's horn, a marrow bone, or, maybe, none of these things.

Animal horns and large shells were certainly used to make loud and terrifying noises at a very early period in the history of mankind, but it is no less certain that the collateral trumpet acquired some degree of refinement much sooner than the horn. Long before the dawn of the Christian era it had become the instrument of religious solemnities and ceremonial parades, and was to be found in the company of princes, prelates, and pro-consuls: the Ancients deemed it worthy of the lips of angels. The horn, on the other hand, only began to emerge from a state of the most primitive simplicity some four hundred years ago. The company it kept was rough and boisterous: the hunter, the forester, the night watchman. Not without reason was it considered the instrument *par excellence* of devils, and there are no doubt plenty of players today who will agree that the influence of 'Old Hornie' has not yet been entirely exorcized, even from the most modern double horn. The aphorism of that distinguished horn player Bruno Jaenecke, 'God in His wrath created the horn', has a deal of truth in it.

In the Middle Ages, when ox-horns and oliphants—horns made of ivory and often very handsomely decorated—were used for a variety of purposes, the horn moved up occasionally, though not musically, into more dignified circles. An ancestor of the present writer, Samuel Pegge the elder, contributed to the journal *Archeologia* (Vol. VII—1775) a paper entitled 'Of the Horn as a Charter or Instrument of Conveyance'. In it he describes such horns as being of four sorts: drinking horns, hunting horns, horns for summoning the people, and horns 'of a mixed kind' which could be used either for blowing or drinking, a stopper being provided for the latter purpose. The paper deals chiefly with two such: the Pusey horn and the Foxlowe horn. The first, by virtue of which the Pusey family held the village of the same name in Berkshire, was given originally to one William Picote by King Cnut (1016–36). Ownership of the Foxlowe horn carried with it the hereditary stewardship of the royal manors of East and West Leake in Nottinghamshire, as well as certain other public offices. Probably the best known of all the 'charter' horns is that reputed to have been given, together with all his lands and revenues, by Ulphus the Dane to the Minster of York about the year 1030.[1] It was by no means unusual for a king or a noble to accompany a grant of land with the gift of a horn, which served as a deed of transfer.

Many places in England still have the 'Burgh-mote' horns that were used in olden days to summon the people, among the more familiar being those at Dover, Folkestone, and Canterbury. Well known, too, are the Watchman's horn at Saffron Walden, and the Wakeman's horn at Ripon. This last is still used to blow a nightly nine o'clock curfew, pursuant to a thousand-year-old custom.

None of these has the smallest claim to be considered a musical instrument, nor indeed have any horns made of or modelled after animal's horns. No more, therefore, will be said about them.

In antiquity there were two bronze instruments having some analogy with the horn, as well as definite musical potentialities. These were the Scandinavian *luur*, in its heyday between 800 and 400 B.C., and the *buccina* of the Roman Empire. Luurs, shaped like mammoth tusks, were always made in perfectly matched pairs, one being curved to the right and the other to the left. The tube, usually in the neighbourhood of 2 m. in length, was of conoidal bore, increasing from about 7 mm. at the proximal to about 55 mm. at the distal end which had no flared bell but was simply embellished with a flat ornamental disk. The mouthpieces of these remarkable instruments were very like those of the modern trombone, some being in cup form and others cone-shaped; some even had an appreciable 'choke'.[2] Many specimens of various sizes have been found in Denmark, but the approximate dimensions given above strike a fair average.

The *buccina*, in appearance, was not unlike a very small-bore helicon bass. It encircled the body and was blown with the bell pointing over the shoulder, one of the player's hands grasping the mouthpiece and the other holding the wooden crosspiece provided to give the instrument the necessary rigidity. Several reproductions of a specimen discovered in the ruins of Pompeii have been made: a description of one will be found in Mahillon's catalogue of the Brussels Conservatoire collection (Vol. I, p. 459; there is an illustration on p. 30 of Vol. II), and of another in N. Bessaraboff's *Ancient European Musical Instruments* (p. 174).

Although the *luur* and the *buccina* could have been used in part harmony, the consensus of opinion among the leading authorities is that they never were, but were always played in unison. These instruments had no connection with each other, and each vanished with the civilization of which it was a product.

Before passing on to the true parent of the French horn, the 16th-century helical horn, something must be said about a very curious drawing by Sebastian Brandt (1457–1521). This drawing, reproduced on Plate I, 1, is one of a number of woodcuts used to illustrate two editions of Virgil's works, one published by Grüninger (Strasbourg, 1502) and the other by Jacobus Sacon (Lyons, 1517). The illustration shows two men-at-arms, one blowing a field trumpet and the other a three-coil horn-like instrument which, except for the playing position, closely resembles the present-day French *trompe de chasse*. It is necessary to examine this problem in some detail, for it led Miss Schlesinger—the author of the important article on the horn in the eleventh edition of the

Encyclopædia Britannica, where this horn player is reproduced—to draw certain conclusions which, if proved correct, upset all previous ideas as to the origin of the French horn. 'These horns', says Miss Schlesinger,

> were not used for hunting but for war in conjunction with the draw-trumpet. Brandt could not have imagined these instruments, and must have seen the originals or at least drawings of them; the instruments probably emanated from the famed workshops of Nuremberg, being intended for use in Italy, and had not been generally adopted in Germany.

In the absence of any concrete evidence to support them these very definite views must be regarded with great caution. To begin with, the trumpet, illustrated in the original woodcut but omitted from the *Encyclopædia Britannica* reproduction, is no draw-trumpet (i.e. sackbut), but an ordinary field trumpet very similar to that figured in *Musica Instrumentalis* of Martin Agricola (1529). It is indeed a moot point whether the draw-trumpet could ever have been used in war, for which its delicate construction would have rendered it particularly unsuitable. The chief, if not the only, purpose of the sackbut up to the end of the 17th century was to serve as bass in consorts of cornetts or hoboys.

The horn in the illustration appears to have a tube length in the region of 4 m. or a little more, which would give a pitch approximating to that of a present-day horn in E-flat, and a bell about 17 or 18 cm. across, which is nearly twice as wide as the bells of the helical horns made three-quarters of a century later than Brandt's drawings. Apart from very short bell and mouthpiece sections the bore appears to be cylindrical rather than conical, in which case the instrument would be more properly described as a bass trumpet. That, however, is a minor point, for the drawing, like all the drawings of musical instruments of that period, is not sufficiently precise to allow it to be determined with any certainty. One thing is quite evident, and that is that such an instrument would be far too costly, too vulnerable, and too difficult to repair for it to find a place in the rough-and-tumble of the medieval battlefield.

It is difficult to understand why the artist could not have imagined such an instrument. Did not Brandt's more illustrious contemporary Leonardo da Vinci imagine and draw a flying machine? Yet who would be so bold as to assert that aircraft existed in the early 16th century? If such a horn, with all its musical potentialities, had really been in use in Brandt's time, it is surely very odd that no mention of anything remotely like it occurs in the works of such writers as Agricola or Virdung, Praetorius or Mersenne. So far as the writer is aware there exists neither a specimen nor a sculptural representation of any such instrument, nor indeed any other picture of it.

Until, and unless, corroborative factual evidence of its existence comes to light the only possible conclusion is that this instrument, like Leonardo's flying machine, was indeed a prophetic figment of the artist's imagination.

It was in the course of the 16th century that the primitive buglehorn underwent the first of the transformations that were to lead it gradually away from the raucous din of the Satanic host to the position of the most refined and poetical voice in the symphony orchestra. This transformation consisted in taking the large arcuate hunting horn of the period and making it in close coiled or helical shape. Once this compact form had been realized, an increase in length, and therefore in musical potentiality, was the logical outcome. Pictorial representations of these helical horns occur in the painting in the Prado in Madrid by Jan Breughel (1568–1625) entitled 'Allegoria dell'udito', and in two etchings by Wenzel Hollar (1607–77), one of which is reproduced on Plate I, 2. Two very early examples of the actual instrument, the earliest, we believe, to which attention has been drawn as yet, were in the Hunting Equipment department of the Dresden Staatliches Historisches Museum (Plate I, 3a and b); their fate is uncertain, since they were lost or destroyed during World War II. They were noticed by the late W. F. H. Blandford while he was on a visit to the continent in 1934, and his expert knowledge of the horn enabled him at once to grasp their significance in the evolution of the instrument. The notes he made on the spot are now in the possession of the present writer.

The smaller, and older, of the two has the words GOTT IST MEIN HELFER V.S. ZV DRESEN (*sic*) MACHT inscribed round the rim of the bell: from the style of the lettering the museum curator estimated its date as about 1572. It is coiled in four complete circles, the greatest width across the coils being 16·5 cm. and across the slightly flared bell 10 cm. The mouthpiece, which Blandford was convinced was original, is decorated with an incised pattern and, like the old Roman *buccina*, fits over instead of into the mouthpipe. The pitch of this horn, estimated during an admittedly hasty trial, was found to be A-flat, a tone below the modern cornet.

The larger horn, which is without mark or inscription of any kind, is also coiled in four complete circles, the greatest width across the coils being 21 cm. and the bell diameter 11 cm. It is pitched in D, in unison with the old D trumpet and an octave above the present-day *trompe de chasse*: Blandford was of opinion that it dates from the very early years of the 17th century.

That the use of these horns was never very general, at all events in the actual hunting field, is not surprising. In the first place their weight would no doubt have been considered a serious disadvantage, and as they were carried slung from baldricks, would have been extremely uncomfortable at the gallop; then, perhaps an even greater disadvantage, there would be the difficulty of sounding them properly. Once the hoop-like, body-encircling horn had been evolved and the inconvenience of carrying an instrument long enough to enable a large number of notes to be produced had been eliminated, it became the fashion, on the continent if not in England, for the highest in the land to adopt them, even if the skill of these players in sounding fanfares was not always that of the expert. In France the helical horn was well known under the name of *cor à plusieurs tours*. Mersenne in *Harmonie universelle* gives very rough drawings of four kinds of hunting horn which he calls respectively *le grand cor*, a large arcuate horn; *le cor à plusieurs tours*, the helical horn; *le cor qui n'a qu'un seul tour*, a slender crescent-shaped horn with one smallish coil in the middle, which is sometimes called the *cor Dufouilloux* from the name of the author of *La Vénerie*, a work on hunting dedicated to Charles IX (1560–74) in which there is a drawing of it; and lastly *le huchet*, a very much smaller version of *le grand cor*. Mersenne gives neither measurements, pitch, nor compass for any of these horns, but he does say that some huntsmen could cover a range as great as that of the trumpet.[3] This statement tacitly implies the existence of horns at least as long as the contemporary trumpets: that is to say, not less than about 2·25 m., which must have been of the helical type since any other would have been too unwieldy. The name of one virtuoso huntsman has been preserved for posterity, for La Borde, in *Essai sur la musique*, written nearly a century and a half later than *Harmonie universelle*, tells of one Livet, or Olivet, who lived in the reign of Louis XIII (1610–43) and who, he says, sounded the horn better than any had done before him, excelling particularly in fanfares.

Mersenne's *cor à plusieurs tours* has six complete circles, and a bell without any flare. Estimating the length of the instrument to be 42 times the diameter of the bell, and supposing the bell to be 10 cm. across, we get a tube length of 4 m. 20 cm. which gives us a horn in E-flat. The drawing, however, is so crude that it is difficult to form any idea as to how long the larger examples might have been in the early part of the 17th century, but it is not unlikely that helical horns 5½ metres in length were occasionally made before 1650. None of these 16th- or 17th-century helical horns appear to have found their way into collections of musical instruments, with the result that their importance in the evolution of the musical horn has not been sufficiently recognized: a search through the hunting accoutrements in the museums of Germany and Central Europe might prove very rewarding.

The French historian of the *trompe de chasse*, the late Commandant Gaston de Marolles, in an interesting paper entitled *Trois questions relatives à l'historique de la trompe de chasse*, quotes Maricourt as writing in 1627 that horns with five or six coils had been in use in the past,[4] but says that in his own opinion what he calls the *trompe Maricourt* was in reality the *Jäger Trommet* illustrated by Praetorius.[5] Marolles was, of course, unaware of the existence of the Dresden helical horns, which could not under any circumstances be described as trumpets.

It certainly looks as though helical horns must have been used for the performance of the horn parts in Cavalli's opera *Le nozze di Teti e di Peleo* given in Venice in 1639, and in Lully's *divertissement*-ballet *La Princesse d'Elide* produced at Versailles in May 1664, about which there has been so much speculation. Marolles, *grand chasseur* but, alas, no musician, asserts in another paper, *Monographie abrégée de la Trompe de Chasse*, that the Lully parts were played on the first model of the hoop-like horn, the direct parent of the French horn. He describes this as having two-and-a-half coils that measured 20 cm. across, a tube length of about 2·27 m., and as sounding in unison with the contemporary cavalry trumpet in D. This will not do at all, for the score requires horns in B-flat, one of them in B-flat basso. This problem will be dealt with fully in Chapter 5.

Helical horns, though quite exceptional once the body-encircling model had come into its own, continued to be made at least until the early years of the present century. An early example is illustrated on Plate II, 3. This curious horn, by an anonymous though probably English maker, is in E-flat by present-day standards and is said to have remained in the hands of one family since the time of Queen Anne (1702–14). It was acquired some years ago by the late W. F. H. Bland-ford and is now in the Horniman Museum (Carse Collection No. 254). It has twelve coils measuring 16 cm. across and—a most unusual feature for a horn of so early a date—a detachable 26·5 cm. bell. A horn of this model is probably what is described in the inventory made in 1768 of the instruments in the Cöthen Capelle as 'a pair of hats [*Hüthe*] containing A horns'. This was apparently an English speciality, for Mattheson mentions one J. G. Gleichmann, of Ilmenau, who kept for sale amongst other things 'English *cors de chasse* which are concealed in hats so that one can put them on and wear them'.[6]

Is the term 'French horn' a misnomer? Did the hoop-like horn in fact originate in some country other than France? It is a pity the *Encyclopædia Britannica* article already mentioned in connection with the Brandt woodcut has never been reprinted in a more accessible form, for it is one of the best documented and most authoritative papers ever published about the horn. Because of its importance, and because its author refuses to admit even the possibility that the French horn originated in France but insists that it came in the first instance either from Germany or, more probably, from Italy, the arguments adduced in support of such a view must be examined in some detail.

Briefly these arguments are: absence from museums of early (i.e. 17th-century) horns by French makers; no mention anywhere of the horn being used in such musical establishments as the *Chapelle Musique* or the *Grande Ecurie* of Louis XIV; no reference to the invention or improvement of the instrument in the sketchy article on it in the *Encyclopédie*; that the account in Gerber's *Lexikon* of how Sporck found the horn being played in a superior manner in Paris, and how he liked it so much that he introduced it into his native Bohemia on his return home, makes no mention of any invention, or even improvement, of the actual instrument; and lastly that the term 'French horn' only gained currency after the publication of the Sporck story by Gerber (1792).

To the first of these arguments it can be objected that there are no known 17th-century Italian specimens extant, and that even in the case of Germany the number of authentic 17th-century horns that have survived does not appear to exceed half a dozen or so. Three only have come to the writer's notice, and he has not seen any of these: their authenticity is guaranteed by the dates on them. There may be others in existence, but it would be unwise to accept an undated instrument as being 17th century without a very careful examination of it. The three known dated horns are a single-coil *Jagdhorn* in A by Wilhelm Haas of Nuremberg, dated 1682 (No. 15 in the musical instrument department of the Historisches Museum in Basel), an anonymous single-coil *grosses Jagdhorn* in B-flat dated 1689 (No. 1661 in Kinsky's small catalogue of the Heyer Collection), and a single-coil *Waldhorn* in B-flat alto by Hans Leonhard Ehe of Nuremberg, dated 1698 (in the Pfälzisches Gewerbe-Museum in Kaiserslautern, museum number unknown). There is, however, an English example of a much more advanced type than any of these German instruments. Formerly in the Galpin Collection, and now in the Horniman Museum (No. 307 in the Carse Collection), this magnificent copper and brass horn was made by William Bull of London and bears the date 1699. It is coiled in three complete circles and is pitched in E by present-day standards (Plate II, 2).

That French specimens should be practically non-existent is less surprising when it is remembered how much destruction was wrought during the Revolution of property considered to have the aristocratic taint, and what could possibly have been more tainted than any object connected with that preserve of the Court and nobility, the punctilious *chasse à courre*?

Before World War II the writer had the opportunity to examine and photograph a single-coil *trompe* in private ownership in Paris (see Plate II, 1). Though it bears no maker's name, it may well be French, for it corresponds in every respect with the *trompes* depicted in two pictures now in the Versailles museum and painted about 1688 by J.-B. Martin. Its pitch lies between D-flat and C (trumpet pitch), which would be the D of the period. Its dimensions approximate closely to those given by Marolles[7] for the *trompe* in current use between 1680 and 1705, after which the larger model sounding an octave lower began to supersede it. Dated French instruments are quite exceptional, and the only 18th-century example known to the writer is a large two-coil *trompe Dauphine* —so called because it made its appearance in the year of the birth of the Dauphin—marked FAIT A PARIS EN 1729 PAR LE BRVN ORDINAIRE DU ROY (Plate II, 4). There are also a few dated instruments, most of them orchestral horns, that belong to the first quarter of the 19th century and are the work either of Raoux or one of the Courtois. *Trompes de chasse* are by their nature exposed to considerable risk of damage, so that even without the depredations of the Revolution, 18th- and *a fortiori* 17th-century horns would have been rare enough.

The absence of the horn from Louis XIV's musical establishments should cause no surprise. It was regarded in France as an instrument of the chase pure and simple, whose harsh tones were offensive to sensitive ears indoors. And not only to French ears, for in a letter from Vienna to her friend Lady Rich, dated 1 January 1717, Lady Mary Wortley Montagu, after describing the magnificent public balls given there during the carnival festivities, says: '. . . the music good, if they had not that detestable custom of mixing hunting horns with it, that almost deafen the company'.[8] Even in Germany the horn was not introduced into the orchestra until within ten years of the death of Le Roi Soleil, while its musical development was virtually confined to Bohemia and Saxony until about the middle of the 18th century. Then, and only then, did France make the acquaintance of the orchestral horn, after the wealthy dilettante Riche de la Pouplinière had imported from Germany two horn players and two clarinettists for his own private orchestra. These players also performed on occasion at the Concert Spirituel and, according to the *Mercure de France*, a *symphonie à cors de chasse*, by Guignon, was played in December 1748 and again in September the following year by 'les deux nouveaux cors de chasse allemands'. The Paris Opéra did not have a regular pair of horns until 1759.

That horns did, however, make exceptional appearances with orchestra at a considerably earlier date is clear from the mention, in the *Mercure de France* of 23 April 1728, of a concert lately given at which was performed a concerto for trumpets, *cors de chasse*, oboes, and timpani with orchestral accompaniment, 'which gave great pleasure'. The wind instruments would, of course, have been used purely in what may be called their 'outdoor' capacity, very different as far as the horns were concerned from the refined style of playing that was even then being cultivated in Bohemia.

The unresponsiveness of the French for so long to the musical potentialities of the horn is, however, no valid reason why the hoop-like instruments, so obviously conceived in the interest of the mounted sportsman, could not have originated in their country: many things invented in France were developed in other countries before returning to the land of their conception. Nor is the fact that the so-called 'invention' of the hoop-like horn is not claimed for France in the *Encyclopédie* at all singular; no early encyclopædia credits it to any particular country. 'Invention' is in any case the wrong word to use in connection with the hoop-like horn which is after all simply a transformation of the helical horn, the invention of which has never been claimed for France, into something like the German *Jäger Trommet*, the bore being considerably fined down in the process. There are no grounds for supposing that such a transformation could not have taken place in France, and indeed it is by no means unlikely that one of the Crétien dynasty, the foremost French makers of hunting horns, trumpets, and kettledrums throughout the 17th century, was responsible for it.

In his account of how Franz Anton, count von Sporck imported the horn into Bohemia from France, Gerber's silence in the matter of the instrument's place of origin in no way rules out the possibility of France being its birthplace. From other sources we know that when Sporck did the grand tour of Europe commonly undertaken by the rich young aristocrats of that day, it was in Paris he first met with the new type of hunting horn. His biographer, von Stillenau,[9] without mentioning its country of origin, leaves us in no doubt that it was a complete novelty to

Sporck, who must surely have heard it in Germany or Italy had it been in use in either of those countries. Another writer, Prochaska, says the art of sounding hunting horns had scarcely been invented in Paris when Sporck, delighted with the sweetness (*suavitas*) of their sound, had two of his retainers instructed in the art of blowing them, and that this was the origin in Bohemia of an art in which the Bohemians are reputed to excel.[10] The two retainers, we are told by a later writer, Hirsching, whose names were Wenzel Sweda and Peter Röllig, instructed other Bohemians on their return home from Paris.[11] Thus, although there is no mention anywhere that France was the country of origin of the improved hunting horn, at least we must conclude that at the time of Sporck's tour in 1680–82 it was unknown elsewhere except, as we shall presently see, in the country he apparently did not visit, England. Which brings us to the last point, that the term 'French horn' never gained currency until after the publication of Gerber's *Lexikon*.

The falsity of this surmise is evident from an advertisement which appeared in *The Loyal Protestant & True Domestick Intelligence*, issue No. 126 of 7 March 1681/2, and which reads as follows:

> William Bull, *one of His Majestie's Trumpeters-in-Ordinary and Trumpet-maker, is removed from the* Trumpet and Horn *in Salisbury-Street near the* Strand, *to the* Trumpet and Horn *at the lower end of the* Hay-market *near the* Pall-mall-end; *where any gentlemen may be furnished with* Trumpets, *French* Horns, Speaking Trumpets, *and* Flasks *of all sorts both Silver and Brass.*

From this it seems reasonable to assume that the French horn was by then well acclimatized, and under that name: had it been an unfamiliar novelty it might be expected that some sort of description of the instrument would have been given. Furthermore, it is known, from the Talbot manuscript in the Library of Christ Church, Oxford, which covers an unspecified period between 1685 and 1700, and to which attention was drawn by A. C. Baines in the Galpin Society's Journal No. 1 (March 1948), that Bull was making French horns that were 10 feet long (about 3 m.), and that other unnamed makers were making them from 8 to 16 feet in length, or from C alto to C basso. The instrument must, on the face of it, have been known for a considerable time to have reached such a degree of development, and no comparable advance in its manufacture on the continent has so far come to light. It does, therefore, seem that the French horn, under that name, was well known in England long before Sporck set foot in Paris. The English, however, made no noticeable contribution to the musical development of the instrument, so the

Bohemians, who did, got the credit for being the first to discover it in Paris.

As far back as 1661 there is an entry in the accounts of the Royal Household, dated 20 February, which reads: 'Warrant to deliver to Gervice Price, Esquire, his Majesty's Sergeant Trumpeter, two silver hornes after the same manner and fashion as he shall inform you'.[12] Is it stretching the imagination overmuch to surmise that this was the new type of hoop-like horn which, according to Marolles, came into use in France about the middle of the 17th century? Such a horn would not have escaped the notice of Charles II during his exile, and he may well have wished to introduce a similar model when the Royal Buck-hounds, suppressed under the Commonwealth, were re-established in 1661. This view is strengthened by a further entry in the accounts, dated 20 March 1667/8: 'Warrant to prepare and deliver to Gervase Price, esquire, sergeant trumpeter and yeoman of the bowes and guns, one silver hunting horn of the quantity of 40 ounces or thereabouts, being a guift from his Majesty'.[13] The silver trumpets used by the trumpeters-in-ordinary of the time weighed five ounces less than this, so the horn, whose extra weight would be accounted for by a larger bore—it would not have the ornamental ball with which trumpets were embellished—would appear to have been of the same length as the trumpet and would therefore have needed the skill of a trained trumpeter to sound it properly. Such a length would approximate closely to that of the French two-coil hunting horn, measuring about 2·270 m., which Marolles says was in use between 1660 and 1689.

In spite of Marolles's assertion that the preference in France between 1680 and 1705 was for the single-coil trumpet-length horn, it seems more likely that the longer instrument pitched an octave lower was already in existence, if not in general use, at the time of Sporck's visit to Versailles: there would have been little of the 'suavitas' that so attracted him in a trumpet-length horn. The large, single-coil, horn with its hoop diameter of c. 0·730 m. must have been a little difficult to manage on horseback; nevertheless the celebrated marquis de Dampierre throughout his career would use no other, although, according to Marolles, a two-coil model made its appearance by, or before, 1710. These horns were made in various sizes: there is, or was before World War I, a single-coil *trompe* in the Paris Conservatoire Museum by Crétien, *Ordinaire de la Musique du Roy*, with a hoop diameter of one metre and pitched in B♮ basso. The museum then had a picture-postcard of it held by a soldier; unfortunately I never bought one, for after the war neither instrument nor postcard was available.

The English seem to have outstripped their continental rivals in early constructional improvement of the instrument, and to have anticipated the French in admitting it into the orchestra, but they did nothing whatsoever to advance the playing technique beyond that of the contemporary trumpet, in which guise it is by no means always an unmixed blessing. Such later mechanical improvements as crooks, tuning slides, and valves—Clagget's 'Cromatic Trumpet and French horn', which is described in Chapter 3 (pp. 26–30), can be discounted—all came from the continent. As far as we know, Handel was the first to introduce the horn into the orchestra in England in his *Water Music* (*c.* 1717), subsequently using it in operas, oratorios, and a few instrumental pieces that include a trio for two clarinets and a horn, and two concertos for four solo horns in F with orchestral accompaniment. It will not be forgotten that, as a young man, Handel had worked in Hamburg under Reinhard Keiser, whose opera *Octavia*, produced in 1705, is believed to be the first orchestral score to include two horns. The fact that in the score the horns are called *cornes de chasse* is surely, at this early date, a strong piece of evidence that the instrument could hardly have been of Germanic or Italian origin.

It is doubtful if in England French horns were ever used, as they were in France, in the actual course of the chase. It seems more likely that their function was confined to the enlivenment of the company at the meet and to welcome them back after, let us hope, a good day's sport. Indeed this is in a measure implied by Ned Ward in *The London Spy*[14] where he says, after he and his companion had paid a visit to Bridewell:

> turned into a Neighbouring Coffee-House, where glancing upon an old Flying-Post, we put ourselves in Mind of my Dame *Butterfield's* Invitation to her *Essex Calf* and *Bacon*, with her Six *Brass Horns* to Accomodate *Sportsmen* with the Delightful Harmony of *Hunting*.

In the field the use of the French horn was normally confined to stag hunting, but at least one pack of foxhounds, the Old Charlton, carried it on their establishment.

But if they were little used for the chase proper, it is likely that even as early as the later years of the 17th century, French horns were being played as a popular attraction on high days and holidays. During the 18th century they were a regular feature at such public playgrounds as Ranelagh and Vauxhall Gardens, where they performed while the elegant supped: French horns playing aboard barges on the water also gave much pleasure. The rich and powerful often included French horn players in their retinues to precede their equipages and to entertain their guests at home. More will be said about this aspect of horn playing in Chapter 5.

When first introduced into the orchestra the instrument was just the ordinary hunting horn able to give only the sounds germane to its tube length; this necessitated a different horn for each key. To overcome the disadvantages of having to have several instruments a system was devised whereby the horn itself was made in two coils with a very much reduced hoop diameter, while the fixed mouthpipe was replaced by a socket into which could be fitted rings of tubing of assorted lengths, so that one instrument could be put into a number of different keys. These rings of tubing, technically known as 'crooks', were usually made up in sets of six, two of them of conical bore and the other four cylindrical, known respectively as 'master crooks' and 'couplers'. Only a master crook would take the mouthpiece, so one of these had always to be used: the couplers, when required, fitted in between the master and the instrument itself, and could be used singly or in any combination (see Plate III, 1). This is the earliest known type of French horn crook.

The application to the horn of the crook principle, already in use with the trumpet and sackbut for more than a century, was hitherto thought to date from about 1715,[15] but has now been shown by Fitzpatrick (op. cit., p. 32) to date from the earliest years of the 18th century and to be definitely due to Michael Leichnambschneider. He has found a bill to the abbot of Kremsmünster which contains an item that reads '4 new double Crooks [*Krumbögen*] . . . 7 Gulden'. The bill, dated 1703, is in Leichnambschneider's own handwriting.

The combination crook system continued in use in England until the mid-19th century. The writer owned a horn (Plate VI, 3) with a detachable set of two valves that was made about 1840 by one of the leading London makers of the time, Thomas Key: it has a crook equipment composed of two master crooks, one a single-coil and the other a double-coil, and no less than seven couplers. With the valves withdrawn and replaced by an ordinary slide the horn can be crooked in every key from C alto to G basso! Another equally well-known and even more progressive London maker, John Köhler, was using the same system with his 'Patent Lever' French horns as made in 1851.

When, some time in the 1750s, Hampel of Dresden introduced his hand stopping technique (see Chapter 5) he found the multiple crook system unsatisfactory, since the distance between mouthpiece and bell varied with each crook change. He therefore redesigned the instrument on lines more suited to using the hand in the bell; the new model, first made by Hampel's fellow townsman, Johann Werner, became known as the *Inventionshorn*. The alteration consisted in restoring the original fixed mouthpipe, cutting one coil of the hoop, and bending the cut ends towards the centre of the circle; the cut ends were then fitted with sockets into which the crook, provided with corresponding tenons, was inserted.

Over the signature of Karl Bargans, then first trumpeter to the king of Prussia, there appeared in the *Harmonicon* an article[16] in which reference is made to certain unsatisfactory features of the earliest *Inventionshörner*. In spite of the almost meaningless jargon into which some person with no practical knowledge of brass instruments has translated the article, it is clear that the crooks did not slide on and off, as they did in later models, but fitted on to the horn by a tenon-and-socket arrangement of the kind used for terminal crooks. What may be perfectly satisfactory for a single connection, however, does not necessarily work equally well for two parallel connections, and the instruments were soon jarred to pieces by frequent changes of crook. Bargans wrongly ascribes the original invention to 'an artist in Hanau' and the subsequent improvement effected by the substitution of a five-inch slide for the tenon-and-socket arrangement to 'makers in Vienna and Dresden'. Actually the original *Inventionshorn* was, as we have said, made in Dresden, while the improved method of fitting the crooks by means of a slide was due to Johann Gottfried Haltenhof, of Hanau-am-Mayn, one of whose horns is illustrated on Plate IV, 1. This beautifully made instrument has crooks for B-flat alto, A, G, F, E, E-flat, D, and C, and a long graduated tuning slide. The higher crooks, down to and including the F crook, have an independent mouthpipe whereby one coil of the horn itself is cut out. For the statements concerning Werner and Haltenhof we have the unimpeachable authority of Heinrich Domnich,[17] professor of the horn at the Paris Conservatoire from the opening of that institution until 1817, and the author of the first scientific horn tutor ever written. Domnich, the son of a horn player in the service of the elector of Bavaria, was born at Würzburg, which is no great distance from Hanau: he is likely to have got his information at first hand not only on this account but because he was also a pupil of Hampel's star pupil, Punto.

This weakness in the original *Inventionshorn* is also referred to by W. Schneider[18] when describing a further improvement, suggested, it is said, by Carl Türrschmidt and carried out by the Paris maker Joseph Raoux and his son Lucien-Joseph about 1780. The improvement consisted in a further lengthening of the branches on to which the crooks fitted, and crossing them at the point where they curve towards the centre of the hoop; this gave a considerable gain in strength. Freer blowing was also claimed on the ground that the arcs described by the curves of the branches were wider, but this really seems to be a selling point on paper rather than a genuine advantage. The new Raoux model, expressly designed for the concert soloist, was built to take five crooks only—G, F, E, E-flat, and D—which sufficed for solo and most chamber music playing. For this reason it became known as the *cor-solo*, and was probably more widely used than any other model by the hand horn virtuosi. Raoux is known to have made silver horns of this model for Punto, Palsa, and Türrschmidt, and the fact that the Raoux *cor-solo* was also used by such eminent virtuosi as Dauprat, Puzzi, and Gallay is no mean testimony to their excellence. Of course, it was not suitable for the general run of orchestral playing, where B-flat alto, A, C, and low B-flat crooks would often be needed, but then it was not intended for orchestral work. The *Inventionshorn*, on the other hand, was an all-purpose instrument designed to take the complete range of crooks. The difference in layout between the French and German models will be clearly seen by comparing the Haltenhof horn (Plate IV, 1) with the Raoux version (Plate IV, 2). Other makers in Paris, notably members of the Courtois dynasty, followed the Raoux lead and turned out some very fine horns of the *cor-solo* model: the two horns shown at Nos. 3 and 4 on Plate IV were made respectively by Courtois *neveu* and Courtois *frère*. At least one Paris maker, Cormeri, of whose horns La Borde speaks highly, made instruments of the *Inventionshorn* model, for there is one in the Arts et Métiers museum in Paris that is an exact copy of the Haltenhof horn. It was, however, probably made before Raoux had brought out his *cor-solo*, since the address on the instrument is 'Rue Mercier à Paris', an address which Cormeri left to go to 'Rue des Prouvaires' in 1786.

Orchestral horns with a complete range of individual terminal crooks were probably first introduced in France towards the close of the 18th century, though it has not yet been possible to establish this with certainty. Until about 1830, when an A-flat crook was added, the standard set comprised crooks for B-flat alto, A, G, F, E, E-flat (nearly always marked DIS on Raoux crooks), D, C, and a coupler to put the horn in B-flat basso. A separate crook for B-flat basso did, however, exist but is very seldom met with: the writer is fortunate in possessing one by L.-J. Raoux. A *cor d'orchestre* by Courtois *neveu aîné* is shown on Plate III, 6.

If the French preferred the terminally-crooked *cor d'orchestre* and the Germans their *Inventionshorn*, the English remained faithful to the primitive Viennese multiple system of master crooks and couplers. They do seem, however, to have adopted the tuning slide at a very early date, for in the days when horns were still generally made without this necessary adjunct, those that were so provided were known in France as *cors à l'anglaise*. In his *Essai sur la musique*[19] La Borde draws particular attention to *cors à l'anglaise* 'which', he says, 'have slides that serve to vary the overall length of the horn, so that it can readily be tuned with the other instruments in the orchestra, and in any key. Horns without slides', he continues, 'are less expensive, but they are far less convenient'. Dauprat[20] also points out that horns with tuning slides were called *cors à l'anglaise* but adds that 'nobody seems to know why'. It can only be supposed that some English maker, whose name we do not know, was the first to see the advantage of Haltenhof's slide on the *Inventionshorn* and to adapt the principle to the terminally-crooked horn.

From this point on the development of the horn is intimately linked with that of the valve. This, and that curiosity the omnitonic horn, are dealt with in separate chapters.

NOTES

[1] Some doubt is cast on the authenticity of this version by Mr Cyril Blunt in an interesting illustrated pamphlet *The Horn of Ulph*, published in York. The horn is actually a drinking horn.

[2] 'Choke' is the constriction at the point where the cup of the mouthpiece joins the stem.

[3] Mersenne, *Harmonie universelle* (Paris, 1636), Proposition X. 'Quant à l'estenduë de leurs tons, elle est différente selon l'adresse et l'habileté de celuy qui en sonne, car il se rencontre des Chasseurs qui leur donnent autant d'estenduë comme à la Trompette, dont ie parleray après'.

[4] Messire René de Maricourt, *Traicté et abrégé de la chasse du lièvre et du chevreuil, dédié au roy Louis tresiesme du nom*. . . . Edité par Bouis (?). 'Le temps passé on portoit des trompes tournées à cinq ou six tours'. It is presumed that the quotation, for which Marolles gives neither chapter nor verse, is from this work which appeared during the first half of the 17th century. It has not been possible to consult Maricourt's treatise.

[5] Praetorius, *Theatrum Instrumentorum*, Table VIII.

[6] J. Mattheson, *Critica Musica*. Hamburg, 1722.

[7] G. de Marolles, *Monographie abrégée de la Trompe de Chasse*. Privately printed. n.d.

[8] *The Works of the Right Honourable Lady Wortley Montagu*. Edition published in London in 1803. Vol. 2.

[9] G. C. von Stillenau, *Leben. . . . Herrn Franz Antoni . . . von Sporck*, 1720.

[10] Faustinus Prochaska, *De Saecularibus Liberalium Artium in Bohemia et Moravia fatis commentarius*. Prague, 1784.

[11] F. C. G. Hirsching, *Historisch-litterärisches Handbuch berühmter und denkwürdiger Personen*. Leipzig, 1809.

[12] H. C. de Lafontaine, *The King's Musick*. London, 1909.

[13] ibid.

[14] Ned Ward, *The London-Spy compleat in Eighteen Parts*. London, 1700. Reprint London, 1924, by the Casanova Society.

[15] From J. Rühlmann, *Neue Zeitschrift f. Musik* (Leipzig, 1870), we learn that in 1718 a pair of Viennese concert horns with six crooks apiece were purchased in Dresden for 50 thalers each. Prior to Fitzpatrick, *The Horn and Horn-playing and the Austro-Bohemian Tradition: 1680–1830* (Oxford, 1970) this was believed to be the earliest mention of horn crooks.

[16] The *Harmonicon*, Vol. 8, 1830.

[17] H. Domnich, *Méthode de Premier et de Second Cor*. Paris, 1808.

[18] W. Schneider, *Historische-technische Beschreibung der musikalischer Instrumente*. Leipzig, 1834.

[19] J.-B. de La Borde, *Essai sur la musique*. Paris, 1780, 1781. 'Il y a différentes espèces de cors. A l'anglaise, avec des coulisses, qui servent à allonger ou à racourcir [*sic*] la totalité du cor, et par ce moyen à s'accorder facilement dans tous les tons avec les autres instruments de musique. Les cors sans coulisses sont moins chers, mais aussi bien moins commodes'.

[20] L.-F. Dauprat, *Méthode de Cor Alto et Cor Basse*. Paris, 1824.

CHAPTER 3

Valves

IT IS NOW well over a century and a half since, by the addition of valve mechanism, the horn was made fully chromatic without the necessity of any stopping of the bell with the hand.

The valve is a device whereby the air-stream may be instantly deflected through an additional loop of tubing in the case of the usual *descending* valve, or by a short cut towards the bell in that of the exceptional *ascending* valve, the overall length of the air-column thus altered creating a new fundamental with its ancillary partials. Three dependent valves[1] that lower the pitch respectively by a semitone, a tone, and three semitones suffice for the production of a complete chromatic scale from six semitones below the second harmonic upwards. Their actual effect is set out in tabulated form in Appendix 1.

Simple enough in conception, the valve itself is no more than a two-way spring-controlled tap operated by the finger: it may nowadays have either a piston or a rotary action. Before the device could become really satisfactory, however, serious mechanical problems had to be overcome, among the most important being those of making it air-tight and of avoiding sharp bends and constricted air passages, as well as that of ensuring perfect smoothness and efficiency in the working parts.

In the first instance applied to the horn, and then to the trumpet, it was not long before valves began to be fitted to instruments of the bugle-horn family. These last, especially in the field of light music where they met a long-felt need, had an immediate success. New families of brass instruments came into being and quickly proved themselves of the greatest value in the wind band. The *cornet à pistons* or cornopean, as it was called in England in its early days, was soon a popular favourite as a solo instrument in dance bands, at promenade concerts and the like, and in a very few years had ousted the key bugle from its place as chief soprano soloist in military and industrial bands.

The valve horn and trumpet, on the other hand, did not readily gain acceptance either by performers or by the public or even by composers. Since the decline of 'clarino' playing about the middle of the 18th century, the trumpet had been relegated to a secondary position in the

orchestra, its legitimate sphere being now confined to the fanfare, together with such original uses as a composer could contrive while keeping strictly to the 'in-tune' harmonics. The only use of valves, which
tended to spoil the tone, appeared to be to save the player the trouble of
changing crooks, and so they were not viewed in a favourable light. The
hand horn, however, was much esteemed as a solo instrument, and in
their early imperfect state valves affected adversely not only the tone but
sureness of attack as well. There was, too, about the hand horn an elf-
like atmosphere that is completely foreign to the more prosaic and
assertive *cor à pistons*.

The earliest attempt to make the horn chromatic by mechanical
means appears to be that of a Bohemian named Kölbel who, about 1760,
invented an instrument he called *Amor-Schall*. Accounts of this instrument are lacking in precision, but it seems to have been a horn with two
closed keys near the bell, so placed that one of them raised the pitch a
semitone and the other a tone. Over the bell itself was a sort of pepper-
pot lid the purpose of which, presumably, was to minimize as far as
possible the disparity in tone colour between the bell notes and those
obtained by means of the keys. This was not, of course, the first use of
keys to cover side-holes in lip-reed instruments, for the larger *cornetti*
had been provided with them at least a century and a half earlier.

Quite original, however, was the idea of the Irish inventor Charles
Clagget, who patented his 'Cromatic Trumpet and French horn' in
1788. In the rare pamphlet *Musical Phenomena*, published by him in
1793, Clagget expatiates on the defects of natural horns and trumpets
arising out of the gaps in the natural harmonic series, and says:

> The Patentee was almost discouraged from attempting this im-
> provement; but, it occurring to him that the third and fifth might
> become the second and fourth to another trumpet of a different
> pitch, the difficulty resolved itself, in a great measure, into this
> problem; that, by combining tubes of different lengths, properly
> proportioned, and by applying such a machine as should give the
> performer an absolute command of either at his pleasure, it would
> be advancing a considerable length; and this, with a tempering
> power, which is given by the same machine, perfects these instru-
> ments.

Although clarity in his writings was not among his virtues, and
though he seems to have merited the judgement passed on him that it
was the misfortune of his life 'to have ideas theoretically sublime, but
deficient in practical utility',[2] Clagget must be recognized as the first to

propound and make use of the principle on which the modern valve is based.

According to the specification[3] the instruments consisted of two horns or two trumpets a semitone apart, united at their mouth pipes 'in such a manner that the same mouthpiece may be applied to either of them instantaneously during the time of performance, as the music may require'. From the wording, purposely nebulous one may suspect, both in the specification and in *Musical Phenomena*, as well from the very poor drawing in the last of a 'cromatic trumpet',[4] the contrivance was made up of two instruments whose mouthpipes were somehow united inside a horizontally placed cylinder into the side of which the mouthpiece fitted. The mouthpiece was connected with a joint

> by means of a piece of elastic, gum or leather, or otherwise, so that the point of the mouthpiece may be directed to the opening of either of the horns or trumpets at pleasure, at the same time that another piece of elastic, gum or leather, or other proper material, stops the aperture of the horn or trumpet which is not in use.

Unless it has some connection, not explained, with the mysterious 'tempering power', alluded to in the pamphlet but not so much as hinted at in the specification, this last refinement would appear to be superfluous. A small pin projecting from one end of the cylinder operated the switching motion.

We are told in the pamphlet that 'The valve which occasionally opens one or other of the instruments, also tempers the tune of that which sounds; by this means the performers produce such harmonious proportions on their instruments that must delight the most critical ear, and . . . in all keys'. How this 'tempering' is supposed to be accomplished is nowhere disclosed. The late Canon Galpin held the view that in addition to switching the mouthpiece from one instrument to the other the valve, by a further turn, would lower the pitch of either by a whole tone. There is, however, no sign discoverable by the present writer in the specification or elsewhere of the extra lengths of tubing without which any such lowering of the pitch is impossible. That no such device did in fact exist seems all the more likely since Clagget ignores every sound below the fourth harmonic. But even if the 'tempering' really could be satisfactorily accomplished, or supposing that either horn could be *shortened* to the extent of a whole tone—a more likely possibility, we feel, than Canon Galpin's suggestion—the odd appearance of the bells waving like Brobdingnagian daffodils in a breeze must have been sufficiently mirth-provoking seriously to jeopardize any chance of success the contraption might otherwise have had.

Clagget's explanation of how a scale might be played is as follows:

> Let us suppose one horn to be in D, and the other in E-flat; then if we play in D major the second is corrected in the D horn. The third, F-sharp, is good in the nature of the instrument, as all sharp thirds on well-made trumpets and horns are: the fourth, or G, on the D horn would be very imperfect, as mentioned above, which sound has always been exceedingly offensive to correct ears; but being taken on the E-flat horn, is in perfect tune, as all major thirds are, G being the major third to E-flat, as is well known to every person acquainted with the common elements of musick; the fifth, A, is good on the D horn, as already observed, the sixth is tempered by the valve.
>
> We thought it best to explain as familiarly as possible how the several intervals are produced in a major key: but as the minor modulations were never heard upon these instruments, it is necessary to give a plain idea of the production of the minor thirds; and to preserve uniformity let us suppose the key of D minor, the second then is as before, but the third, F, is a second tempered in the E-flat horn, and the remainder of the octave, ascending, is the same as in D major; but the seventh descending is the tempered sixth in the E-flat horn; and the sixth descending is perfect, being the fifth of the E-flat horn.
>
> As additional evidence that the powers of modulation in Trumpets & Horns are extended to a very great degree of perfection see the minor part of Mr. Haydn's Air in Musical Plate No. 1 where the seven notes are all flattened:[5] not produced, as on common harpsichords, by playing G-sharp for A-flat, B-natural for C-flat, etc., etc., but they are flattened by the tempering power or cylinder already described; and it has been publicly proved that these instruments are as finely in tune as the Violins and Violoncellos which made the responses and which were a certain means of detecting any errors in the intonation, if such errors existed.

Not a very lucid exposition, and in the absence of all knowledge of the mysterious 'tempering power', one can only wonder how this duo can possibly have been made acceptable even to the most undiscriminating ears. The juxtaposition of the eleventh and thirteenth harmonics produces an effect that is quite excruciating; the bare thought, even, is

enough to set one's teeth on edge. A glance at the music will quickly disclose other combinations almost as bad.

The three scales taken from *Musical Phenomena* and quoted below
contain some curious features which, so far from helping us to understand what the inventor has previously written, only add to the general
confusion. The first is a chromatic scale of two octaves and a semitone,
apparently from the fourth harmonic of

'The Practitioner will find the tones chang'd require sometimes a lesser pressure, particularly where the figures
appear ¼: no extract rule can here be given, but he must be
governed by his ear and his embouchere [*sic*]'

D major scale

Those notes that are white are 'produced from
the E-flat horn'

D minor scale

the D horn to the sixteenth of the E-flat instrument. In the second
(D major) and third (D minor) the range seems to be from the eighth
to the sixteenth harmonic. If our surmise is correct, these scales are
written an octave lower than the actual sounds.

There are several points here that call for comment. In the first place
there is no mention of any 'tempering' by the valve, nor is the oddly
placed ¼ the equivalent, as far as can be judged, of a 'tempered' note
since none of the notes marked 'tempered by the valve' in the major and

minor scales have it over them in the chromatic scale. Next he replaces F-sharp in the lower octave by G-flat, which is marked $\frac{1}{4}$, though it would have been quite satisfactory as F-sharp, good on the D horn 'as all sharp thirds . . . are': truly Clagget's reasoning is hard to follow at times. The C-natural (marked $\frac{1}{4}$) and the D-flat (not marked) in the first octave would both normally be played as seventh harmonics which, though rather flat normally, can nevertheless be played pretty well in tune by a competent player.

Clagget greatly overestimated the possibilities of his invention, but a few public performances on the 'cromatic horns' did take place at the New Rooms, Bath, as well as one in Hanover Square, London. Both the duettists, Messrs Milgrove and Henrard, appear to have been Bath men; neither figures among the horn players in Doane's 1794 *Musical Directory*, though Milgrove is shown as 'composer—Bath'.

A good deal of space has been devoted to what, after all, was only an abortive experiment. Abortive, perhaps, but it was the very first known attempt to make a brass instrument chromatic by altering the effective tube length otherwise than by side-holes, never really satisfactory, or by a slide which is applicable only to an instrument whose bore is mainly cylindrical.

And so, from the fantastical to the practical, we come to the invention of the valve proper.

Which of the two, the Saxon Heinrich Stölzel or the Silesian Friedrich Blühmel, who jointly took out a ten-year patent for valves in Berlin in 1818, was actually the first in the field will now probably never be known, for even their contemporaries were unable to agree about it. Piecing together the story from such sources as have been available to the writer, the probabilities seem to favour the theory that Stölzel was the first to produce a valve of any kind but that Blühmel made the first more or less satisfactory one. Quite a lot is known about Stölzel but about Blühmel we are very much in the dark. He is usually described as a 'Berghoboist', only too often translated as 'mountain-hoboy player'— whatever a 'mountain-hoboy' may be; the correct translation of Berghoboist is mine bandsman, or in other words he was simply a member of a mining company's works band. What instrument he played has never, so far as we know, been disclosed, but it is unlikely to have been a reed instrument. Stölzel, on the other hand, was a horn player attached first to the private band of the prince of Pless, and then to the Royal Opera orchestra in Berlin, from which he retired with a pension in 1829. He was also a Royal Chamber Musician and instrument repairer to King Frederick William III of Prussia.

The first that is heard of Blühmel is his signature on the specification that accompanied the application for the patent to be taken out jointly in the names of himself and Stölzel: nor does anything seem to be heard of him again until after the partners had separated and the patent expired. In the meantime he had invented another valve which he sought to patent, but the Prussian Patent Office would not accept. He thereupon asserted that he himself was the original inventor of the valve and that he had sold a valve horn in 1817 to Stölzel which the latter had passed off as his own invention. This does not agree at all with certain known facts, so in spite of his protestations the Patent Office remained adamant.

As we shall see, Stölzel was certainly in Berlin in the early part of 1815 with a valve horn purporting to be his own invention, and had made contact with the well-known firm of instrument makers Griessling & Schlott—not 'Schott' as is sometimes stated—who readily took up the invention.

In an article entitled 'Cors à pistons'[6] Fétis gives a plausible account of the origin of the invention. He tells how, about 1815 or 1816, a free-lance horn player named Stölzel got so tired of carrying a lot of crooks about with him that he set to work to try and evolve some type of horn that would obviate this. He thought out a scheme for making an instrument on which he would be able to play in every key and took his blue-print to Schlott who tried to turn it into a practical proposition. At this time Christoph Schunke, principal horn in the grand duke of Baden's orchestra at Carlsruhe, chanced to be in Berlin, and realizing the latent possibilities of the valve persuaded the Carlsruhe maker Schuster to try and improve the new invention. This story, pieced together for Fétis by Dauprat, professor at the Conservatoire, and Meifred, the French protagonist of the valve horn, though perhaps fanciful here and there, certainly gives a reasonably accurate impression of the genesis of the valve, though there is no mention whatever of Blühmel or of the patent taken out in 1818.

Over the signature of G. B. Bierey there appears a short notice in *Allgemeine musikalische Zeitung* for 3 May 1815, to the effect that by adding a simple mechanism to the horn Stölzel had succeeded in endowing his instrument with a chromatic scale of nearly three octaves, every note of which was pure, full, and in tune. Without giving any clue from which the nature of the mechanism might be deduced Bierey nonetheless affirms his conviction that the idea is an excellent one, and that it might with great advantage be applied to the trumpet and bugle-horn, without, however, having as yet seen it himself fitted to any instrument but the horn. In the same periodical, in the number dated

26 November 1817, there is an article by Friedrich Schneider stating that Stölzel, by dint of patient labour, had succeeded in providing the horn with two spring-controlled valves, the effect of which was better than anything obtainable from brass instruments with keys. In neither article is there any mention of Blühmel.

The patent taken out by Blühmel and Stölzel in 1818 was for a square piston valve. In the catalogue of the Brussels Conservatoire museum Mahillon tells how he procured from Berlin a copy of the specification, which was signed by Blühmel alone, but that as the drawings that should have accompanied it had been lost it was quite unintelligible until a lucky chance put him in possession of a trumpet with two square valves that exactly fitted it. Schuster of Carlsruhe, as we know, made this type of valve, so it is highly probable that Blühmel acted as his technical adviser. At all events the specification which Blühmel signed fits the Schuster valve. Nothing is known about the form of Stölzel's first valve: it may well always have been tubular but less efficient than the square model of Blühmel which figured in the patent. The tubular valve was improved in due course by the Paris makers, notably Labbaye and Halary, but Stölzel's name has always been associated with the type of valve the bottom of which serves as a windway. It completely eclipsed the square model, and up to 1914 very cheap cornets with Stölzel valves were still being made in France.

It looks as though Blühmel's claim to have been the original inventor of the valve was exaggerated by biased partisans, for according to Rode[7] it was only in 1817 that he sold to Stölzel the valve horn the latter is alleged to have passed off as his own invention, yet Stölzel had been demonstrating his instrument to Bierey two years earlier. Had Blühmel had any hand in that, surely his name would not have been left out of the notices of 1815 and 1817. On the face of it it seems not unlikely that before, and perhaps after, they joined forces each was working on independent lines, Stölzel with Schlott in Berlin and Blühmel in Carlsruhe with Schuster. The manufacture of tubular and square valves continued side by side for some years before the last were abandoned.

In France, where a solution to the loose crook problem was being sought on 'omnitonic' lines, valves seem to have been unknown before about 1826, in which year Spontini, then chief Kapellmeister to King Frederick William III of Prussia, sent some valve instruments to Paris. One of these, a trumpet with three Stölzel tubular valves, went to Dauverné, then first trumpet at the Opéra and later professor at the Conservatoire, who tells us[8] it was unsatisfactory both in tone and intonation. In collaboration with Meifred, the first Frenchman to make a serious study of the valve horn, the Paris maker Jacques-Charles Labbaye set about the task of improving these valves and produced a horn that won a silver medal at the Paris Industrial Exhibition of 1827. Fig. 1 shows the instrument as redesigned by Meifred and made by Halary, together with the Schuster valves as fitted to the German horn. Fig. 2 overleaf shows in diagrammatic form the Stölzel valve as improved by the addition of slides to the valve loops, but in other respects similar to the first tubular valves seen in Paris.

In that same year, 1827, Dauprat, professor of the horn at the Paris Conservatoire, procured a horn with square valves, made by Schuster,

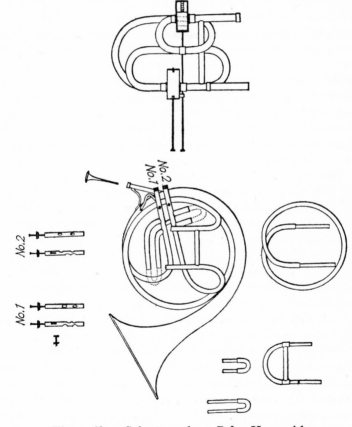

Fig. 1 *Above* Schuster valves. *Below* Horn with
Meifred-Labbaye improvements
From *La Revue Musicale de Fétis* (tome II, 1828)

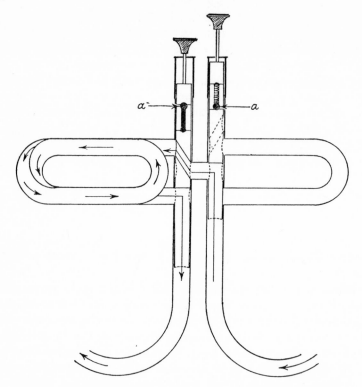

Fig. 2 Small screw that passes below the spring through a
window in the valve itself: it screws into the far side of the
valve casing and acts as a guide to keep the valve in position.
In early English-made valves of this description the screw is
replaced by a small projection on the valve running in a groove,
a system still in use on modern pistons

from Carlsruhe. Fig. 3 shows the layout of this system in detail. Meifred
says in his monograph on the construction of brass instruments[9] that
this square valve was better than the tubular model in the sense that the
windway was more direct and some of the sharp angles were eliminated.
It was the tubular type, notwithstanding, that Meifred decided to adopt
and improve. The square valve model was very heavy, and as the instrument was built as a unit in F without any sort of tuning slide, it was impossible to make use of crooks. Dauprat, unable to accustom himself to
its weight and other drawbacks, gave up all idea of using it. It is much
to be regretted that Dauprat did not leave this instrument to the Paris

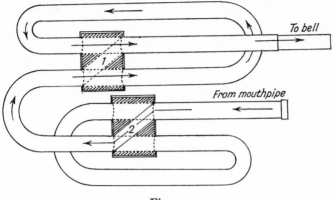

Fig. 3

Conservatoire museum as well as his *premier prix* received in 1798 (Plate IV, 2).

Meifred remodelled the original Stölzel layout so as to provide tuning slides for the valve loops, and at the same time incorporated a main tuning slide on to which could be fitted, *cor-solo* fashion, crooks for E, E-flat, and D, the instrument being primarily in F. That the Germans considered valve instruments as chromatic units in a fixed tonality is perhaps reason enough, at all events on paper, for dispensing with tuning slides as such, but their absence sadly complicates the minor though necessary operation of getting rid of the moisture that inevitably collects in the valve loops after a spell of blowing. Meifred saw to it that this defect was remedied on French instruments, and thereafter valve slides became a standard refinement on brass instruments of every kind.

Meanwhile a most interesting valve had been invented in England by a Derbyshire farmer, one John Shaw, of Glossop. It was patented by him in 1824[10] under the name of *Transverse Spring Slides*. This ingenious device incorporated three absolutely original features that owed nothing whatsoever to any continental valve then known, though continental makers later made use of all three in a modified form. These innovations were: *twin pistons*, seen again in the so-called *Wiener-Ventil*; *independent valves*, used by Adolphe Sax for the six-valve instruments he produced in the 1850s and by Prager for his six-valve omnitonic horn; and *ascending valves* which, when depressed, raise the pitch instead of lowering it, utilized by Jules Halary for his horn with an ascending third valve in 1849, and also by Sax for his six-valve instruments.

Shaw's system required four *spring slides*, three of them ascending

Horn with four transverse spring slides

D O 1 2 3   D O 1 2 3 D   O 1 2 3 Q O 1

2 O 1 2 3 D O 1 O 1 O 1 2 O 1 2 3 O O
or   or or or or   or or
D   D D D D   D D

Horn with two Stölzel or Schuster valves

1.2 1 2 0   1.2 1 2 0   1.2 1 2   0 1.2 1 2 0

1 2 0 1 1.2 1   2   0 2 0 2 0 1 2 0 1.2 1.2 1 2 0

The white notes are not playable as valve notes pure and
simple; O=open note (i.e. no valve depressed): D=descend-
ing spring slide: 1, 2, 3 valves 1, 2, and 3, valve 1 being nearest
the mouthpiece.

and one descending for horn or trumpet, and six, five ascending and one
descending, for bugle-horns and trombones. Each ascending valve
raised the pitch progressively by a semitone, and the descending valve,
always that nearest the bell, lowered it by a semitone. Thus the ascending valves, working from the one next to the descending valve towards

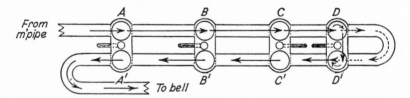

Fig. 4. With all the valves 'up' the air goes straight through A,
B, and C, but at D it crosses via the staple to D′ whence it re-
turns to the bell. If one of the valves A, B, or C is depressed,
the air travels across to A′, B′, or C′ as the case may be and then
on to the bell, thus cutting out the appropriate section of tubing. If valve D is depressed, the air follows the path indicated
by the dotted arrows

the mouthpiece, raised the pitch respectively by a semitone, a tone, and three semitones, and in the case of the six-valve instruments, two tones and five semitones. If the system was ever actually applied to the horn, the instrument would have had to be built in E-flat in order to cover the same ground as the German two-valve horn in F. A glance at the comparative fingering chart for the two systems, both instruments being built in F, will make this clear.

The German system allows the horn to be put into E, E-flat, and D, while Shaw's gives the tonalities of E, F-sharp, G, and A-flat. If the composer calls for horns in E-flat or D, two of the most widely used keys in the music of the late 18th and early 19th centuries, with Shaw's system it would have been impossible to produce the extremely important pedal C or the G above it (second and third harmonics) in either of these keys. This alone makes Shaw's instrument useless in the orchestra or for chamber music—unless built in E-flat—though it might serve with good effect in a wind band.

An attempt has been made in Figs. 4, 5, and 6 to show the working of these valves in an intelligible form from the long-winded patent specification, no actual specimen having, so far as is known, survived. Fig. 4 shows diagrammatically the path followed by the air in the arrangement for horn or trumpet. Figs. 5 and 6 combine in a single sketch the essential components of the ascending and descending valves as depicted in the many drawings that accompany the specification. It should be remembered that these valves are all independent and therefore cannot be used in combination.

We are told by Messrs Russell and Elliot[11] that Shaw's spring slides were made by an obscure Birmingham brass instrument repairer by name Battee, George Metzler being appointed London agent. Fourteen years later Shaw, who by then was making his own valves, patented an entirely different action which he called his *swivel valve*. This device was taken up by the London maker John Köhler, who exploited it in a modified form with some success for several years under the name of *Patent Lever Valves*. This valve will be examined in detail in due course.

To revert to Germany. In 1827, Blühmel brought out his *Drehbüchsen-Ventil*, presumably the one for which the Berlin Patent Office refused him a patent on the ground of its similarity with that for which a ten-year patent had already been granted. Little can be deduced from the complex names given to the many types of valve that now began to emerge as to the precise nature of their mechanism, but because of this one's name the general assumption has been that it was the first rotary action. If so it is difficult to understand why the patent was refused; but

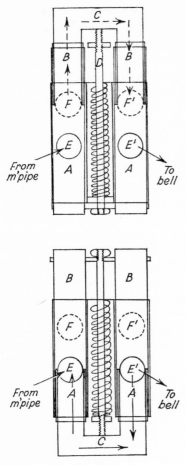

Fig. 5 *Ascending valve*

AA is the valve casing; BB are sliding legs linked by mitre joints to tube C to form a 'staple'; D is the piston rod, part of which carries a spring enclosed in its own casing. The piston rod is held in position by nuts and screws which serve to regulate the movement of BCB, and the valve is operated by a finger lever (not shown) attached to one of the nuts. E and E′ are inlet and outlet holes bored right through BB, and F and F′ holes bored through the near side only of BB. Depression of the valve brings holes FF′ opposite holes EE′ and the air is diverted via C, thus cutting out all further tubing through which the air would have travelled with the valve 'up'

Fig. 6 *Descending valve*

The construction is the same as that of the ascending valve except that it works upside down. Here it is holes E and E′ that are bored on the near side only and F and F′ that go right through

if, as Adam Carse has pointed out,[12] Wieprecht's *Stecherbüchsenventil*, which appears to have had a piston action, was, as he alleged, an improvement on Blühmel's valve, some doubt arises as to whether the latter was in fact a rotary valve.

According to Rode[13] the *Blühmel'schen Büchsen-Ventil* found favour in Vienna, Pesth, and Prague where, in 1829, they were much improved as the result of suggestions made by Joseph Kail, professor of the trumpet at the Prague Conservatory. Kail, who had formerly enjoyed some reputation as a soloist on the valve horn, was one of the very first to interest himself in the development of chromatic brass instruments.[14]

In 1830 the Viennese maker Leopold Uhlmann was granted a *k. k.*

Privilegium for his twin-piston mechanism which was to prove so successful in Central Europe under the name of *Wiener-Ventil* or, as Rode calls them, *Wiener-Schub- oder Stechbüchsen Ventil.* One can only assume that Uhlmann's valve was an improved version of one already in existence, for a similar kind of mechanism was being made before 1830 (Figs. 7 and 8). There is in the Crosby Brown Collection (Metropolitan Museum of Art, New York) a trumpet marked on the bell rim *Michael Saurle in München. Dem K. Landwehr Jäger Bataillon gehörig,* and with the date 1829, surrounded by a decorative festoon, engraved on the valve plate. This instrument has two twin-piston valves of the earliest known type. Another instrument, a horn with three valves of similar model, is marked *Mainz bei B. Schott Söhnen*—not, however, made by them: Schott's Söhnen were never actually makers[15]—and is in the Brussels Conservatoire museum (catalogue no. 1314). The effect of the actuating mechanism in both cases is unusual in that it drives the pistons upwards instead of downwards, which has led to the misleading remark in the Crosby Brown catalogue that they are *ascending* valves, which they are not.[16] The fact that in this early model the pistons actually protruded through their casings when the finger levers were depressed, of course made them extremely vulnerable to dust and grit, which seriously impaired their efficiency. This drawback was overcome, presumably first by Uhlmann, by the use of external connecting rods, the pistons themselves remaining completely enclosed.

It has often been alleged that the Vienna valve was merely an improved version of Shaw's spring slides, but in point of fact they have but one common feature, twin pistons. Shaw's slides were placed at right angles to a double windway, while in the Vienna valve the pistons are set one behind the other on a single windway; Shaw used a combination of ascending and descending valves as against two, or three, descending Vienna valves; Shaw's valves were independent and the Vienna valves dependent.

Johann Strauss the elder was, it seems, the first to introduce horns and trumpets with *Wiener-Ventil* mechanism to Berlin, when he and his orchestra visited that city in 1835. Later the system was taken up by Belgian makers, especially for trumpets and trombones: so much so, in fact, that in Paris it was commonly known thirty or forty years ago as 'le système belge'. Of late years single-piston and rotary actions have completely swept the board, and the last stronghold of the *Wiener-Ventil* —and even there it is now losing ground—is Vienna itself.

The rotary valve is believed to have made its first appearance about 1832, for in that year Joseph Riedl, also of Vienna, was granted a *k. k.*

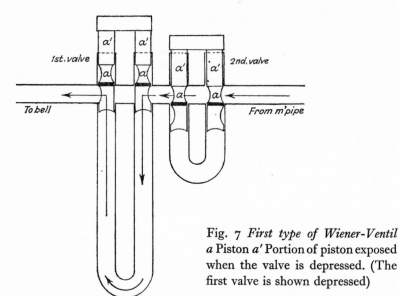

1st. valve   2nd. valve

To bell   From m'pipe

Fig. 7 *First type of Wiener-Ventil*
a Piston *a'* Portion of piston exposed
when the valve is depressed. (The
first valve is shown depressed)

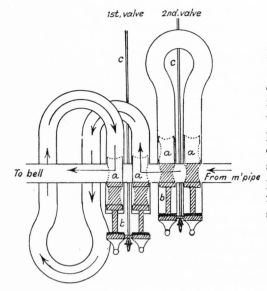

1st, valve   2nd. valve

To bell   From m'pipe

Fig. 8 *Uhlmann im-*
proved Wiener-Ventil
a Piston *b* Connecting
rod exposed when the
valve is depressed. The
piston itself remains
entirely enclosed *c* Actuating spring-controlled
push rod operated by the
finger. (The first valve is
shown depressed)

Privilegium for his *Rad-Maschine*. Apart from the actuating mechanism, apt to be rather complicated, this is the simplest and most efficient of all valves; the rotor and its casing remain the same today as when this valve itself consists of a brass or German silver rotor bored with two parallel channels and housed in a brass casing with four windways, two of them main and two subsidiary. When the valve lever is in the 'up' position there is unbroken continuity between the mouthpiece and the main windway to the bell; when the lever is depressed the rotor makes a quarter turn and the air-stream is diverted through the valve loop before regaining the main windway to the bell.

Operating mechanism was for long the subject of experiment. Probably the earliest was a simple form of articulated crank, similar to that depicted in Fig. 9, such as is seen on the horn by Kersten (Plate VI, 1); this, in a slightly more complex form with an additional articulation, is still by far the most widely used. About the middle of the century direct-acting cranks with a piston-like action were tried out and Higham in Manchester patented such a device in 1857[17] (see Fig. 10). This action was copied by Alphonse Sax in Paris (see Plate VII, 5), but it cannot have been very satisfactory since it was abandoned almost immediately. The American string action (Fig. 11) which, in effect, is really a simplified and more flexible type of direct-acting crank, appears to have been first put on the market by the Schreiber Cornet Manufacturing Company of New York; it was patented by them in 1866.[18] The articulated crank, in some versions of which the articulation takes the form of a ball-and-socket arrangement, and the American string action have now superseded all other actions.

The earliest and still most widely used spring for rotary mechanism is a watch spring coiled inside a small drum, sometimes with an external device to regulate the tension. Most horns, and many other instruments, of the best class are now, however, fitted with simple unenclosed helical springs.

For some reason the rotary valve never found favour in England, France, or Belgium, though every other country adopted it on a large scale almost immediately. A few Paris makers, notably Antoine Courtois, Adolphe and Alphonse Sax, and Gautrot, as well as Distin in London, Higham in Manchester, and Mahillon in Brussels, all made a small number of rotary instruments, but they never seem to have caught the fancy of the players. It is only within the last thirty-five years or so that any rotary instruments were seen in England, but fashion—and comparative ease of playing—have dictated a radical change-over from the French to the German horn with its rotary valves. In France, where the

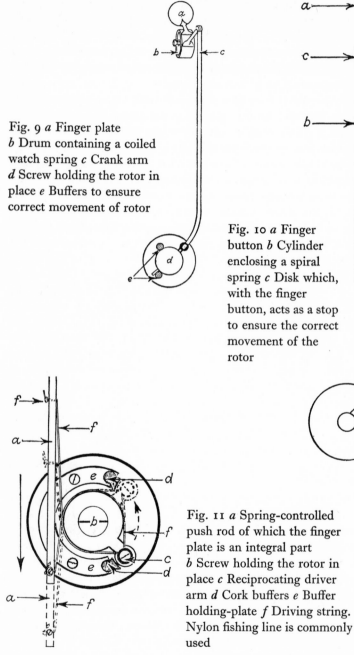

Fig. 9 *a* Finger plate
b Drum containing a coiled
watch spring *c* Crank arm
d Screw holding the rotor in
place *e* Buffers to ensure
correct movement of rotor

Fig. 10 *a* Finger
button *b* Cylinder
enclosing a spiral
spring *c* Disk which,
with the finger
button, acts as a stop
to ensure the correct
movement of the
rotor

Fig. 11 *a* Spring-controlled
push rod of which the finger
plate is an integral part
b Screw holding the rotor in
place *c* Reciprocating driver
arm *d* Cork buffers *e* Buffer
holding-plate *f* Driving string.
Nylon fishing line is commonly
used

double horn is also now widely used, they have evolved their own model which retains the piston action. Belgium appears to have adopted the French instrument.

Ever since the second half of the 18th century when some anonymous, presumably English, maker was the first to provide terminally crooked horns with a tuning slide (*cors à l'anglaise*), the English have never successfully produced an original model of horn. After a few abortive attempts by Key and Köhler, English makers have in the main been content to copy (not without considerable skill, be it said) the models of the continental makers. Until the late 1920s, when musical taste in England suddenly veered round from the once so much admired French horn to the hitherto no less despised German instrument, they not only copied the superb Raoux model but proudly advertised the fact. Since about 1930 England has gradually transferred her allegiance from Paris to Mainz, from Raoux to Gebr. Alexander, so the makers now have to

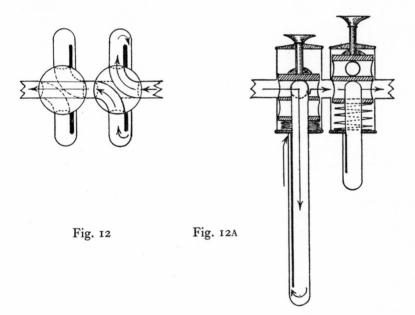

Fig. 12   Fig. 12A

copy the German lay-out, rotary valves and all. There is no question but that the German instrument is not so difficult to master as the smaller-bore French model, and, in these days when a cracked note is considered a heinous crime, this is no mean advantage. Moreover, horns are nowadays expected to be as agile as bassoons.

The first really big step forward in the improvement of the piston valve occurred in 1835 when Wieprecht, soon to become bandmaster-in-chief of the Prussian Guards, in collaboration with the Berlin maker G. W. Moritz, brought out the valves that became known as *Berliner-Pumpen* (Figs. 12 and 12A). They were short and of very large diameter, and the bottoms of the valves no longer served as windways. All the windways lay in the same plane, thus combining to some extent the advantages of rotary valves (ease of blowing and purity of tone) with the mechanically simpler piston action. Adolphe Sax, when he set up in Paris in 1843, owed much of his initial success to this valve which he 'borrowed', with or without permission, from Berlin, for he used it on his early cornets, saxhorns, and saxotrombas. It was without question a great improvement on the slender Stölzel valve with which most makers everywhere were then equipping their instruments, for the 1839 Périnet valve had not as yet proved its superiority.

John Shaw, the English inventor of the *transverse spring slides* already described, took out a second patent[19] in 1838 for what he called his *Patent swivel valves for brass instruments*, the London maker J. A. Köhler immediately acquiring the sole right to exploit them for a term of years. In a modified form this valve enjoyed a measure of success for twenty-five years or so, but it was found impossible in the long run to keep them air-tight and the principle had to be abandoned.

In its original form (Fig. 13) the invention consisted of two plates, in shape not unlike a section of a railway metal, one of them fixed and the other movable, joined together by a central pivot. The fixed plate had two holes to which were attached the leads from the mouthpipe and to the bell, while the movable plate had four holes and carried, in addition to the valve loop, a short bow connecting the inlet and outlet holes in the fixed plate when the valve was not depressed. The inventor states in his specification, however, that the plates may be made circular 'so as never to expose their internal surface to dust or other injury', and it was in the circular form that Köhler made what he called his *Patent Lever* valves. Two trumpets by Köhler with the original circular type of *Patent Lever* valves were exhibited at the Royal Military Exhibition held in London in 1890, and the system is accurately described in detail in Day's catalogue under No. 405.

After making instruments with valves of this model for a year or two Köhler introduced a much-improved version which he called *The New Patent Lever*.[20] The disks of the first model were retained, but this time it was the fixed disk, now also provided with four holes, that carried the valve loop while the movable disk had only two very short bows which, according to the up or down position of the finger button, directed the air-stream either straight to the bell or via the valve loop (Fig. 14). This arrangement made the valve very much lighter in action, and theoretically it was now everything that could be desired, but in spite of a last-ditch effort in the form of a spring arrangement intended to take up automatically any wear due to friction, it still could not be kept air-tight. It is not impossible that Shaw or Köhler, whoever was responsible for the substitution of disks for plates, got the idea from a disk valve invented in Paris by Halary in 1835. From a drawing in Meifred's 'Notice sur la

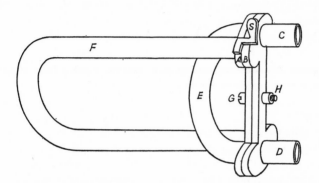

Fig. 13 A Movable plate perforated with holes corresponding with each end of each tube. B Corresponding fixed plate to which are soldered the main windways C and D. E Bow ensuring continuity of windway when the finger plate is not depressed. F Supplementary tubing brought into the circuit in place of E when the finger plate is depressed. G Screw pivot fastening A to B. H Nut to hold A and B in their correct positions. S Finger plate. The spring is a flat one attached by two screws to the far side of B. It is not visible on the drawing
(From the drawing with the patent specification)

fabrication des instruments . . . en cuivre' the Halary system appears to be practically identical with the Köhler *Patent Lever*. Several authorities say Halary patented his device, but they never give a patent number, and diligent search in the French patent files has failed to reveal any trace either of a patent or of provisional protection. In any case Halary never followed up this idea: possibly he foresaw the trouble that finally overcame Köhler.

A large number of these 'patent lever' instruments were supplied to the British army, and eighteen of them were sold to the band of the Crystal Palace when that institution was opened in 1854. A hand-bill issued by Köhler on the occasion of the Great Exhibition of 1851 quotes £33 12s. as the price of a pair of 'patent lever' French horns (Fig. 15) as against £31 10s. for a pair with ordinary, i.e. Stölzel, valves. Horns made about this time and rather earlier, especially in England, sometimes had the valves so arranged that it was the first valve that gave the semitone and the second the whole tone (see Plate VI, 1 and 3): as will be seen from Fig. 15 this was the case for the 'patent lever' horn.

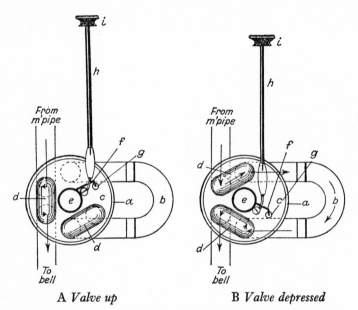

A *Valve up*   B *Valve depressed*

Fig. 14 *a* Fixed back plate carrying the valve loop *b c* Movable plate carrying two short bows *d d e* Spring-box containing coiled watch spring *f* 'Finger' fixed to the revolving outer part of the spring-box and engaging in a ring *g* on the movable plate *h* Push rod *i* Finger button

Before leaving the subject of valves of a more or less experimental nature which, for one reason or another, were either not exploited commercially or did not stand the test of time, there are three others worth a mention, though only one of them was ever put on the market. The first, invented by the horn player Meifred and a Paris mechanic

named Deshays, was patented in 1834.[21] The device, highly ingenious
and original in conception, consisted of twin conjugated wedge-shaped
shutters, called *valvules* by the inventors, working inside the windway
and diverting the air-stream as required through the appropriate valve
loop. The object of this system was to obviate the repercussion of air
caused by the constricted bore and sharp angles inherent in the Stölzel
valve then in general use. But as Meifred himself pointed out,[22] 'the
cost of this system is such as to leave little hope that it can ever be put on
the market'. It never was.

Next in chronological order is the device known as *finger slides*
patented by Samson in 1862.[23] This system, as improved by their
technical adviser Charles Goodison, was made and sold by Rudall, Rose,

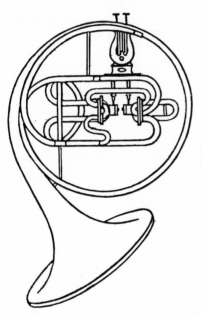

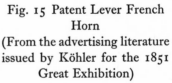

Fig. 15 Patent Lever French
Horn
(From the advertising literature
issued by Köhler for the 1851
Great Exhibition)

Carte & Co. under the name of 'Prize Medal Valves', after the system
had gained an award at the International Exhibition of 1861. The 'finger
slide' is, like the *Wiener-Ventil*, a valve that works entirely inside the
windway, for what appears to be the piston case in fact contains only the
push rod and connection that transmit the up-and-down movement to
the actual valve. The makers listed most classes of brass instruments
with these 'Prize Medal Valves', but as they cost rather more than those
fitted with a modified Périnet valve, which by then was not only quite

satisfactory but also much easier to dismantle for cleaning and lubrication, they were not very successful commercially and specimens are
seldom met with.

The last of these experimental types, like the Meifred/Deshays patent,
was never produced commercially. It consisted of an ingenious and
intricate arrangement in which trombone-like slides could be extended
to the desired length by suitable pressure on a finger button: it was
patented by E. Ford in 1869.[24] Although in theory the perfect compensating system, Ford's device was of far too delicate and complex a
nature to be of practical value, while as far as the horn is concerned, any
mechanical device for correcting the sharpness inseparable from the use
of valves in combination is quite superfluous since the horn player has
always the resource of the hand in the bell to correct his intonation.[25] It
is therefore not necessary to go into any of the ordinary compensating
systems, so many of which found their way into the patent files during
the second half of last century—with a single exception, Gautrot's
système équitonique. This is interesting because it contains the germ of
the modern double horn, and it will be dealt with in due course.

The present-day piston valve is basically that brought out in 1839
by the Paris maker François Périnet. Considering the importance of his
valve, and also the fact that he perfected the *trompe de chasse* by deter-
mining the ideal proportions of its bell, it is surprising how little is
known about Périnet. He worked in the first instance for Raoux but
appears to have set up on his own account in the early 1830s, producing
his valve in 1839 and the model of *trompe de chasse* that is known by his
name in 1855. His name, indeed, is as closely bound up with the *trompe
de chasse* as is that of Raoux with the French horn, and it is still kept alive
by a small Paris firm of specialists making only *trompes de chasse* and,
true to the Périnet tradition, beating out the bells entirely by hand.

The Périnet valve, in diameter midway between the Stölzel and
Berliner-Pumpen types, had air passages that were far less constricted
than those of the former, which resulted in greater ease of blowing and
considerably improved tone. This valve was improved subsequently by
Gustave Besson and Antoine Courtois in France, and by Dr J. P. Oates
in England. It is every bit as efficient as the rotary action besides possessing the advantage of simpler mechanism. For horns it is now being
discarded in England, the inflexible fashion of the day having decreed
that since the large-bore German horn, which has superseded the more
distinguished French type, is made in its native country with rotary
valves, English-made horns must follow suit.

The double horn, now far more widely used than any other for symphony and opera work, combines the tonalities of F and B-flat alto independently in a single instrument. In order to be able to use either section chromatically, double sets of valve loops and valves bored with dual windways are provided. The normal lay-out is made up of a valve, worked by the thumb, which directs the air-stream through the F or the B-flat section at will and three valves that function in the normal way and lower the pitch by two, one, and three semitones; they can, of course, be used in any combination. The amount of additional tubing necessary to lower an instrument by a tone, a semitone, and three semitones is, respectively, about one-eighth, one-fifteenth, and one-fifth of its basic tube length. Loops correct for the F horn (approximately 3·751 m.) and measuring about 0·461 m., 0·225 m., and 0·711 m. would be far too long for a horn in B-flat (approximately 2·812 m.) which needs only loop lengths of 0·343 m., 0·166 m., and 0·531 m. Hence the necessity of two sets of valve loops.

Double horns exist in two versions, the 'full double' and the 'compensator'. The first, as its name implies, has two completely independent sets of valve loops, one set tuned for the F horn and the other for the B-flat, while the second has a primary set tuned for the B-flat horn and a secondary set so tuned that their lengths, when added to those of the primary set, are right for the F horn. The lay-out of the compensating type is shown at Fig. 16. One advantage of the compensating type is an appreciable diminution in the weight of the instrument.

Although the double horn as we now know it dates only from the end of last century, valves with dual windways made on the compensator principle had been invented in Paris as long ago as 1858. A device called *système équitonique* was patented by Gautrot and Marquet in France in 1864, and a year later in England under the name of Brooks.[26] This was one of the earliest of the 'compensating systems' whose object was to correct the sharpness arising out of the simultaneous use of two or more valves—a bane that is particularly noticeable in the case of large instruments of the tuba class. As has already been pointed out, however, the horn player has no need of compensating devices as such, but the *système équitonique* was applied to the horn for quite a different purpose. This is explained by Louis-Adolphe de Pontécoulant in a report on the musical instruments in the International Exhibition held in London in 1861.[27]

'This system', says Pontécoulant,

> can be applied with advantage to the French horn. French horns, as everybody knows, are built in *B-flat* and the valve slides, being tuned for this pitch, have to be re-set for every downward change of

crook: by the time the *E* crook is reached the slides have been pulled out as far as they will go. With the double-acting piston the slides are now pushed home again and a rotary valve is operated, which makes the air pass through a secondary set of valve slides placed at the back of the pistons: the combined length of the two sets of slides gives the correct tuning for the *E-flat* crook. The slides are then pulled out to the requisite extent for every crook down to B-natural basso.

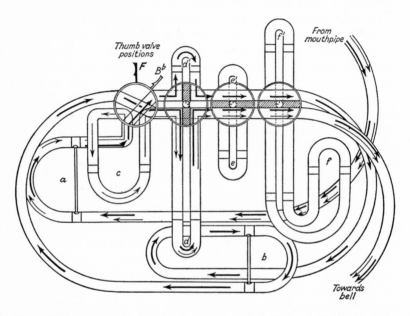

Fig. 16 Diagrammatic sketch of the mechanical lay-out of a double horn in F and B-flat built on the compensating principle.Purely diagrammatic and not to scale, it is merely intended to show the path of the air-stream according to whether the instrument is being played in F or in B-flat

Thick arrows show the path of the air-stream in the F horn.

Thin arrows show the path of the air-stream in the B-flat horn.

The 1st valve is shown depressed

a General tuning slide *b* Tuning slide for F section *c* Tuning slide for B-flat section *d e f* 1st, 2nd, and 3rd valve slides tuned for B-flat *d' e' f'* Supplementary loops to give the correct tuning for F horn *Note* Loop e' is so short that in practice it is hardly ever provided with a tuning slide

However superfluous the device in this form may appear to horn players of the present day, the fact remains that it does embody, and for the first time, the principle on which the modern F/B-flat horn works.

In its present guise the double horn was first put on the market about 1898, and was the fruit of the collaboration of the Erfurt horn maker Fritz Kruspe with a nephew of Friedrich Gumbert, the famous Gewandhaus horn player, professor at the Leipzig Conservatory, and compiler of the ten volumes of the *Solobuch für Horn* which contain difficult and solo passages from repertory works and are an indispensable part of the horn student's library. On the original Gumbert/Kruspe double horn the change from F to B-flat, and vice versa, was effected by means of two small valves connected by a rod and operated by a thumb lever. This arrangement did not prove entirely satisfactory: it was, as Anton Horner[28] puts it, 'rather temperamental in operation', and in 1900 Kruspe replaced it by a single valve in all essentials similar to that in use today. In this same year Schmidt in Berlin produced a double horn with a thumb-operated piston for the change from F to B-flat. This model also had a measure of popularity and was fairly widely used in the United States, but to some hands, including that of the writer, the piston proved awkward to manage.

In 1912 D. J. Blaikley patented a piston-valve F and B-flat horn modelled after the Raoux type of instrument then in universal use in England. It was built on the compensating principle, the valve lay-out being very similar to the Gautrot/Marquet patent of 1864. It met with scant success, however, for London players had not as yet yielded to the blandishments of comparatively new German double horns and only made very exceptional use of the high B-flat crook; when they felt they needed a high crook they nearly always used an A-natural crook. Moreover, these high crooks, especially the B-flat, are apt to sound hard and 'bugley' when used with a small-bore horn.

With very few exceptions the French players have refused to allow themselves to be inveigled into the now prevailing fashion for German horns, and have evolved their own particular model of double horn. Though larger in bore than the old Raoux instruments, they are smaller than the German horns, and have a bell diameter midway between the two. They are provided with the usual French ascending third valve which puts the F horn into G and the B-flat into C alto. Like the Blaikley instrument of 1912, from which its designer, the late Louis Vuillermoz, drew his inspiration, the French double horn is built on the compensating principle and has piston valves. It was first made and marketed about 1930 by the Paris maker Thibouville-Lamy, but was subsequently taken up by other makers, and a rotary thumb valve has been substituted for the piston thumb valve of the original version. Whether it is due to the use of the high B-flat and C tube lengths with a comparatively small bore or to some other factor, it cannot be denied that much of the present-day French tone tends to sound 'saxophoney'.

The rotary and piston actions are now equally efficient, but in the early days the rotary valve was superior to the piston as regards air passages, but not in the matter of its actuating mechanism. The French, English, and Belgian makers, however, devoted their ingenuity to suppressing awkward angles and constricted windways, their efforts ultimately proving completely successful.

Piston valves are certainly far simpler mechanically than rotary valves, but they need frequent lubrication and cleaning: it is, however, a very simple matter to dismantle them. Rotary valves, on the other hand, seldom require attention, but they are bedevilled by a multitude of tiny screws: should one of these work loose and fall out during a performance it is well-nigh impossible to do anything about it on the spot. With the so-called American action a string will occasionally break; this can be fraught with dire consequences if, as happened on one occasion at Covent Garden Opera House, the performer in the wings had just put his instrument to his lips to sound the Siegfried horn call. . . . Such accidents, fortunately, are very few and far between, but it is nevertheless advisable, to say the least, to check strings and/or little screws—these last abound on all types of rotary mechanism—fairly often. It once happened to the writer—also at Covent Garden—that one of these small screws came adrift during a performance, and it was only thanks to a lynx-eyed colleague that it was finally recovered.

NOTES

[1] The only use of independent valves other than by Shaw for his *Transverse Spring Slides* of 1824 was by Adolphe Sax for his six- and seven-piston instruments.

[2] See Busby's *Concert Room and Orchestra Anecdotes*, Vol. 2, p. 175.

[3] Br. pat. No. 1664 of 1788, item vi.

[4] Reproduced in F. W. Galpin's *European Musical Instruments* (London, 1937) and in Birchard Coar's *The French Horn* (Ann Arbor, 1947).

[5] See Appendix 2.

[6] *Revue Musicale de Fétis*, tome II, 1828.

[7] *Neue Berliner Musikzeitung*, 1860.

[8] F.-G.-A. Dauverné, *Méthode pour la trompette*. Paris, 1857.

[9] J. Meifred, 'Notice sur la fabrication des instruments en cuivre'. Paris, 1851.

[10] Br. pat. No. 5013 of 1824.

[11] John F. Russell and J. H. Elliot, *The Brass Band Movement*. London, 1936.

[12] Adam Carse, *Musical Wind Instruments*. London, 1939.

[13] Th. Rode, *Neue Berliner Musikzeitung*, 1860.

[14] There is said to be an edition of three quartets for four chromatic horns composed by Dionys Weber (1771–1842) that contains a drawing of the valve horn as used by Kail. It has so far proved impossible to trace a copy of an edition with this picture. These quartets have recently been reprinted under the editorship, we believe, of Kurt Janetzsky, *Kammervirtuos* of Leipzig, but even he has not come across the drawing.

[15] Dr Walter Bergmann, of the London branch of Schott's, very kindly obtained this information for the writer from his firm's headquarters in Mainz. The horn in question is illustrated in Day's Catalogue, Pl. XI.

[16] The curator of the Crosby Brown Collection, Dr Emanuel Winternitz, was good enough to send the writer a photograph of this trumpet (Cat. No. 89.4.1098) together with a sketch of the piston mechanism, which shows conclusively that these valves are ordinary half- and whole-tone descending valves.

[17] Br. pat. No. 123 of 1857.

[18] Br. pat. No. 2468 of 1866.

[19] Br. pat. No. 7892 of 1838.

[20] That Köhler should have changed the name 'Patent Swivel' into 'Patent Lever' evidently ruffled Shaw, for in 1855, after the expiry of the licence, he published an open letter announcing that he could now supply the trade generally with his 'Patent Swivel' valves 'by him, Mr. Köhler, unaccountably called *The Patent Lever Instruments*, in the same detached state as they have during the term of the patent been supplied to Mr. Köhler'. (Rudall Carte's *Musical Directory* for 1855.)

[21] Fr. pat. No. 4002 of 1834.

[22] J. Meifred, *Méthode pour le Cor Chromatique ou à Pistons*. Paris, 1841; supplement on ascending third valve c. 1849.

[23] Br. pat. No. 1245 of 1862.

[24] Br. pat. No. 3165 of 1869.

[25] The following is the explanation of the rise in pitch inevitable when valves are used in combination:

Horn in F measures 3·751 m.
To lower this a semitone needs 0·225 m.   Horn in E=3·976 m.
To lower this one tone needs 0·461 m.   Horn in E-flat=4·212 m.
To lower this 3 semitones needs 0·711 m.   Horn in D=4·462 m.

If we put the horn in E-flat by depressing the first valve, we have a tube length of 4·212 m., but to lower this a further semitone we need an additional 0·250 m. as against the 0·225 m. provided by the second valve slide as tuned for F horn. The discrepancy is still more marked in the combinations 2+3 and 1+3 (respectively horn in D-flat and C basso), for the valve combinations give us only 4·687 m. and 4·923 m. as against the required 4·726 m. and 5·006 m. The players get round the occasional necessity of using these combinations by suitable use of the hand in the bell. As regards the third valve, the foregoing remarks do not, of course, apply to instruments with the French ascending third valve.

[26] Br. pat. No. 741 of 1865.

[27] '. . . Ce système s'applique avantageusement au cor d'harmonie. Les cors sont, on le sait, construits en *si-bémol*, les coulisses des pistons sont accordées sur ce ton, on est donc obligé de les tirer pour chaque ton de rechange que l'on ajoute à l'instrument; lorsqu'on arrive au ton de *mi*, les coulisses sont entièrement tirées et il est impossible de les accorder avec le ton de *mi-bémol*, tandis qu'avec le piston à double effet, lorsqu'on est arrivé à ce ton de *mi*, on rentre les coulisses et on ouvre un cylindre qui fait passer l'air dans le second jeu de coulisses placé derrière les pistons; ces coulisses réunies donnent la longueur nécessaire pour s'accorder avec le ton de *mi-bémol*, et on les tire ensuite graduellement pour chaque autre ton de rechange jusqu'au *si-naturel* bas'.

[28] The writer is indebted to Mr Osbourne McConathy, of the Boston Symphony Orchestra, for the information about the earliest double horns which he was kind enough to obtain from that distinguished Germano-American horn player and teacher Anton Horner. Horner, who retired some twenty-seven years ago from the Philadelphia Symphony Orchestra, of which he was principal horn for twenty-six years, was himself a pupil of Friedrich Gumbert at the Leipzig Conservatory. He was the first prominent horn player in the United States to use a double horn, having acquired his first Kruspe in 1899, when he was first horn of the Pittsburgh Orchestra under Victor Herbert.

CHAPTER 4

Omnitonic Horns

WITH THE GENERAL adoption, in the latter part of the 18th century, of individual crooks for every key, the horn became a very cumbersome affair to transport with its heavy wooden box fitted to take the instrument and anything from nine to fifteen crooks. This did not bother the virtuoso soloist. His concertos and *airs variés*, as well as any chamber music he was likely to play, were always written for horn using one or other of the best solo crooks—F, E, E-flat, or D—with the E-flat crook as the most favoured by the classical composers, so that he needed to carry but four crooks and could, if he so wished, put the lot in a bag. Moreover, if he was one of the great stars, he would probably have had a manservant to carry his instrument for him.

The less fortunate and far more usual type of orchestral player was in a very different case. With a diversity of engagements for which he would require a minimum of nine crooks—B-flat alto, A, G, F, E, E-flat, D, C, and B-flat basso—it can have been neither easy nor pleasant to have to struggle along dark, narrow, dirty streets carrying an awkwardly shaped box weighing, maybe, twenty or twenty-five pounds. His need for some device that would eliminate the necessity of loose crooks was therefore a very real one. It was this need that led to the practically simultaneous invention of the valve in Germany and the omnitonic horn in France. Both types did away with the loose crook, but there was an essential difference between them: the action of the valve was instantaneous, that of the omnitonic horn was not.

The early German valve horns were built in F as a unit, and had no provision for loose crooks: there were just the two spring-controlled valves with rigidly fixed valve loops which enabled the performer to switch his instrument at will from F to E, E-flat, or D and back again. Players could, and for a long time did, confine themselves almost entirely to hand technique in the four keys at their disposal, but they could also play in other keys by transposing their parts as we do today. The second harmonic (written as pedal C) in the keys of D-flat, C, B-natural, and B-flat basso could not be played as a true valve note, but the satisfactory performance of any of these would have been no obstacle to a properly trained second-horn player.

The omnitonic horn, of French origin but manufactured sporadically in other countries, carried, on the other hand, enough incorporated tubing to enable it to be put into a wide range of keys. The crook change was effected by setting a graduated plunger, rotary tap, or other equivalent mechanical device, but the operation, while quicker and quieter than loose crook changing, was not instantaneous like the action of the valve and a scale of open notes at any useful speed was quite out of the question. The valve horn always could be, and today generally is, played without the smallest knowledge of hand technique, but the omnitonic horn relied exclusively on hand-horn methods.

That any maker should have persisted in trying to produce improved types of omnitonic horn once the valve horn had got properly into its stride—the perfect example, if ever there was one, of flogging a dead horse—may at first sight seem strange. Up to about 1845, however, there was a perfectly good reason.

During the first half of last century the hand horn was greatly esteemed by musicians generally, and any mechanical device to increase its scope was looked upon askance, not only by competent critics but also by the large body of uninformed concertgoers on the ground that its character was being changed and its quality debased. The difference in shade between open and stopped notes as well as between one stopped note and another was deemed to give the horn a peculiar quality and charm possessed by no other instrument. Many feared, rightly as events were to prove, that general adoption of the valve horn would lead to the complete disappearance of the older instrument, and that the music conceived for it by the classical composers would no longer be played as the composer had visualized. Quite a lot of attention was paid, too, to the subtle differences in tone colour between the high, medium, and low crooks, and the early valve horn, being confined to the medium crooks, could offer neither the hard brilliance of the first nor the velvety warmth of the last. Added to all this was the mechanical imperfection of the early valves: sharp angles and constricted windways impaired both the tone and the freedom of emission. There was also, perhaps not unnaturally, some hostility on the part of skilled hand-horn players in the fear, only too well founded, that their positions might be jeopardized by the valve horn, in some respects easier to play, which opened up such tremendous new possibilities to the composer by freeing him from the tyranny of the natural harmonic series. So strong, in fact, was the prejudice against it in France that when Meifred, for whom a valve-horn class had been instituted at the Paris Conservatoire in 1832, retired in 1864, the class was suppressed and the instrument absolutely barred from that institution until it was tentatively re-introduced by Brémond in 1897, even so becoming the official instrument exclusively only in 1903.

The photograph on Plate V, 1, shows what appears to be the first omnitonic horn ever made. Clearly an experimental model, it was made by J.-B. Dupont of Paris about 1815, and the only known example is preserved in the museum of the Paris Conservatoire. It has eight independent tube lengths, each complete with its own mouthpipe: by setting a graduated slide at the back of the instrument and placing the mouthpiece in the corresponding mouthpipe the horn could be put into B-flat alto, A, G, F, E, E-flat, D, or C, as required. Its weight is formidable, considerably more than that of a modern double horn, and this alone would have made it unacceptable to players who only a few years later were to find the weight of a two-valve horn unduly fatiguing.

In May 1818 Dupont took out a patent[1] for a much more advanced model (Plate V, 2), but seems then and there to have disposed of all the rights in this invention to the Paris maker J.-C. Labbaye who, in the following year, was producing the instrument as his own. In the Bottin directory for 1820 Labbaye describes himself, amongst other things, as the producer of a mechanized French horn giving nine tonalities, from B-flat alto to B-flat basso, without changing a crook or removing the mouthpiece, 'modulating into any tonality, like an ordinary horn but in less than a second'.[2] Unfortunately part of the notched slide as well as the spring catch are missing from the specimen in the photograph, so in order to show how the mechanism works a reproduction of the drawing that accompanies the patent specification is included here (Fig. 17).

A more conventional type which, though evocative of a forkful of spaghetti, was far superior to either of the foregoing, was brought out in 1824 by Charles Sax in Brussels. It is made like an *Inventionshorn*, but in place of a single crook the slide carries several loops of tubing which suffice to give the same nine keys as those available on the Labbaye horn. Like every other instrument of its class, except Dupont's first experimental model, it is built on the compensating principle, the only way to avoid excessive weight. A graduated central plunger ensures that the right amount of tubing for the tonality required is incorporated into the main windway. The system was patented in France in 1826 in the name of one Stuckens, not a maker, so presumably a patent agent. The reproduction of the drawings accompanying the specification included here explains the working of the mechanism (Fig. 18). A noteworthy feature is the provision of a water-key, the prototype of that fitted nowadays to brass instruments of almost any kind. There is no doubt that Sax's ingenious omnitonic horn had a considerable measure of success,

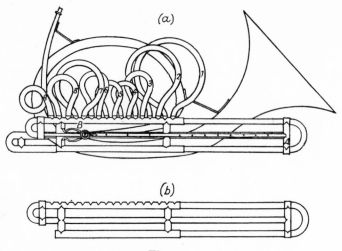

Fig. 17

(from Dupont's 1818 patent specification)

Fig. *a* Side view of the horn
Fig. *b* Sectional view of the slide

The instrument can be put into any one of nine tonalities
like an ordinary horn: *viz.*, B-flat, C, D, E-flat, E, F, G, A,
and B-flat alto, in accordance with the numbers 1, 2, 3, 4, 5,
6, 7, 8, and 9, shown in the drawing. To change the tonality
the slide is pushed into the appropriate position and fixed by
means of the spring catch B

and Fétis gave it a favourable notice in *La Revue Musicale de Fétis*.[3]
Other makers copied it, presumably under licence, among them being
Sautermeister of Lyons. The slide carrying the omnitonic mechanism
could be replaced by a lighter version giving only the tonalities of F, E,
and E-flat, the keys most often needed by the soloist (see Plate V, 3).

Another omnitonic horn somewhat on the same lines was brought
out by the Dutch maker Embach. It had the same changes of tonality as
the Sax and Labbaye instruments, the changes being obtained in this
instance by a graduated milled wheel at the base of a large cylinder.
There is a specimen in the Brussels Conservatoire museum (No. 2721),
described by Mahillon on page 392 of Vol. IV of the catalogue. There is
another in the collection of the Berlin Hochschule für Musik (No. 3022),
and an illustration of it will be found in Curt Sachs's catalogue.

Several clever versions of the omnitonic horn were patented by P.-L.

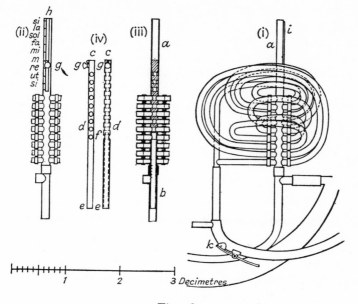

Fig. 18

(from the Stuckens 1826 French patent specification)

Fig. i   Front view of complete mechanism

Fig. ii Back view, convoluted tubing removed

Fig. iii Sectional view, convoluted tubing removed

Fig. iv Cylinder by which changes of tonality are made

The mechanism is composed of a straight tube *a* to which are soldered nine loops corresponding with each other. The junction of one or more of these loops can be interrupted by the tube shown, in front and side views, at Fig. iv and at *b* in Fig. iii. Eight of the holes bored in this tube go right through, but the ninth *f* is bored on one side only. This tube slides into tube *a*, and by its position one or more loops are brought into play so as to give the total tube length necessary for the desired tonality. An indicator-plate, graduated as shown in Fig. ii, is fixed to the top of tube *a*, and a pointer operated by the knob *g* attached to tube *b* enables the instrument to be set as required.

The prototype of the present-day water-key is shown at *k* (Fig. i)

Gautrot, whose pioneer work in the improvement of brass instruments has been rather lost sight of in the blaze of publicity and official patronage that surrounded every word and deed of his contemporary Adolphe Sax.[4] Many of his inventions were extremely ingenious, even if they were not always practical. His first omnitonic horn, patented in 1847, had three rotary quick-change taps and a double tuning slide. It possessed the advantage over previous horns of this type of allowing for as many as twelve crook changes, namely B-flat, A, A-flat, G, F, E, E-flat, D, D-flat, C, B-flat basso, and A basso. The complicated adjustments of slides and taps required to switch from one tonality to another seem, at any rate on paper, to be quite as lengthy a process as changing an ordinary crook, and this, together with what, for a hand horn, must have been an excessive weight, no doubt accounts for the fact that it attracted little notice in professional circles. A few years later Gautrot produced a couple of omnitonic models with valves, and these will be noticed later. His last valveless omnitonic horn—probably the last instrument of this class ever made—appeared in the 1870s. It was made by M. Miramont, who died in 1935 after having been with the firm for sixty-five years. This very odd, octopus-like instrument has a single central rotary tap from which radiate eight windways (Plate V, 5). Only six tonalities are available: B-flat alto, A-flat, G, F, E-flat, and D-flat, from which it is evident that this horn was intended for the wind band and not for the orchestra.

For all their ingenuity Gautrot's many ideas were, with two notable exceptions, in the main still-born. The shadow of Adolphe Sax, thanks to that influence in high places that assured him the monopoly of supplying all the French official bands, hung heavily over the brass instrument industry of Paris during the 1840s, '50s, and '60s, and obscured many an invention that might otherwise have attracted far more attention than it did. The two exceptions were the *système équitonique*, already mentioned in Chapter 3 as the basis of the modern double horn, and a matter of industrial policy.

This policy was the manufacture, on mass-production lines and under one roof, of brass, woodwind, and stringed instruments of the cheaper sort. True, Gautrot's predecessor and erstwhile partner Guichard had already inaugurated the era of 'factory-built' brass instruments of the class known in France as *pacotille*,[5] as well as turning out others of a superior class, and by 1844 was employing as many as 210 workmen. In the following year Gautrot bought out his partner, took over the firm, and became the first European musical instrument maker to introduce divisional labour and steam-driven machinery into his factory.[6]

This was really the first step towards the replacement of the artist-craftsman, often a professional player of good standing, by industrial processes governed by the drawing board and remote control: the business tycoon and the scientist in place of the artist. Two of the artist-craftsmen of last century who immediately come to mind are Marcel-Auguste Raoux, one-time principal horn at the Théâtre Royal Italien (Paris), and Jules Halary, who was one of the horns in the Paris Opéra orchestra. These artist-craftsmen are still to be found in Germany, a case in point being the well-known Erfurt maker Ed. Kruspe, whose head for many years was George Wendler, a former principal horn of the Boston Symphony Orchestra. This industrialization is, in some ways, no doubt a good thing, and in keeping with the present age. To the more sensitive player, however, the factory-built instrument for all its scientific perfection, will always lack an indefinable 'something' that only the artist-craftsman who has conceived it and nursed it through from sheet metal to finished product can put into it.

As far as is known the only omnitonic horn ever produced in England was the 'Radius French horn', designed by John Callcott and almost certainly made by Thomas Key of Charing Cross (Plate V, 4). Callcott, who was for many years third horn in the opera orchestras at the King's and His Majesty's theatres (London) under Spagnoletti, Costa, and others, issued, on the occasion of the Great Exhibition of 1851, a prospectus in which he describes his instrument as follows:

> The novelty of this invention is in dispensing with loose crooks, by making (within the hoop of the instrument) a continuous tube, which is divided into semitone lengths, at each of which a portion of tube leading from the bell to the centre of the hoop, turns there to any of the above-mentioned divisions (which divisions produce the different keys) and there receiving the wind carries it to the bell.

At each semitone division there is a valvelet that diverts the wind into the appropriate tube length and into which fits an articulated 'goose-neck' directly connected with the mouthpipe. The idea is an extremely ingenious one, and the horn can be crooked in every semitone from B-flat alto to B-flat basso inclusive. It came too late to be commercially successful, for by that time the valve had got well over its teething troubles and the valve horn was everywhere fast superseding the hand horn. So, in spite of the most flattering testimonials from prominent London players (among them Puzzi, who by then had given up active horn playing to devote himself to his business as an impresario, Charles Harper, and Kielbach), it did not meet with the success it would surely have commanded had it made its appearance twenty years earlier. Of all the known types of omnitonic horn without valves it is assuredly by far the best designed. It figured in the 1854 price list of Rudall, Rose & Carte, its cost being £14 10s.

If we do not hear of any German omnitonic hand horn, the reason no doubt is that the Germans made regular use of valve horns at a very much earlier date than the French, the Belgians, or the English. Nor has the writer knowledge of any Italian omnitonic horn.

Omnitonic Horns with Valves

1. Gautrot

The first to combine an omnitonic system with three ordinary valves was apparently P.-L. Gautrot aîné who took out a patent for such an instrument in 1854.[7] The omnitonic system was made up of two quick-change rotary taps, the larger bored for ten windways and the smaller with four. The small tap, like its modern counterpart, made only a quarter turn and served exclusively to lower the pitch of the instrument a semitone. The large tap, provided with a pointer, was marked B-flat alto, A-flat, F, E-flat, D-flat, and B-flat basso, which were the tonalities available with the small tap closed; with this open the horn could be put into A, G, E, D, and C. But the valve loop of the smaller tap has an impossible task, since it can neither be made short enough to give a proper A nor long enough for a good D or C, though, of course, these last tonalities, as well as B-natural basso not otherwise obtainable, could be had with the ordinary valves. Small wonder, then, that Gautrot brought out in the following year a revised version much simplified, with only one rotary tap,[8] the semitones now being obtained by means of the ordinary valves instead of by the small rotary tap. Ten crook changes were available with this model as against eleven with the original version, the missing tonality being the important one of B-flat alto.

Gautrot obviously expended a great deal of ingenuity as well as a lot of money in his quest of the needless, but his perseverance in the experimental field did lead him a few years later to his système équitonique which, as was shown in Chapter 3, was the true parent of the compensating double horn. There could be little point in cluttering up with heavy rotary taps and their concomitant tubing a three-valve horn which could be put into any key from F to B-natural basso—or perhaps it would be better to say into any of the six semitones below the basic pitch of the instrument—by valve combinations alone: the higher crooks, assuming a horn built in F, could have been made available with one rotary tap and quite short lengths of tubing. This was actually done later, though by another maker and with different mechanism, as will be seen when we come to the Prager horn. Gautrot pursued the mirage of a horn that could be played chromatically with the valves, irrespective of the crook: he seems to have been quite oblivious of the fact that the use of valves, even if they could be tuned properly, with the lower crooks results in such excessive tube lengths that the air-column becomes virtually uncontrollable.

2. Chaussier

Henri Chaussier (1854–?) was a virtuoso hand-horn player who enjoyed a certain reputation as a soloist but was less successful as an orchestral performer. Engaged for a season in Berlin with the Bilse orchestra, he found he was expected to play everything on a valve horn in F, in conformity with German practice.[9] Accustomed always to playing his part on the crook for which it was written he found himself suddenly confronted with transposition problems that gave him a great deal of trouble, and his rather unfortunate experiences on that occasion led him to design a horn on revolutionary lines. Chaussier's horn had four valves (Fig. 19) with which he could put it into any key from B-flat

Fig. 19 The Chaussier
omnitonic horn

alto to B-flat basso, but to play a chromatic scale called for fingering totally different from that of the long-standardized three-valve instrument.

Valve lay-out of the Chaussier horn

Open horn stands in F.

Valve 1 lowers pitch 1 tone, gives horn in E-flat.

Valve 2 raises pitch $\frac{1}{2}$ tone, gives horn in F-sharp.

Valve 3 raises pitch 2 tones, gives horn in A.

Valve 4 (thumb) lowers pitch $2\frac{1}{2}$ tones, gives horn in C.

Valves 1+3 raise pitch 1 tone, give horn in G.

Valves 1+2+3 raise pitch $1\frac{1}{2}$ tones, give horn in A-flat.

Valves 2+3 raise pitch $2\frac{1}{2}$ tones, give horn in B-flat alto.

Valves 1+2 lower pitch $\frac{1}{2}$ tone, give horn in E.

Valves 1+2+3+4 lower pitch $1\frac{1}{2}$ tones, give horn in D.

Valves 1+3+4 lower pitch 2 tones, give horn in D-flat.

Valves 1+2+4 lower pitch 3 tones, give horn in B-nat. basso.

Valves 1+4 lower pitch $3\frac{1}{2}$ tones, give horn in B-flat basso.

Mahillon criticizes[10] the Chaussier horn seemingly without having given it much thought. After giving the valve lay-out he draws attention to the fact that the first valve is expected to lower the A horn to G as well as the C horn to B-flat basso, and that the second (ascending) valve has to raise the pitch from A to B-flat alto and also from B-flat basso to B-natural.[11] Expressed thus, the system appears absurd, and Mahillon dismisses it with a snort of contempt. But on the face of it a horn player with a reputation as a virtuoso to safeguard would be unlikely to waste time and money on an instrument that could not be played in tune, and a somewhat closer study of the system reveals a large number of different ways of getting a required note by a different harmonic of a different tube length. Such are the pitfalls that may ensnare the most erudite person if he—or she—is not an experienced player of the instrument criticized.

When we look at Chaussier's own fingering chart, which he calls *Doigté rationnel de la gamme chromatique*, we find that valve 4 is never used except for the pedal note (second harmonic) of the D, D-flat, C, and B-natural horns. These low notes are very flexible and can be brought into perfect tune with the lip without loss of quality. We see also that there are alternative fingerings for every note that lies higher than No. 6 in the harmonic series of its tube length. Lastly, pedal B-flat (second harmonic of the B-flat basso horn) is not played on the B-flat basso tube length but as the fundamental of the B-flat alto combination. Chaussier further gives a warning that when the instrument is to be used as a hand horn in one of the lower tonalities, say for a solo, the main tuning slide and the slides of the descending valves (valves 1 and 4) must be pulled out sufficiently to cancel out the sharpness arising from the combination of valves.

Chaussier's *Doigté rationnel de la gamme chromatique* is given below, his fingerings being shown above the notes. The alternative fingerings given below the notes are not included in the *Doigté rationnel*; they serve to show some of the many possible ways of keeping the intonation under control.

Doigté rationnel de la gamme chromatique

The above scale is in actual sounds, Chaussier's idea being to treat the horn as a truly chromatic instrument, like the piano or a stringed instrument. The transpositions necessary to play parts for horns in various keys would be effected by reading them in the appropriate clef—mezzo-soprano clef for horn in F, bass clef for horn in E or E-flat, alto clef for horn in D, etc., etc., adding in the sharps or flats as the key may require. This would offer no difficulty to a player properly trained in *solfège*.

Provided the performer has studied the instrument with intelligence there is no reason why the intonation of the Chaussier horn should not be every bit as good as that of the standard three-valve instrument, in spite of certain valve combinations theoretically preposterous but in practice used only in exceptional circumstances and after suitable adjustment of the tuning slides. That, in fact, it was seems pretty clear from the report of a comparative trial of the Chaussier horn, an orthodox three-valve horn, and a hand horn that was held on 11 April 1891. The contest was between the Chaussier horn, played by Chaussier himself, and the three-valve horn in F played by Garigue *fils*; the hand horn, played by Henri Gruyer, principal horn of the Châtelet (Colonne) concerts, served merely as a standard of comparison for the performance of old works written expressly for that instrument. It took place in the presence of ten well-known French musical personalities, among them being Théodore Dubois, Principal of the Paris Conservatoire, Vincent d'Indy, Paul Vidal, Ernest Chausson, and Constant Pierre. As the result of the voting shows—nine in favour with one abstention—Chaussier came through with flying colours. A detailed account of the trial was published in a special report by the periodical *L'Orphéon*, on whose premises it took place. The instrument cannot therefore have been as defective as Mahillon would have us believe.

Though there might be some objection—actually more valid on paper than in practice—that to switch from a high to a low crook in the course of a single passage would cause undesirable inequalities of tone colour, the chief obstacle to its general acceptance was the different fingering. Players being what they are, and since the advantages of the Chaussier horn really only amounted to the ability to use it as a hand horn with twelve instantaneous crook changes, they completely rejected it. The days of the hand horn, even in France, its last stronghold, were by then numbered, and Brémond himself, stalwart champion of the hand horn though he was, would have none of it. Full details of this interesting and ingenious experiment are given in Chaussier's *Notice explicative sur les nouveaux instruments en UT* (Paul Dupont, Paris, 1889) as well as in Constant Pierre's *La Facture instrumentale à l'Exposition de 1889* (Librairie de l'Art Indépendant, Paris, 1890).

3. *Prager (Zurich)*

The photograph on Plate V, 6, shows a remarkable instrument which, for lack of a more appropriate place, may serve to conclude the procession of omnitonic horns, although it cannot in truth be classed as one. Any possible use of it as a hand horn that can instantly be crooked in any key does not appear to have been in its inventor's mind—it is really too heavy for such a purpose—and the underlying idea was, no doubt, the provision of safe alternative means of getting high notes that are apt to be uncertain or even downright bad on an ordinary three-valve horn in F. The inventor of this system was Hermann Prager, a retired Zurich musician whose hobby it was to devise, in collaboration with August Knopf of Markneukirchen who actually made the instruments, complicated mechanisms comprising valves that could either be *ascending* or *descending* according to whether the thumb valve was up or down. These instruments he patented under the name 'Siegfried' horns.

Edgar Knopf, son and successor of August Knopf, has very kindly informed the writer that, from correspondence between his father and Prager, it transpires that the primary object was to construct a horn on which a chromatic scale could be played either by raising or by lowering the pitch of the open notes. Since Prager was an old gentleman of eighty the last time he visited the Knopf factory, in 1937, and August Knopf died during the war, it is unlikely that much further information on the subject will be forthcoming. Edgar Knopf very kindly enclosed in his letter photographs of the first five models of the Prager horn, and although it is impossible to tell from them the precise function of each valve—never fewer than six—it is clear that at least four of these models could be played as an ordinary three-valve horn in F with, of course, the possibility of using all the open notes of the shorter tube lengths up to B-flat alto. None of these models is quite like that pictured on Plate V, 1, though the differences are differences of detail only. Each successive model—some ten or a dozen of these horns were made, mostly between 1933 and 1937—would have embodied improvements not necessarily discernible on a photograph.

The writer's first-hand acquaintance with these horns is limited to two. The first of them he saw for a few moments in a Geneva instrument repairer's shop more than thirty years ago; it completely mystified him. The second, that shown on Plate V, he had in his keeping for a day or two and was thus able to examine it at leisure.

The valve lay-out of this last is as under:

(a) *Thumb valve not depressed.* The valves are independent. The pitch of the open horn is F.

Valve 1 raises the pitch $\frac{1}{2}$ tone giving horn in F-sharp.

Valve 2 raises the pitch 1 tone giving horn in G.

Valve 3 raises the pitch $1\frac{1}{2}$ tones giving horn in A-flat.

Valve 4 raises the pitch 2 tones giving horn in A.

Valve 5 raises the pitch $2\frac{1}{2}$ tones giving horn in B-flat alto.

(b) *Thumb valve depressed.* The valves become dependent and the instrument is transformed into a chromatic three-valve horn in F with the valves lowering the pitch by one tone, a semitone, three semitones, two tones, five semitones, and three tones according to the normal three-valve practice. Valve 5 acts as a muting valve with the chromatic horn.

It is difficult to see what advantage this complicated system could be supposed to have had over the standard F/B-flat double horn, which offers everything the Prager instrument could give, with, in addition, a fully chromatic horn in B-flat. It is included here for its curiosity value as showing to what lengths human ingenuity will sometimes go to find a different solution to a problem already satisfactorily solved.

There may have been, and probably there were, other omnitonic systems that do not happen to have come within the writer's purview, but, whatever the system, always they were just sporadic curiosities which never gained general acceptance. Their *raison d'être* utterly ceased once the valve had got over its early mechanical troubles. They do, how-ever, provide a picturesque backwater in the development of the modern horn, and as such are well worth preserving whenever specimens are found—which will not happen very often.

NOTES

[1] Fr. pat. No. 892 of 1818.

[2] 'Auteur d'un cor d'harmonie mécanique portant neuf tons depuis le si-haut jusqu'en si-bas sans changer de ton ni d'embouchure, modulant dans tous les tons en moins d'une seconde, dans le même système que le cor ordinaire'.

The 'si-haut' and 'si-bas' here mean B-flat alto and B-flat basso, and not, as they would today, B-natural. The Germanic origin of the orchestral horn was still near enough for French makers to use German markings fairly often for crooks: the E-flat crook, for instance, was often marked 'DIS'. B-natural was never a standard horn crook, and the 'si' here is simply the equivalent of the German B used to indicate B-flat, B-natural being written H.

[3] *La Revue Musicale de Fétis.* 1833 (p. 172).

[4] For particulars see Fr. pats. No. 3170 of 1 July 1847, and *certificats d'addition* dated 20 Sept. 1847, 11 Feb. 1848, and 6 May 1851; No. 11407 of 22 July 1854, and *certificat d'addition* dated 15 Jan. 1855.

[5] *Pacotille* is more or less equivalent to the English Brummagem.

[6] See Constant Pierre, *Les Facteurs d'instruments de musique*, pp. 363 and 364.

[7] Fr. pat. No. 1407 of 22 July 1854.

[8] *Certificat d'addition* dated 15 Jan. 1855.

[9] H. Chaussier, *Notice explicative sur les nouveaux instruments en UT*. Nouvelle édition, Paris, 1889.

[10] V.-C. Mahillon, *Catalogue . . . du Musée Instrumental du Conserva-toire Royal de Musique de Bruxelles*. Vol. 2, p. 495.

[11] Approximate supplementary tube lengths required:

To lower pitch from A to G add 36 cm.
To lower pitch from C to B-flat basso add 63 cm.
To raise pitch from A to B-flat alto subtract 16 cm.
To raise pitch from B-flat basso to B-natural subtract 32 cm.

It is therefore evident that a supplementary tube length in the first case of 46 cm. (normal length of first valve slide on F horn), and in the second of 22 cm. (normal length of second valve slide on F horn), cannot appear otherwise than ridiculous on paper. In practice, however, the performer, should he want to play a passage with hand-horn technique in one of these keys, would take the precaution of adjusting his valve slides so that his instrument was in tune over the required harmonic series. If he were playing the same passage by valve-horn methods, he would use his valves in the knowledge that he could avail himself of one of several alternative fingerings for nearly every note in the instrument. For instance, he is not obliged to use the B-flat basso tube length in order to play a concert B-flat; the note can be had on the E-flat, D-flat, A-flat, and F-sharp tube lengths. It would, in fact, be possible to play a better enharmonic scale on the Chaussier horn than on an ordinary three-valve instrument.

CHAPTER 5

The Evolution of Playing Technique

OF ALL WIND instruments with a place in the modern orchestra none, as far as its playing technique is concerned, has had so varied an existence as the horn. In the three hundred-odd years that have elapsed since composers of standing began to take notice of it, the manner of playing it has passed through no less than three major phases, the last of which is again divisible into three sub-phases. Each of these phases and sub-phases has involved a more or less complete revision of the technique previously in favour.

The first phase covers the musical horn in its simplest form, which gradually increased in length, as the players in skill, from the latter part of the 16th century down to about 1750. Rather more than half-way through this period the technique branched out in two different directions. One of them remained the hunting horn pure and simple, finding its ultimate expression in the fanfares composed by the marquis de Dampierre, *gentilhomme des chasses et plaisirs* at the Court of Louis XV, which are still used and have never been surpassed:[1] the other, embracing the technique of the coeval trumpet, became the orchestral horn and reached its apogee in the works of J. S. Bach and his contemporaries.

The second phase covers a period of just about one hundred years, roughly from 1750 to 1850. Then it was that the horn achieved the 'personality' that gave it its unique position in the orchestra. The value of the low register was recognized and appreciated by musicians generally, hand-horn technique budded, flowered, and withered, and the horn proved itself not only an ideal blending agent between the different orchestral groups, but also a picturesque, if occasional, soloist in symphonic music. It was the golden age of the virtuoso as well as that during which the horn acquired its not wholly undeserved reputation of being the most difficult of all instruments to master.

Phase three was ushered in, very tentatively at first, by the invention of the valve during the first quarter of the 19th century. The overlap from phase two was, however, considerable, for the cult of the hand horn persisted in most places until about 1850, and in France, as we have already seen, right up to the beginning of the present century. In the first of the three subdivisions, which lasted only a comparatively short time, the two valves with which the horn was originally provided were considered essentially as a quick and easy way of changing crook, hand technique being retained throughout except where a note required so much stopping that it was ineffective, in which case advantage was taken of the valves. The leading early protagonists of the valve horn were Kail in Prague, Meifred in Paris, and the brothers E.-C. and J.-R. Lewy in Vienna. A Strasbourg correspondent of the *Harmonicon* (Vol. V, 1827) writes as follows of a performance given in that city by E.-C. Lewy: 'In a concert given by Mr. Levy, hornist, from Vienna, this artist delighted a numerous audience by his admirable performance on the keyed-horn,[2] in which taste and science, sweetness and power were admirably blended'. At the first concert ever given by the *Société des Concerts du Conservatoire*, on 9 March 1828, Meifred played a valve-horn solo, this being the first occasion on which it was heard by a Paris audience. The next subdivision is that of the development of the fully chromatic horn, made possible by the now widespread adoption of a third valve, with Wagner pioneering an entirely new way of writing for it. Schumann's *Adagio und Allegro* for horn and piano (op. 70), composed in 1849, is a well-known example of the treatment of the horn as a fully chromatic instrument over its entire range: this work cannot be played satisfactorily on a two-valve instrument. No doubt there are earlier and less well-known German examples in a similar vein, for in Germany regular use was made of the three-valve horn many years earlier than in France or England. This subdivision culminated in the works of Richard Strauss, which make such heavy technical as well as physical demands on the player that something had to be done about it. That something, which brings us to the last subdivision, was the introduction, about the turn of the century, of the F/B-flat double horn, and the gradually increasing abandonment of the F horn in favour of the B-flat/A instrument by habitual first- and third-chair men. With the exception of the French version all these double horns and single B-flat/A horns are made after the large-bore German model with rotary valves: they have now completely superseded the older small-bore type except in some English military bands.

Each of these phases has had, and has, its own peculiar qualities and defects. As we may gather from that letter of Lady Mary Wortley Montagu quoted in an earlier chapter, the sound of the horn played in the manner of phase 1 was not everybody's idea of the sound beautiful, though the best players of that day no doubt extracted from their instruments a brilliance as unfamiliar to modern ears as the sound of the shawm.

When hand technique came into fashion it, too, was severely criticized in certain quarters. We read, for instance, in *New Instructions for
the French Horn*, published by Longman, Lukey & Co. between 1772
and 1779:

> Should you want to make the cromatic tones . . . one hand must
> be within the edge of the Bell ready to put into the Pavilion or Bell
> of the Horn as notes require; . . . Mr. Ponto[3] . . . constantly
> uses this method, by which means the half tones are expressed,
> which is not to be done by any other method: but it is deemed by
> Judges of the Horn that the principal beauty, the tone, is greatly
> impaired thereby.

Again in Rees's *Cyclopædia*, Dr Burney, who contributed the article
on the horn (written in 1803), says:

> It must, however, be discovered by every discriminating hearer,
> that the factitious half notes that are made by the hand in the mouth
> of the instrument, are sounds of a different quality from the natural
> tones of the instrument. We have often thought that Ponto,[3] with
> all his dexterity, produced some of these new notes with similar
> difficulty to a person ridden by the night mare, who tries to cry out
> but cannot.

Nevertheless, it was to hand technique, and especially to the improved
quality of tone due to the retention of the hand in the bell even for the
production of notes in the natural harmonic series, that the horn owed
its initial success as an orchestral instrument. Many of the virtuosi,
particularly those of the early 19th century who usually composed their
own solos—of the 'Fantasia' or 'Air and Variations' order as a rule—
greatly overstrained the legitimate resources of hand technique, thereby
bringing it into disrepute. Even so fine an artist as Puzzi, considered by
many competent judges to be the finest horn player of his day (the first
half of last century, when solo horn playing was in its heyday), drew a
damning criticism from a correspondent to the *Musical World*.[4] The vast
number of laudatory notices of Puzzi's playing, however, puts this uninformed criticism where it belongs and amply justifies his international
reputation. It is nevertheless true that the intrinsic qualities of the horn
show up to much greater advantage in movements of moderate tempo
than in efforts to compete with the clarinet in a *prestissimo*.

The appearance of the valve gave rise to much adverse criticism on
the ground of its deleterious effect on the tone. This was undoubtedly
quite justified at a time when the mechanism was still very imperfect

and the valves were being used mainly as a quick way of crooking the horn in a fresh key. The constricted passages and sharp angles in the windway were bound to jeopardize sureness of attack, and at the same time give a tone that compared unfavourably with that of the freer-blowing natural horn. Even after mid-century, when the mechanism left little or nothing to be desired, there were still diehards to whom the valve horn would always be anathema.

Today we are inclined to decry the tone of the now ubiquitous German horn as 'wooffy' in F and 'bugley' in B-flat. This criticism is often, though not always, justified, especially to ears old enough to remember the beautiful quality of the true French horn in the hands of such masters as Paersch and the brothers Alfred and Aubrey Brain in England, or Edouard Vuillermoz and Emile Lambert in France, who assuredly cracked no more notes than their peers of today. The German horn is, of course, more powerful, and it is a good deal easier to play. Its general adoption has been of immense benefit to the less gifted performer owing to its near-immunity from that bugbear of the old instrument, the cracked note. In the greater facility of execution, however, there lurks the danger of allowing technique to become an end rather than a means. It should never be forgotten that the finest qualities of the horn show up to much greater advantage in a movement of moderate tempo, such as, for instance, the Nocturne from *A Midsummer Night's Dream* exquisitely played, than when it seeks to rival the agility and speed of the clarinet, however masterly the rendering.

Another danger to tonal quality and perfect intonation is the present tendency to neglect the many and varied uses of the hand in the bell, apart from the production of what we now call 'stopped notes': even here we find only too often a mute being substituted for the hand.

It would be a great pity to let the horn, with all its unique tonal resources, degenerate into something that was little more than a brass-band baritone which, for all its admirable qualities in its own sphere, is no substitute for true French-horn tone in the orchestra. Imagine the famous horn quartet in the overture *Der Freischütz* played on four baritones!

PHASE I (*up to mid-18th century*)

This phase is almost entirely pre-orchestral, for it was not until the early years of the 18th century that the horn began to be used, very tentatively at first, as a true member of the orchestra. So, in considering the evolution of the instrument's technique, we must perforce deal at some little length with the hunting horn.

Until the latter part of the 17th century the recognized field signals—elaborate codes date at least from the 14th century—were confined to a single note of indeterminate pitch sounded in conventional rhythmic patterns. The oldest code known to the writer is to be found in a curious little book on hunting written in 1349 by Hardoyn, seigneur de Fontainnes Guérin, entitled *Le Livre du Trêsor de Vanerie*; it was first printed and published in Metz in 1856 by H. Michelet. This work, illustrated with woodcuts, is entirely in verse and contains fourteen different calls or *cornures* written out in a very odd notation and accompanied by descriptive couplets. In his monograph *Le Cor de Chasse*[5] H. Kling draws attention to this book, quoting all the calls and some of the descriptive verse. He gives his interpretation of Hardoyn's signs in modern notation, which appears quite logical as given below:

■	mot sengle	♩
☐☐	demi double de chemin	♫
☐☐☐☐	double de chemin	♫♫
■☐☐	mot double de chasse	♩ ♫
■■	long	♩ or 𝅝
■☐☐	mot de chasse et d'apel	♩ ♫♩

No English code as old as this is known to the writer, but in an unusual and valuable paper he read before the Royal Musical Association in 1954[6] Eric Halfpenny gave an account of Turberville's *Noble Art of Venerie*, which was published in 1575 and contains an elaborate code of seventeen calls. This code, with slight variations and 'Marsh's additions' which appear to date from about 1650, was in regular use in the English hunting field until about the middle of the 18th century. In France Dufouilloux published a code in 1560, or thereabouts, that was in use there for a century and a half, and Mersenne quotes ten of his calls. There is no resemblance whatever between the Dufouilloux and Turberville codes beyond the fact that in the first instance the Turberville code was written down in the musical notation of the time, as was that of Dufouilloux. By 1700 or shortly after, the hooped *cor de chasse* had attained a sufficient tube length to warrant an entirely new and musical code, of which the marquis de Dampierre was the chief architect, the shorter horns being then completely abandoned.

From about 1600 and for as long as the Marsh code was in use English calls were set out in certain conventional signs, instead of in musical notation, thus:

The ancient Hunting Noats with Marsh's additions.
Names of Noats[7]

/—/ tone, ⌢ ton, ȯ tavern, ô ton-tavern, ö ton-ton-tavern, etc.

Then follows a series of eighteen calls. At the bottom of the 'Sculpture' we read: 'These Noats are taught & Sould by Michaell Marsh at ye Huntsman at Holbourne Bridge'.

In musical notation these signs would probably be the equivalent of something like this:

/—/ tone .	.	.	.	♩
⌢ ton	.	.	.	♩ or ♪ (but not used by itself)
ȯ tavern .	.	.	.	♫
ô ton-tavern	.	.	♫ ♩ (♪)
ö ton-ton-tavern	.	.	♬

The earliest known example of this method of setting down the different calls is a manuscript sheet entitled *Directyones to Wynde the Horne*, which is signed by one Henry Sayer and appears to date from the early years of the 17th century. The credit for drawing attention to this almost unknown piece belongs to Eric Halfpenny, who reproduces a fragment of it in his R.M.A. paper.

By the dawn of the 18th century the hooped hunting horn capable of sounding upwards of twelve harmonics was everywhere making headway. In Central Europe it found its way not only into the hunting establishments of kings and lesser potentates but also into the theatre orchestra. The French made it a necessary apanage of the hunt in all its forms, and it became a very essential part of the pageantry and court etiquette that ruled the royal hunt of Louis XV.

In England, where it was already well known—indeed judging by an extant 17th-century specimen the English were in advance of the continental makers—it found many and varied uses, although it was never generally adopted in the hunting field where the straight or slightly curved horn about 20 inches long was preferred. It was, however, much employed for popular open-air entertainment. The rich and powerful often numbered French-horn players among their retainers to lend panache to their equipages and give pleasure to their guests at home as, for instance, when the duke of Newcastle was host to Queen Caroline at Claremont in 1729 and they 'walked till candle-light, being entertained with very fine French horns'. Many of these French horn players were negroes, and the notorious Lord Barrymore had four such in his retinue.

Another negro, Cato by name, was in the service first of Sir Robert
Walpole and then of the earl of Chesterfield. When, in the summer of
1738, the prince and princess of Wales and their children arrived at
Cliefden, they received as a present from Lord Chesterfield 'Cato (his
Black), who is recon'd to blow the best French horn and Trumpet in
England'. The prince of Wales appointed Cato head gamekeeper first at
Cliefden and later at Richmond Park. Cato's portrait, in a group of
hunting celebrities, was painted by Wooton.[8]

Typical of the kind of music they played are the five pieces for two
French horns given in Appendix 3 (a to e). These are all taken from one
or other of the two editions of *The Compleat Tutor for the French Horn*,
the earlier one published by John Simpson *c.* 1746 and the other about
ten years later by Peter Thompson. The completely valueless instructions for playing the instrument are believed to have been the work of
'Mr. Winch[9] and other eminent Masters', and are almost word for word
the same in both editions, though the selection of duets is entirely
different. Identical text will be found again in *Instructions for the French
horn* in *The Muse's Delight, or Apollo's Cabinet*, a compendium of instructions for a number of different instruments, published in Liverpool
in 1757. The type of horn used would have been the ordinary French
horn without crooks, similar to that shown in Plate II, 5. The tutors tell
us that: 'There are several sizes, and different pitches, as G, F, E, D and
C; but most Masters allow a D Horn to be the best to begin with'. It is
likely that the duettists used horns in F in preference to any other key.
The five pieces for two French horns, which will be found in Appendix
3 (a, b, c, d, e), show that technique had already reached a fairly high
standard, though with a single exception—but a notable one—it was the
technique of the trumpet. The exception (e: '*Minuet* by Mr. Festin')[10]
provides a very early instance of the use of the pedal notes of the horn,
then to all intents and purposes completely ignored, as well as a manner
of writing for the instrument much favoured by later composers. 'The
Early Horn' (see Appendix 3 f) seems to have been a very popular
virtuoso number, often performed by 'request'. All these pieces are said
to have been edited by Mr Winch.

A few English and French hunting calls of different periods, but of
much the same sort of meaning, are quoted below. It is presumed that
all signals used in the hunting field before the latter half of the 17th
century were sounded on one note with horns of the simplest possible
nature.

Four early 18th-century fanfares for *cor de chasse* will be found in
Appendix 3 (g).

Hardoyn (1394)

Cornure de Chasse

Un demi-double III-mos sengles
Et III-doubles de chasse sengles
D'un trait puis V-mos chascun double
Dont ceste ystoire oste le trouble.

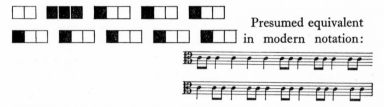

Presumed equivalent
in modern notation:

Dufouilloux (1560)

Si les Piqueurs se trouuent au deuant de la meute, et qu'ils voyent
le cerf a veuë, ils doyuent forhuer[11] et sonner de la Trompe
plusieurs fois, en motz longs ainsi:

Tran   tran   tran   tran tran tran tran

Antient Hunting Noats with Marsh's additions (c. 1650)

Presumed equivalent
in modern notation:

To uncouple the hounds:

/—/o̊ o̊ o̊ o̊ o̊ o̊̂/—/

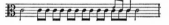

Compleat Tutor for the French Horn (Simpson edition, c. 1746)

The View

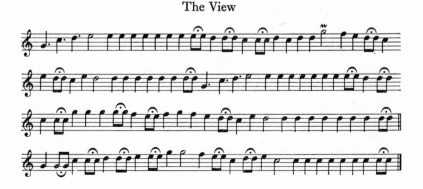

Diderot et d'Alembert, *Encyclopédie* (1767)

Ton pour la première vue

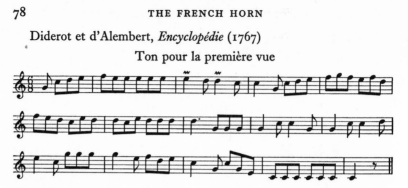

In 'The View' the recurrence will be noticed of two quavers with a pause sign over them, reminiscent of *ton-tavern*: the following is the explanation given in the three instruction books of how they are to be played.

'When you meet with the following Notes which are slur'd ⌒ they must be expressed after a jirking manner'.

ton nah ton nah ton nah ton nah ton nah ton nah ton nah ton nah

'Observe to sound the four Minims in one Breath and jirk the two last only'.

ton   ton non   ton   ton non non   non   nah ___

The explanation, no doubt obvious to the author's contemporaries, is by no means clear today. It can only be supposed that the first quaver is to be tongued and the second produced by a sharp exhalation without intervention from the tongue. There would appear to be some analogy between our anonymous author's 'jirked' notes and an indication given in a couple of lines in de Salnove's *La Vénerie Royalle* (Paris, 1655), which reads: '. . . et sonnez, si vous voulez, le premier ton de gresle, et les autres entrecoupez du gros ton, en cette sorte: Ton hon, Ton hon, Ton hon'. The *ton de gresle* would be a note sharply attacked with the tongue, and the *gros ton* one obtained by simple exhalation.

Many French hunting calls have for a long time past been played in the style known as *tayauté*, the notes to be played in this manner having a sign ⌒ placed over them:

played thus

It was in Italy that the orchestra first began to take shape, and so, not unfittingly, it is in the works of Italian composers that we first find the horn included in orchestral scores. Two well-known examples are quoted below, one from Cavalli's opera *Le nozze di Teti e di Peleo*, first produced at the Teatro San Cassiano in Venice in 1639, and played again in Paris in 1654; the second, still better known, is from Lully's incidental music to Molière's comedy *La Princesse d'Elide*, which was part of the first large-scale fête given at Versailles. This consisted of a grandiose spectacle called *Les Plaisirs de l'Ile enchantée*, which lasted for three days, Lully's music being performed on the second day, 7 May 1664.

Both examples are simple fanfares: the first may be intended for four horns only with the fifth part played on a bass viol, but the second clearly requires five horns.

Attention was drawn to the Cavalli example by Hugo Goldschmidt in a paper entitled 'Das Orchester des Italienische Oper im 17 Jahrhundert', which appeared in *Sammelbände der Internationalen Musik-Gesellschaft* (2 Jahrgang, 1900–01). The author, transcribing the musical examples from the original score, uses the now seldom seen soprano and mezzo-soprano clefs as well as the treble, alto, tenor, and bass clefs, so overleaf, for convenience, the parts are given in the treble and bass clefs only.

It is generally assumed that the execution of this fanfare requires two horns in C alto (2·50 m.) and two in C basso (5 m.): the fifth part, if played on a horn, could be equally well played by either. The C basso horns are considered essential on account of the E's in the first and last bars of the third horn part and in the last two bars of the fourth horn part. This E is the fifth harmonic of the five-metre horn and, theoretically at any rate, it cannot be produced on an instrument half this length. In practice, however, it can be done, though not without some difficulty. Dauprat, in his *Méthode*, devotes part of *Leçon XIV* to its production without the aid of the hand in the bell. In the writer's experience it is a note that 'speaks' more readily on some instruments than on others, but in any case a lot of practice and a flexible embouchure

Le nozze di Teti e di Peleo
Atto 1, scena 1. Chiamata alla Caccia

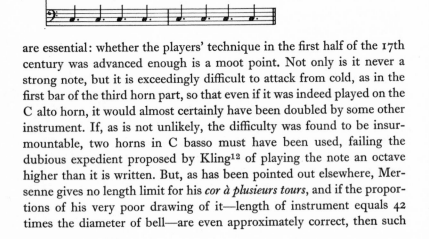

are essential: whether the players' technique in the first half of the 17th
century was advanced enough is a moot point. Not only is it never a
strong note, but it is exceedingly difficult to attack from cold, as in the
first bar of the third horn part, so that even if it was indeed played on the
C alto horn, it would almost certainly have been doubled by some other
instrument. If, as is not unlikely, the difficulty was found to be insur-
mountable, two horns in C basso must have been used, failing the
dubious expedient proposed by Kling[12] of playing the note an octave
higher than it is written. But, as has been pointed out elsewhere, Mersenne gives no length limit for his *cor à plusieurs tours*, and if the proportions of his very poor drawing of it—length of instrument equals 42
times the diameter of bell—are even approximately correct, then such

2. 'Air des Valets de Chiens et des Chasseurs
avec des Cors de chasse'

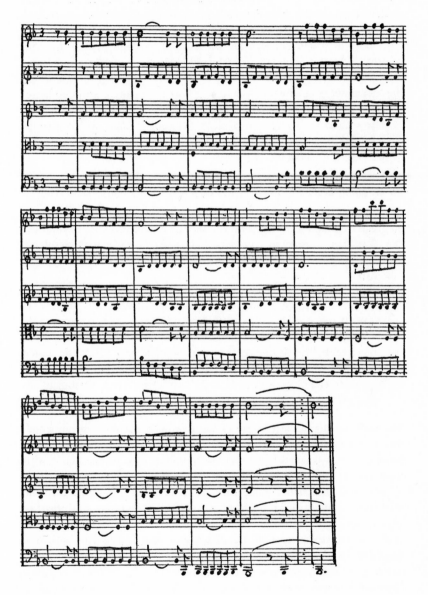

an instrument with a 12 cm. bell would have a total tube length in the region of five metres, which would meet the case of the longer horns. The problem of manufacturing a five-metre horn with the narrow tubing characteristic of the true French horn would probably have overtaxed the resources of the makers of that day in any case, but the comparatively large-bore helical horn, well known from the second half of the 16th century, at least in its smaller sizes, would have presented no insuperable difficulty. Pending further evidence we are forced to the conclusion that the instruments used were four helical horns, two small and two large: the large ones might well have been specially made for the occasion.

The second example, from Lully's *Princesse d'Elide*, which is given on page 81, is taken from a copy of the manuscript of Philidor *l'aîné* in the Paris Conservatoire Library.

The three highest parts, written in these clefs in the original, are here given in the ordinary treble clef.

Although this fanfare is a trifle more ambitious than that of Cavalli, no greater demands are made on the skill of the performers, beyond the fact that they appear to combine their horn blowing with acrobatic dancing. A note in manuscript which precedes the music reads as follows:

> Lyciscas s'estant levé avec toutes les peines du monde et s'estant mis à crier de toute sa force plusieurs cors et trompes de chasse se firent entendre, et concertés avec les Violons commencèrent l'air d'une entrée sur laquelle six valets de chien dansèrent avec beaucoup de justesse et de disposition reprenant à certaines cadences le son de leurs cors et trompes. C'estoient les sieurs Paysant, Chicanneau, Noblet, Bonard et la Pierre.[13]

The names are evidently those of the five horn players, the unnamed sixth being a dancer only. How le sieur la Pierre, who presumably played the fifth part, managed to intersperse moments of capering about with great neatness and zeal with adequate performances on an eighteen-foot horn of any kind defies conjecture. It is, of course, possible that the horns were actually blown off-stage, as they would be today, and that the dancers simply went through the motions.

The instruments required for this fanfare are all in B-flat, with one the length of a modern cornet, three the length of a horn in B-flat alto, and one the length of a horn in B-flat basso (i.e., 5 metres or 18 feet). This last is needed on account of the D in bars 9 and 10, unless one or other of the alternative methods already discussed was employed: in that case the part could perfectly well be played on a horn in B-flat alto, using the fundamental, which 'speaks' readily on all horns pitched in G or higher, for the pedal note in the last bars.

Theatrical and symphonic works employing horns in a purely illustrative manner were heard from time to time in France during the first half of the 18th century. Morin's[14] *La Chasse du Cerf*, performed before Louis XIV at Fontainebleau on 25 August 1708, and a *Concerto de Trompetes, Cors de Chasse, Hautbois et Tymbales*, given at a Concert Spirituel on 23 April 1728, are cases in point. It was not before about the middle of the century, however, that the horn got a regular seat in the orchestra in France, and that only after the music-loving *fermier-général* Riche de la Pouplinière had imported for his own private band players from Germany with instruments provided with crooks.

What appears to be the first use of horns as an integral part of the orchestra occurs in Reinhard Keiser's opera *Octavia*, produced at Hamburg in 1705, when Handel was connected with the Hamburg Opera-House. Shortly afterwards horn players began to be engaged at more and more of the important musical establishments in Central Europe, though for the next fifty years or so the technique was essentially that of the coeval trumpet. The range was from the fourth harmonic to the eighteenth or even higher, irrespective of the key of the horn—Bach, in Cantata No. 14, takes the B-flat alto horn up to the eighteenth harmonic —the first horn covering from the sixth harmonic upwards, and the second from the fourth to about the fourteenth. Musically, horns were used like an organ stop, sometimes soli and sometimes doubled by other instruments.

The artistic development of the horn in Bohemia, under the enlightened patronage of count von Sporck, was favoured by the existence of aristocratic hunting establishments with numerous hunt servants skilled in blowing the horn: these could be, and were, drafted into their masters' house orchestras as and when the need arose. The Church, too, encouraged music, and a musical education up to a very high standard was given in various monasteries. In England, on the other hand, the use of the *cor de chasse* was virtually confined to the field of light entertainment. It therefore seems likely that most, if not all, the early English horn players were trained in the first instance on the trumpet, thus acquiring that mastery of the upper register, so necessary for the works of Handel and others. (See Appendix 3a and 3f.) Altenburg[15] carries the trumpet's range up to g′′′. These early parts that were viewed with such trepidation, until perhaps a few years ago when the double horn and the horn in high F became generally known—though even now they are not undertaken without some qualms—would therefore have had few terrors for the trumpeter-hornists of Handel's day. It is extremely probable that most of these old players, whose tone would have been more akin to that of the *trompe de chasse* than to that of the horn as we are accustomed to hear it now, used mouthpieces bearing a closer resemblance to that of the trumpet than those commonly employed at the present time: also they would have played with the 'trumpet embouchure'—that is with most of the mouthpiece on the lower lip—instead of the 'horn embouchure' with most of the mouthpiece on the upper lip. We can only speculate in this matter, for no really informative tutor existed before about 1800; in all probability no detailed instructions were ever put on paper and professors taught their pupils by word of mouth and example alone.

As the century advanced and the knowledge of hand stopping increased, so the art of playing these very high notes gradually fell into desuetude. By 1800 command of the highest register was no longer necessary since elaborate melodic passages between the sixth and twelfth harmonics had now become possible, with results infinitely preferable to the eldritch screech of the stratosphere.

Most players will be familiar with the more exacting of Bach's and Handel's horn parts, if only from the Gumbert and other collections of difficult orchestral passages. But Bach and Handel were not the only composers of their time who wrote in this way for the horn; here are four less well-known examples:

TELEMANN. *Tafelmusik* (1733), *3 Produktion*, No. 3 Concerto à 7 for two horns in E-flat—the horn is here called *tromba selvatica*—strings and continuo. Both horn parts are virtuoso material.

(Miniature score, with a foreword by Walter Bergmann, published by Eulenburg.)

MAURICE GREENE. *Florimel; or, Love's Revenge*, a dramatic pastoral composed in 1737. The ritornello to the bass aria 'Beneath that shade' contains two horn parts characteristic of the writing of that period. The passage in question is quoted in W. F. H. Blandford's paper 'The French Horn in England' (the *Musical Times*, August 1922).

LEOPOLD MOZART. *Sinfonia di Camera* (1755). This work contains a very difficult horn part which goes up to the twenty-second harmonic of the horn in D.

HAYDN. *Divertimento a tre per il corno di caccia* (1767) for horn in E-flat, violin, and cello. The horn part bristles with difficulties of every sort, and covers the enormous range of from the second to the twenty-second harmonics.[16]

Both the Leopold Mozart and the Haydn would extend to the utmost the capacity of any modern player equipped with the most up-to-date instrument although, it must not be forgotten, the works were both written for the simplest kind of horn at a time when hand stopping was in its infancy and still almost unknown. No English chamber music calling for horns appears to have been written at this period, from which it may perhaps be inferred that the musicianship of the English players was not equal to that of their German and Austrian counterparts. Nevertheless, judging by the pieces for unaccompanied horns given in Appendix 3, their technique must have been of a pretty high standard.

Of the players of the first half of the 18th century we know little beyond a few names for, unlike dramatic criticism which was flourishing, musical criticism both in England and on the continent was practically non-existent. Among the few whose names broke through the anonymity of mere orchestral lists are two with the unusual accomplishment of playing two French horns at once. The first of these was one Joachim Friedrich Creta who, at a concert in London in 1729, was announced 'to blow the first and second treble on two French horns in the same manner as is usually done by two performers'. Unfortunately, we have no account of the actual performance, but if we had, it would no doubt be couched in terms very similar to those used by the concert reporter of the *Mercure de France* when, twenty or so years later, a similar phenomenon appeared at a Concert Spirituel in Paris: he writes 'A German, M. Ernst, played single-handed a concerto for two horns, a novelty that proved more curious than pleasing'.[17] As it no doubt did. Mattheson speaks of another remarkable horn player, blind from birth but nameless, who performed at Hamburg 'producing more notes than the organ possesses, though with less precision'.[18] Had he discovered the art of hand stopping fifteen or twenty years before the generally accepted date, or was he the first to produce chords in public? History does not tell us.

Another was that versatile but nebulous personage described in the *Dublin Mercury*, in the announcement of a concert to be given by him on 12 May 1742, as 'Mr. Charles, the Hungarian, Master of the French Horn'. This gentleman, who played horn solos, duets with 'his second', and occasionally trios with his wife as third horn, also performed on the clarinet, the 'Hautbois de Amour', and a mysterious instrument called the 'Shalamo'. At a follow-up concert on 19 May he played 'by particular desire' 'The Early Horn', which is transcribed in Appendix 3 (f). Mr Charles was also the author of *Twelve Duettos for two French Horns or two German Flutes,* which appeared in *The Muse's Delight, or Apollo's Cabinet* published by John Sadler in Liverpool, in 1757. The 'instructions' that precede these duos are not, of course, by Mr Charles, but are taken, practically word for word, from the Simpson and Thompson tutors and, as we have seen, were probably the handiwork of Mr Winch. Mr Winch was himself a soloist of some note in Dublin as well as in London, besides having played in 'Mr. Handel's operas and oratorios for several years'. We hear, too, of the Messings, of whom Burney wrote in Rees's *Cyclopædia* that they were 'the first who pretended to perform in all keys in England, about the year 1740'. The name of Frederick Messing figures in *Mortimer's London Directory* (1763) as a violinist as well as a horn player, but it was in the latter capacity that he took part in the Three Choirs Festival at Worcester in 1755, and again at Hereford in the following year. Lysons refers to him as 'an eminent performer on the chromatic French horn'.[19] It is clear that the references to performing 'in all keys' and 'chromatic French horn' can only mean that Messing used an instrument provided with crooks, which were then a complete novelty in England: hand stopping was first introduced to an English audience when Punto visited London in 1770 or 1771. Lysons also quotes the text of an advertisement for a concert to be given by Messing at the Devil Tavern, which reads:

MR. MESSING

Goes to the Devil this present Thursday, to prepare a polite serenade, both vocal and instrumental, for the entertainment of his well-wishers and benefactors.—To begin at half an hour after six o'clock. Tickets to be had at the place of performance, the Devil Tavern, Temple-Bar; and of Mr. Messing, at the Golden Acorn, in James-Street, Covent Garden. Red, 5s. White, 3s.

Note. One of the vocal parts by a lady who never performed in public.

And so, from the unsophisticated pleasures of mid-18th-century England, we pass on to Phase 2.

PHASE 2 (mid-18th to mid-19th century)

This was essentially the hand-horn phase, when the instrument won its musical spurs and became a permanent and indispensable member of the symphony orchestra. It saw the rise of the internationally famous virtuoso horn player, whose vogue was to endure for upwards of fifty years.

During the first half of the century, under the enlightened impetus of Sporck, the artistic resources of the horn had been explored and developed in Bohemia and Saxony, the culminating point being the discovery, about mid-century, that by placing the hand in the bell, keeping it there, and using it as a shutter to be opened or closed as circumstances might dictate, it was possible to produce a number of notes foreign to the operative harmonic series. At the same time the mere presence of the hand in the bell, by mitigating the instrument's native coarseness, transformed its tone quality and promoted it at one bound from the stables to the drawing-room.

It has been generally assumed that this new use of the hand in the bell was 'invented' by Anton Joseph Hampel, or Hampl, second horn in King Augustus III of Poland's famous orchestra at Dresden.[20] What seems more likely is that Hampel extended and codified a technique about which at least something must have been known much earlier, even if little or no practical use had been made of it, at any rate so far as the horn was concerned. For it is by no means impossible, nor even improbable, that certain trumpet players who used the so-called Italian (circular) trumpet—such, for instance, as Gottfried Reiche, Bach's principal trumpeter in Leipzig—put their fingers in the bell of the instrument in order to improve the intonation of the eleventh, thirteenth, and fourteenth harmonics. It has even been suggested[21] that Fantini, the celebrated Tuscan trumpeter of the first half of the 17th century, used hand stopping to produce the scale stigmatized by the duc de Créqui's trumpeters as 'tonos praedicti tubicinis spurios, confusos et plenitus inordinatos fuisse'.[22] The hypothesis is neither unattractive nor unduly far-fetched.

Although it may be an exaggeration to credit Hampel with 'inventing' hand stopping *totus porcus*, there is not the slightest doubt that he made order out of chaos to such good effect that the outcome of his labours was accepted then and there by the musical world at large. As evidence of this we have only to look at the luxuriant crop of virtuoso soloists, nearly all of them of Bohemian or Saxon origin, who were so much appreciated on the concert platform from about 1760 onwards.

The only detailed account we possess of the origin of hand stopping, which credits the whole discovery to Hampel, is to be found in the historical notice at the beginning of Domnich's *Méthode de Premier et de Second Cor*. Heinrich Domnich, a native of Würzburg and the son of a horn player in the service of the Elector Maximilian III Joseph of Bavaria, probably got his information in part from local hearsay—he was only born in 1767—and in part from Hampel's most brilliant pupil, Punto, under whom he studied.

The passage is worth quoting in its entirety, not only for what it says but also for what it does not say. (The tutor was published *c.* 1808, and was intended for use at the Paris Conservatoire.)

> The Hautboy was then far from the state of perfection it has now reached, and was a raucous, harsh-toned instrument, ill-fitted to accompany a graceful air or for music of an expressive nature. When it was needed for such purposes the custom was to insert a plug of cotton into the bell. Hampl, one of the most celebrated horn players of that time [here a footnote says: 'He lived at the Court of Dresden about sixty years ago'], had the idea of trying this method instead of a mute. The first time he made the experiment he was surprised to find that the pitch of his instrument rose by a semitone. In a flash of inspiration he realized that by alternately inserting and withdrawing the plug he could cover without a break every diatonic and chromatic scale. He thereupon composed some new music for the horn that included notes hitherto foreign to the instrument. Soon afterwards, finding that the plug could be replaced advantageously by his hand alone, he discarded the plug altogether.[23]

So much Domnich tells us. What he does not say is that pitch-raising mutes had been in use with trumpets ever since the first half of the 17th century, so that Hampel's astonishment can scarcely have been caused by a phenomenon of which he must have been well aware, since he was known to have experimented extensively with mutes of various kinds. If we repeat his experiment using, say, a pair of rolled-up socks in place of the cotton plug, of which we do not know the exact nature, we shall find the pitch will be progressively lowered as the socks are pushed farther in until the point is reached when they will go no farther, whereupon the pitch rises a semitone. It was surely this hitherto undiscovered faculty of being able to blow 'hot and cold', so to speak, with one and the same appliance that amazed him when it suddenly dawned on him that here was the germ of an entirely new technique fraught with tremendous possibilities.

In Ersch and Gruber's *Encyclopædia* Frölich recounts that Hampel made some experiments with a view to replacing the horn mute then in use by something better, and to that end made a wooden stopper which closely filled up the opening of the bell. He was surprised—once again—

to find that, while making the tone softer, his stopper lowered the pitch a semitone.

These apparent contradictions have led many dictionary and text-book writers astray, some having favoured pitch-raising and others pitch-lowering, and it is to be feared that even today there are some who should know better who would be unable to say whether stopping the bell raised or lowered the pitch. . . .

Domnich then goes on to say that Hampel, having created what was virtually a new instrument, restricted his own use of hand stopping to movements in slow tempo since he was no longer a young man when he made his discovery, and that it remained for his pupil, Punto, to bring to fruition all the latent possibilities and brilliance of the new technique.

There were, however, others in the field as early as or earlier than Punto, among them being Rodolphe, who introduced hand stopping to a Paris audience in 1765 or perhaps even in 1763; Mozart's friend Leitgeb, of the prince archbishop of Salzburg's orchestra, who played concertos on two occasions in 1770 at the Concert Spirituel in Paris; and Spandau, the Dutchman, who played in London in 1773 and whose stopped notes attracted the favourable notice of Sir John Hawkins. Although all these were players with big reputations, Punto was without question the most brilliant of them all as well as the most outstanding personality. This combination of ability and personality in a solo horn player was never equalled, let alone surpassed, until the advent of the British player Dennis Brain, whose untimely death at the age of thirty-six in 1957 was such a grievous loss to music everywhere.

Of Hampel's own methods we know practically nothing, for his tutor, in its only known form as revised and published by Punto, is by no means informative. For the first fifty years or so of the recognized existence of hand technique nothing explicit seems to have been written about it, so that the student, having acquired some general notion of it, either from a teacher or by hearsay, had to work out for himself the niceties of the business. One may even suspect that the horn players of Bohemia and Saxony, who developed it, regarded the art in the light of a vested interest whose secrets were to be divulged only to an élite and not to be dissemi-nated to all and sundry through the medium of print.

Apart from Hampel himself and his partner Karl Haudek, probably the earliest exponent of hand technique was Jean-Joseph Rodolphe, Punto's senior by eighteen years, who was in the service of Philip, duke of Parma between 1754 and 1760. During that time he played a con-certante horn accompaniment to an air by his teacher of harmony and counterpoint, Tommaso Traetta, and also accompanied motets in churches on the horn. Rodolphe is said to have been the first ever to do this, and he must, on the face of it, have used hand stopping for the event to have been thought worth recording. It was this same Rodolphe who, in 1765 when Punto was still under twenty, introduced the new technique to a Paris Opéra audience when he played an obbligato to Boyer's air 'L'Amour dans ce riant bocage', sung by Joseph Legros, the leading French counter-tenor of his day, who later became director of the Concert Spirituel. It has not been possible to trace this particular obbligato, but another, written six years later, accompanying an ariette in *La Fête de Flore* by Jean-Claude Trial, and also written for Rodolphe, will be found in Appendix 4 (d). Rodolphe is said by Choron to have learned the horn from his father, and as he probably gave this information himself to Choron, it is likely to be correct. There is certainly not the slightest evidence that he ever met Hampel, whom he may even have anticipated, so he must have worked out his hand technique entirely on his own: that it was of a high order is evident from the quotation in Appendix 4. It is much to be regretted that he did not leave behind him a horn tutor as well as his famous *Solfèges*, but so far as is known he did not train any horn pupils. He was for many years a violinist in the Académie Royale (Opéra) orchestra, but was called upon for the *cor de chasse*, as the horn was then designated in French orchestras, whenever there was an important obbligato for that instrument.

Considering his tremendous contribution to the artistic development of the horn, it is quite remarkable how little is known about Hampel's life. Neither the place nor the year of his birth seems to have been recorded; we do not even know where or under what masters he studied. Yet, quite apart from his achievements as an innovator, he was not only the foremost teacher of his day but a renowned virtuoso as well. He left a certain amount of unpublished music, including some trios, the originals of which are in the Paris Conservatoire Library; an autograph book of exercises, *Lection pro Cornui*, to which Miss Schlesinger drew attention in her article on the horn in the *Encyclopædia Britannica*; and a tutor which is now only known as revised by Punto and published in Paris during the last decade of the 18th century. Two extracts from *Lection pro Cornui*, one of the trios, and two duos from the tutor will be found in Appendix 4 (a, b, and c). Of the tutor there appear to have been at least three editions, two of them bearing the name of Naderman as the publisher, the third, according to Fétis, having been published in 1798 by Leduc. The title page of the copy in the Paris Conservatoire Library examined by the writer is transcribed below because it contains the only technical instructions in the whole work, apart from some advice to composers. It will be seen that nothing whatever is said about stopped notes or how to produce them, though many of these occur in the various exercises and duos. It looks as though Punto, at any rate, was unwilling to disclose in print what was still, apparently, the 'closed shop' of the virtuoso. In his paper 'Giovanni Punto, célèbre corniste'[24] Henry Kling quotes the title page of another edition, word for word the same as that of the Paris copy except for the addition of *Dediée à la Convention Nationale par le Citoyen Punto, Professeur de Musique et de Cor* and *Gravée par la Citoyenne Oger*. The dedication on this copy would lead one to suppose that it was published between September 1792 and October 1795—the lifetime of the *Convention Nationale*—and from the publisher's address 1793 or 1794 seems a likely date. This edition is no doubt somewhat earlier than that in the Paris Conservatoire Library, for it is known that when, in 1794, the *Institut National de Musique* increased its teaching staff by thirteen new professors, Punto tried to get taken on the strength.[25] The fact that his application was unsuccessful might well account for the omission of the dedication from later editions, although this might also be due to the fact that after 1795 the *Convention Nationale* no longer existed.

Another curious but little-known work by Punto is his *Etude ou Exercice Journalier*, of which the only copy known to the writer is in his own possession. The *Avertissement* to this vouchsafes a little more technical advice to the student than is accorded in the tutor, but here again there is no mention whatever of stopped notes and their production, although many of them occur in these very irksome exercises (see Appendix 5a).

In the title pages of these two works and the *Avertissement* of the *Exercice* quoted in the following pages the original spelling and syntax have been observed throughout.

Apart from half a page of exercises at the beginning similar to the first two quoted in Appendix 5(a), there are none that contain any sustained notes such as are commonly used to strengthen the lip; but the sole object of this work is to provide stepping stones to the acquisition of an impeccable acrobatic technique, and for this purpose they are admirable. The performer who can play perfectly, in quick tempo, such exercises as those quoted from pages 50 and 51 has nothing to fear in any virtuoso piece ever written for the horn—if we except the production chords, a rather shoddy trick of no artistic value.

SEULE ET VRAIE
METHODE

Pour apprendre facilement les Elémens des

Premier et Second Cors

Aux Jeunes Elèves

Dans laquelle sont indiquer les coups de langue et les liaisons les plus nécessaires pour tirer les beaux son de cet Instrument.

Et pour y parvenir il faut observer,

1. De Prononcer en appliquant son premier coup de langue le mot D A O N en frappant fort avec la langue et diminuant le son ensorte qu'il produise le même effet que le tintement d'une Cloche.

2. Pour bien exécuter le coup de langue sec il est essentiel de Prononcer en appliquant le coup de langue le mot T A.

3. Pour bien appliquer dans les Adagio le coup de langue doux il faut prononcer le mot D A.

Composée par H A M P L

Et perfectionnée par P U N T O son Elève[26]

Prix 15^{11}

A Paris Chez H. Naderman. Editeur, Luthier, Facteur de Harpe et autres Instrumens de Musique. rue d'Argenteuil à Apollon.

ETUDE ou EXERCICE JOURNALIER

Ouvrage Périodique

Pour le Cor

Dédié

AU Cᵉⁿ· M A R C - W Ä I S

Consul de Genes, Nᵍᵗ· à Bordeaux

Composé
PAR PUNTO

Gravé d'apres le Manuscrit original de l'Auteur.

Prix 12¹¹

A LA MUSE DU JOUR DC

Chez Cochet, Luthier, Facteur de Harpe, et Mᵈ· de Musique
Passage du Théâtre de la Rue Feydeau, No. 23.

Nota. Enregistré à la   Bibliothèque nationale, et
Propriété de l'Editeur   d'après le Décret du 19
           Juillet   1793
Chez Jmbault rue Honoré au mont d'or. No. 200 de la section des
Gardes-Françaises entre la rue des Poulies et la maison d'Aligre.

At the top of the page is engraved a man's face surrounded by rays
of the sun. At the bottom, in the gap shown in the publisher's 'Nota',
is a very poor drawing of a 'cor-solo': the engraver is Ribier.

AVERTISSEMENT
ou
Manière d'exercer ces Caprices ou Etude.

Pour parvenir à vaincre toutes les difficultés du Cor et ne pas se trouver embarassé dans aucun trait qui puisse se présenter, il faut en travaillant ces Etudes s'assurer de tous les Coups de langue et Liaisons.

Chaque Coup de langue doit être exactement frappé comme il est indiqué dans les exemples suivans. Il est marqué sur la première blanche pointé, on commencera par frapper vivement et fortement avec la langue le mot D a o n ce qui fait l'effet du marteau qui frappe la cloche et donne le son grave dans le pavillon de l'Instrument on continuera les autres Coups de langue et Liaisons jusqu'à la dernière Triple croche en observant toujours d'executer ponctuellement tels que les Signes l'indiquent.

L'Auteur recommande de ne pas se dégouter d'un aussi long et fastidieux travail; Mais il assure qu'avec de la constance on parviendra aisement à se familiariser avec tous les traits et toutes les difficultés.[27]

Probably the first ever to put on paper any definite instructions concerning the use of the hand in the bell was Othon-Joseph Vandenbroek, one of the horn players in the Paris Opéra orchestra. Besides being the author of the well-known *Traité général de tous les instrumens à vent à l'usage des compositeurs* published by Boyer (Paris) c. 1800, Vandenbroek wrote two horn tutors. One of these, *Méthode nouvelle et raisonnée pour apprendre à donner du Cor, dédiée aux Amateurs,* was published by Naderman in 1797; the other, an unpublished manuscript, is now preserved in the library of the Paris Conservatoire. This last, which contains rather more written matter than the printed tutor, is the more informative of the two; unfortunately, it shows its author, when left to his own devices, to have had but the flimsiest acquaintance with the written language, almost every word being just spelt phonetically without regard to grammar or syntax. It is therefore not worth quoting in the original, but the gist of what he says about various ways of dealing with stopped notes and one of his final remarks are given below. The printed tutor, less discursive on the subject of the hand—the principal hobbyhorse here being a very intricate system of tonguing—does, however, contain a couple of drawings, one showing the open hand, to be held, presumably, with its back against the further wall of the bell, and the other a hand with the tips of the fingers bent downwards for stopped notes. In spite of an added title sheet, written in a different hand, which reads *Suite à la Méthode Nouvelle et Raisonnée . . .*, the manuscript tutor has every appearance of being a first attempt rather than a follow-on.

Holding the hand in the bell

Vandenbroek points out that though there may be several ways of producing semitones (stopped notes) there is, or ought to be, only one correct way. Some professors, he says, when playing open notes keep the thumb down (in the manuscript the operative word may be 'laisse' or may be 'baisse' *le pouce*), bringing it into its natural position, which completely closes the bell, for stopped notes. This method, he adds, is not one of the best. Others again thrust the hand forward into the bell for stopped notes, withdrawing it for natural tones. Yet another, but better, way, and the one recommended in the tutor, is to place the hand in the bell so that its back is in contact with the further wall, flexing the wrist so that the ball of the thumb touches the nearer wall for stopped notes. It must be borne in mind that some notes require less stopping than others. The author adds that this method is not only the most convenient but is also the best for intonation.

The manuscript ends with an *Observation dernière* which includes the following remark, as pertinent today as the day it was written: 'Possession of an excellent sense of pitch is the horn player's greatest asset since he has only his ear to guide him. By no means all horn players are so endowed, while faulty intonation is to some extent inherent in the instrument'.

The absence of any drawing in the manuscript tutor makes it impossible to do more than guess at how the first manner of stopping was supposed to function.

Since the dawn of orchestral horn playing of the best class it had been the custom to segregate the players into two hard and fast categories, since it was held to be impossible for any one performer to cover adequately both extremes of the instrument's compass. These categories were known as 'first' and 'second' horns, but the distinction did not necessarily imply any inferiority on the part of the 'second', who often had solo passages to play as important as, and frequently more difficult than, those given to the 'first'. Towards the end of the 18th century a new category came into being, the 'cor du milieu', as Vandenbroek calls it, or 'cor mixte', as it was more usually called. Their approximate ranges are given below, but the skilled performer both in the 'first' and 'second' categories would be able to extend the upward range on all but the shortest crooks by a number of notes that would vary according to the crook used.

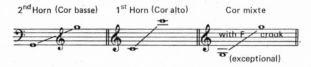

The best early 19th-century teachers rightly condemned the *cor mixte* for students on the ground that a superficial efficiency in its limited range could be too easily acquired without the labour of mastering either the 'first' or the 'second' category, indispensable background to good playing. The great players who, like Duvernoy, came to specialize in the *cor mixte* range were consummate artists and, without exception, thorough masters of whichever category they were best fitted for by nature before they wrote, or had written for them, solos whose range was confined to that part of the compass—about an octave and a half— where they could most effectively disguise the tonal differences between open and stopped notes. It does not, however, follow that everything a front-rank artist may do can be copied with impunity by the neophyte. The predilection of the leading early 19th-century hand-horn soloists for the brighter tone colour of the F crook as against the more sombre but perhaps nobler timbre of the E-flat and D crooks, undoubtedly in-fluenced the adoption of the first as the standard tonality of the valve horn. In Appendix 4 (h) will be found an example of a composer writing an obbligato part for horn in F, although E-flat is not only the key of the piece but that of the accompanying horns as well. The same procedure is again followed by Spontini in his one-act opera *Milton* (Hymn 4). It is pretty certain that for the passage quoted in Appendix 4 (f) (from Steibelt's *Roméo et Juliette*) Duvernoy would have used his F crook in spite of the fact that the part is written for horn in E-flat.

In 1803 Frédéric Duvernoy published his *Méthode pour le Cor*, a work whose author was clearly a man of superior intelligence. Though simpler in its lay-out and less exhaustive than the admirable *Méthode de Premier et de Second Cor* that Domnich was to bring out five years later, it nevertheless embodies all the basic principles on which the superb 19th-century French school of horn playing was founded, while it pioneered the method of teaching that was to find its ultimate expression in Dauprat's monumental *Méthode de Cor Alto et Cor Basse*, a huge volume of some 350 super royal quarto pages, of which more than a hundred are text. Duvernoy's tutor is admirably clear as far as it goes, and is certainly much better suited to the beginner than the more abstruse works of Domnich and Dauprat. He confines his teaching to the 'first horn' and 'second horn' categories, making no mention of the *cor mixte*; from which it may be gathered that this last is outside the province of anyone who has not already made himself master of one or other of the two recognized orders. He was the first to include a chromatic scale over the entire range of the instrument with an indication of the degree of stopping required for each note, and the first to concern himself, to however small an extent, with the musical and artistic development of the student.

If Duvernoy's tutor was addressed chiefly to the beginner, Domnich's *Méthode de Premier et de Second Cor*, published in 1808, was intended for the advanced student. It was approved by the Inspectors of Musical Training in France (Gossec, Méhul, and Cherubini) in 1807 and adopted forthwith as the official Paris Conservatoire tutor. Here every aspect of horn playing is treated in detail, and a historical notice is included which, if not entirely accurate at all points in the light of present knowledge, is nevertheless extremely valuable as our main source of information about the origin of hand stopping.

By far the greatest tutor of them all was that of Louis-François Dauprat, himself the winner of the first *premier prix* ever given for the horn. This *Méthode de Cor Alto et Cor Basse*, which was published in 1824, is divided into two parts, covering every problem, technical and musical, likely to confront the advanced hand-horn student. There is, of course, no mention of valves, for although these had been in existence for ten years or so before the appearance of the *Méthode*, they had not yet crossed the French frontier. No other tutor, however, lays so much stress on the development of good musicianship and taste. Nothing like it, or equal to it, has appeared since, and there is much in it that is still of great value.

Valves have done away with the need of hand stopping as a means of producing semitones, but that does not mean the hand has no longer any useful function to perform in the bell. Far from it. Not only has its position a marked influence on the tone—one has only to listen to a quartet of *cors de chasse* at close quarters to be convinced of this—but as a means of ensuring good intonation it is invaluable. No matter how carefully a horn is built and tuned some harmonics are by nature 'off white' with the tempered scale. Thus the fifth and tenth incline to be rather flat, while the ninth—especially on the F horn—is liable to be a trifle sharp, as is also, on some instruments, the sixteenth. Furthermore, it will generally be found that on the large-bore horn in B-flat fourth harmonics are considerably sharper than the corresponding eighth harmonics. Problems of this kind can be got over in some cases by judicious valve combinations, but the player must ever be on the alert if he is to maintain consistently good intonation. A little skilful hand work will be of enormous help to the lip in overcoming such inherent defects where they exist, for however relatively slight they may be, they can, if left uncorrected, show up most disagreeably in a chord.

The hand position, as laid down by the best French authorities, is this: the hand, slightly cupped and with fingers and thumb in close contact, is inserted into the bell so that the thumb is immediately under or in alignment with the bell stay and the backs of the fingers touch the metal, leaving a gap of about 4 cm. ($1\frac{1}{2}$ inches) between the ball of the thumb and the near wall of the bell: this is the normal position for all in-tune harmonics. Under no circumstances is the hand withdrawn from the bell, the normal 4 cm. gap being reduced by a third, a half, etc., as required, or increased by opening out the hand for notes that would otherwise be flat. All the necessary movements are effected solely by flexing the knuckles and wrist, the elbow remaining as nearly as possible motionless. Flexibility of lip and an acutely sensitive ear are a *sine qua non* of impeccable intonation. The indication 'bells up' sometimes met with in modern music is really a nonsense: complete withdrawal of the hand from the bell would, unless time is given to retune the instrument, result in a noticeable rise in pitch.

With the valve horn, once the tube length has been suitably fixed by the depression of one or more valves, every note in the harmonic series germane to that tube length becomes available, so that hard and fast rules can be laid down for the purely mechanical function of depressing valves. It is far otherwise with the hand horn. Here all sorts of variable factors come into the picture, such as the size and shape of the player's hand and the form of the instrument's throat and bell. How impossible it is to do more than give some sort of indication of the degree of stopping necessary for a particular note will be evident from the comparative table on page 99, which has been compiled from eight of the best-known tutors and covers a period of a little over a hundred years. All their authors were, with one exception, front-rank performers of their day: the exception, Frölich, was a well-known didactic writer who certainly had the help of a fully qualified authority for the horn tutor in his *Vollständige theor.-pract. Musiklehre*, from which his indications are taken. This last, based largely on the methods of Punto and

COMPARATIVE TABLE OF STOPPED NOTES ACCORDING TO EIGHT DIFFERENT AUTHORITIES

Duvernoy 1803
Domnich 1808
Frölich 1811
Dauprat 1824
Mengal 1835
Gallay c. 1845 (?)
Franz, O. c. 1880
Pree, Aug. 1911

○ = normal hand position; ● = fully stopped; Ø = hand opened wide.
Fractions = the amount by which the normal opening is to be reduced.

(a) ¾ in quick time; ○ in slow time.   (d) ● in quick time; Ø in slow time.
(b) ½ in quick time; ○ in slow time.   (e) ¾ in quick time; Ø in slow time.
(c) Not in the instrument.   (f) ½ in quick time; Ø in slow time.

(g) ¾ in sharp keys; ● in flat keys.

X is an alternative, independent of enharmonics.

presumably vetted by a former pupil of his, contains, among other valuable suggestions, a strong recommendation to all horn students to study the methods of the singer, in order to improve his breathing and develop the very necessary sense of accurate pitch. He also gives draw-ings of two different types of mouthpiece, one of them slightly cupped and very similar to the mouthpieces generally used nowadays with German horns. The stopping indications over this period of about a century will be seen to run in a crescendo of complexity which reaches its culmination with Dauprat and Gallay—Mengal's work is of slighter proportions and is intended more for the dilettante than for the ad-vanced student—thereafter becoming simpler and simpler as the valve horn dominates the scene more and more until, with Pree, the inclusion of a hand-horn scale at all is no more than a perfunctory salute to the past.

The last major hand-horn tutor in France was Gallay's *Méthode pour le Cor*, which appeared two or three years after its author had been appointed professor at the Conservatoire in succession to Dauprat (1842). Gallay was by nature a *cor alto*—it was said of him that 'il montait comme un ange, mais il ne pouvait pas descendre'—though Fétis reproaches him with being a *cor mixte*. He disapproved of Dauprat's nomenclature of *cor alto* and *cor basse*, and advocated a more open normal position for the hand in the bell than his predecessors: this meant that stopped notes required rather less occlusion than was needed with the older method, and gave a brighter tone, a gain or a loss according to one's personal view of what the ideal horn tone should be. It is a noteworthy feature of this tutor that none of the exercises goes below 🎼 ,

while the lowest note in any second-horn part in the duos is 🎼 .

Since the uppermost limit is 🎼 and if the solos he played con-

formed to the gamut of his tutor, Fétis's reproach is perhaps not without foundation. Gallay also advocated a curious method of using the tongue for trills, quite unlike any other. In spite of the reservations of Fétis, Gallay was a very distinguished artist, while as a teacher he trained a number of very excellent players, among whom Mohr was probably the most outstanding. Birchard Coar is probably right when he says that Gallay's teaching retarded the acceptance of the valve horn as a standard instrument in France.[28]

As a matter of fact one more full-scale hand-horn tutor did appear in

France after Gallay's, and that was *Méthode de Premier et de Second Cor* by Gallay's pupil and successor as professor at the Conservatoire, Jean Mohr. This tutor, which contains virtually no text, adds nothing to those of Dauprat and Gallay. Indeed it was really out-of-date at the time of its publication (1871), for it makes no reference whatever to the valve horn, familiarity with which was by then everywhere essential— except in the Conservatoire horn class. As a player Mohr had a big reputation, and Ella tells us how, owing to a failure on the part of his first horn, Pasdeloup was obliged to 'engage Mohr, the best horn player in Paris. . . . I ascertained that Mohr plays upon one of the new horns of Sax, and I strongly commend their use in this country'. Elwart says of him that he had a fine tone together with a sureness in the attack that is invaluable in horn entries such as those in the symphonies of Beethoven.[29]

Needless to say, a great deal of thought was devoted to that very important accessory the mouthpiece by the authors of the major tutors. In theory—and formerly in practice—the mouthpiece of the French horn is strictly a truncated cone, and in the old days it was made of sheet metal. This was treated in much the same way as the bell, the sheet being cut to a pattern, shaped on a mandrel, and the edges soldered together. The lip was then turned over to a depth sufficient to provide a rim of the desired thickness. Generally speaking such rims were more rounded and narrower than they were later, when it had become the practice to turn mouthpieces out of solid cylinders of brass or silver, or out of castings in the case of the mass-produced article.

The measurements in the accompanying diagrams (Fig. 20) of mouthpiece openings and rims are from actual specimens in the case of Nos. 1a, 1b, and 6. For the remainder they are those given by the authors of the tutors from which they are taken. To copy a mouthpiece accurately is an exceedingly difficult operation, for although on paper the difference between, say, 2b and 3b—one millimetre for the inside diameter—is barely discernible, so sensitive is the lip that a difference of as little as half a millimetre could be enough to upset a player considerably until he got used to the new diameter. Slight differences in the thickness of the rim are not quite so noticeable.

There are two ways of putting the mouthpiece to the lips: the player may either place the bottom third of it *against* the under-lip, or he may use the so-called 'set-in' embouchure where the lower edge of the mouthpiece is actually set into the red flesh of the under-lip. The 'set-in' position appears to be of Germanic origin, and possibly originates with the Bohemians in the first half of the 18th century. None of the French

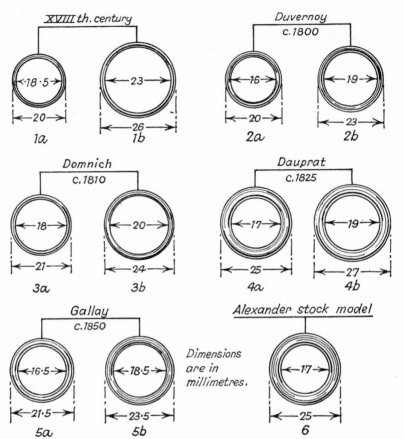

Fig. 20

1a Silver. Exceptionally small by any standards
1b Brass. Exceptionally large by any standards. Possibly made for one
  of the 18th-century negro horn players
2a 'First' horns   2b 'Second' horns
3a 'First' horns   3b 'Second' horns
4a 'Cor alto'   4b 'Cor basse'
5a 'Thin lips'   5b 'Thick lips'
6 Modern German mouthpiece, rather heavily 'choked' and slightly
  'cupped'

authors recommends, or so much as even mentions, it, though the writer
has known a number of French players who used it. Either method seems
equally satisfactory in practice, and the choice of method would appear

to rest solely on what best suits the individual, although some teachers held that the 'set-in' position did not give sufficient power or stamina and would not accept pupils unless they were willing to change it, among these teachers being Gumbert and Horner.

It was the emergence of the soloist as opposed to the duettists, whose vogue declined at the end of the 18th century, that brought into prominence the *cor mixte*, who concentrated all his energies on making the best possible use of the octave-and-a-half that lies between the fourth and twelfth harmonics. This octave-and-a-half, with all its tonal advantages combined with ease of emission, lies comfortably within the range of both first and second horns, so it was possible for either to be principal horn in an orchestra or a concert soloist. Moreover, when an exceptionally gifted artist devoted special attention to this relatively small part of the horn's compass, he was able, at any rate in slow or moderate time, to produce a chromatic scale of very even tone quality though restricted dynamically. But the restricted dynamics together with the almost exclusive use of the F crook undoubtedly resulted in a degree of monotony often criticized by Fétis and other writers of that time.

Probably the three most notable protagonists of the *cor mixte* were Frédéric Duvernoy in Paris, Luigi Belloli in Milan, and Giovanni Puzzi in London. Duvernoy, by nature a second horn and, according to Fétis, self-taught, was one of the first, if not the first, to bring the *cor mixte* style of playing to a high degree of excellence. In 1788 he appeared as soloist in a concerto by Punto—himself also a second horn—at a Concert Spirituel, and two years later was appointed principal second horn at the Théâtre de Monsieur. In 1799 he became solo horn at the Paris Opéra, with Buch, Kenn, Vandenbroek, and Paillard as the regular quartet. Some idea of the position he occupied in the musical life of Paris may be gathered from the poster[30] announcing the first performance of Spontini's opera *La Vestale* for 15 December 1807. On this bill the words 'M. FREDERIC DUVERNOY exécutera les Solos de Cor' are in much larger letters than anything else relating to the performance, nor is the name of any other artist even printed in capitals.

During the first forty years or so of last century horn solos were much in evidence, but as the skill of the players increased, so, in all too many cases, technique tended more and more to become an end in itself instead of a means to an end. Eminent performers, who were rarely gifted composers, wrote musically valueless solos for themselves to show off their virtuosity to the best advantage, and in so doing tried to make the horn accomplish feats for which by nature it was unfitted. It must never be forgotten that the place of mere virtuosity, unless accompanied by great artistry, is the Palace of Varieties or the Circus. The result was that when the established hand-horn soloists reached the end of their careers, the instrument disappeared entirely from the concert platform.

The Romantic period was the golden age of the horn. The differences in the tone quality of the various crooks could then be appreciated in all their subtlety, which is now impossible since with valves the tube length changes from one note to the next. Even a passage played 'hand-horn' on a modern instrument with one or two valves depressed does not seem to have quite the quality of the same passage played on a natural horn with the E-flat or D crook. No longer can we hear that wonderful opening to the *Oberon* overture played as it is written.

Instead of the eighth, ninth, and tenth harmonics of the horn in D, with its veiled and rather mysterious quality, we probably hear harmonics 6 of the G horn, 6 of the A horn, and 8 of the F-sharp horn: a very different sound to the discriminating ear. In the ensuing phrase several notes require some degree of stopping on the D horn, but nowadays it is played entirely with the valves—as often as not on the B-flat horn—without any hand stopping. True, we are unlikely to hear this passage 'fluffed'—and it is more difficult to play well than it looks on paper, even on the modern valve horn—but most of the poetry has evaporated in the process.

Sometimes, however, a passage may be made to sound even better than the way it was written for hand horns by judicious mixture of hand and valve. The writer remembers an occasion, some fifty-five years ago, when he took part in a performance of the *Eroica* Symphony where this was done. In the Scherzo the first horn, M. Reine, then solo horn of the Paris Opéra, crooked his instrument in B-flat alto; the writer, who was playing second, used an E-flat crook and played the passage 'hand-horn'; the third horn, whose part is less colourful, used the customary F crook. The brilliance of the B-flat crook against the velvet of the E-flat and the discretion of the F produced a result that earned very favourable comment both from the conductor and from the members of the orchestra.

PHASE 3 (*c.* 1820 *to the present day*)

We come now to the valve-horn phase, which may be said to start about 1820, for there can have been but few such instruments about before that; the writer has been able to discover very little about it until Spontini sent some valve horns and valve trumpets to Paris in 1826 and Meifred, in the following year, brought out his improved version of the original German instrument.

As has already been said, this phase is really composed of three sub-phases: the two-valve horn in conjunction with some degree of hand-horn technique; the three-valve horn, now a completely chromatic instrument playable without assistance from the hand; and the modern four- and five-valve horns that have now practically superseded all older types. The subject must, however, be treated as a continuous whole, for there is so much overlap from one sub-phase to the next that it is useless to try to apportion into definite periods what is really a process of evolution.

The idea of the inventor of the valve does not seem originally to have gone beyond the mere abolition of loose crooks, so it can only be supposed that his intention was that the hand in the bell should continue to furnish the basic technique. The instrument itself was built in F and its two valves served to 'crook' it in E, E-flat, and D. If other tonalities were called for, it became necessary to have recourse to transposition, using the valves as they are used today. Although it is possible, and indeed probable, that both Stölzel and Christoph Schunke played solos on the new instrument earlier, the first mention of such an event known to the writer occurs in the *Quarterly Musical Magazine & Review* (Vol. V, p. 408) where we learn that at a concert in Berlin in January 1823 one Glazemann performed on a 'chromatic French horn'. The correspondent makes no comment on the performance, from which it may perhaps be deduced that the instrument was by that time quite familiar to Berlin concertgoers. A noteworthy performer on the valve horn in its earliest days was Joseph Kail, of Prague, who interested himself from the first in the mechanical development of chromatic brass instruments. In this he was encouraged by the Director of the Prague Conservatory, Dionys Weber, who appointed him professor of the valve trumpet and valve trombone in 1826: in that same year he became first horn at the Prague National Theatre. Kail is also credited with having invented some sort of echo device, controlled by a valve, which could be attached to any brass instrument, evidently the ancestor of that erstwhile military-band horror, the echo-cornet.

The first front-rank artists to perform on the valve horn were the brothers Eduard-Constantin and Joseph-Rudolph Lewy. E.-C. Lewy studied under Domnich at the Paris Conservatoire, though not as an official student of that institution. A criticism of his playing at a concert in Strasbourg in 1827 has already been quoted, and in the same year the Stuttgart correspondent of the *Harmonicon* reports as follows on the two brothers:

> The most interesting concert of the season was that given by the brothers Lewy, wherein, among a variety of delightful instrumental pieces they gave a duet and variations upon the newly-invented Vienna chromatic horn;[31] the effect produced by the transition from a subject of great tenderness to a sprightly Bohemian air was perfectly magical.

The *Harmonicon*'s Vienna critic also gives high praise to the brothers' performance of a concerto for two French horns by Riotti and Variations for two horns by Dittersdorf, but does not say whether they played on hand horns or valve horns. According to tradition it was E.-C. Lewy who played fourth horn in the first performance of Beethoven's Ninth Symphony, in which case the part was probably played on a valve horn, switching into E for the famous A-flat scale. This does not mean that Beethoven actually wrote the part with the valve horn in mind, but the whole question of this much-discussed passage is exhaustively treated in W. F. H. Blandford's admirable paper 'The Fourth Horn in the Choral Symphony',[32] to which there is nothing to add. It was for J.-R. Lewy that Schubert wrote the horn obbligato to his song 'Auf dem Strom', composed in 1828 and first performed on 26 March of that year at a concert given by Schubert in Vienna: the performers were Tietze, Lewy 'dem Jüngeren', and the composer himself. The horn part contains the following notes, all of them bad or hopelessly bad on the hand horn:

This appears to be one of the earliest, if not the earliest, instance of a major composer deliberately writing for the valve horn.

Unlike his French contemporary Meifred, Lewy left no horn tutor explaining his technical methods. A fairly good idea of his principles may, however, be gleaned from his twelve very difficult studies for chromatic horn in F with piano accompaniment. An extract from Study

XI is given in Appendix 5(b). Like Meifred, who wrote a very excellent tutor,[33] Lewy considered first-rate hand technique to be of paramount importance for the conservation of the finest quality of tone. In the study in question it will be seen that there are indications of crook changes from one bar to the next, and even in the middle of a bar, and that only where 'horn in F' is marked is it permissible to use the valves chromatically. Otherwise their use is to be confined to making the called-for crook changes (first valve E-flat, second valve E, third valve D), the section then to be played hand-horn. From this it may be deduced that he considered all music for horn in F, E, E-flat, or D—the 'solo' crooks —should as far as possible be played by hand-horn technique, though for other crooks the valves would have to be used as they are today. His consistent use of the third valve for D shows that he tuned his valves so as to have each strictly in correct relationship with the horn in F. This rules out, as far as hand-horn technique is concerned, the use of valves 2+3 for horn in D-flat or 1+3 for horn in C, owing to the rise of pitch inevitable with the employment of valves in combination (see above, p. 53, note 25). Transposition would in any case have been necessary for crooks higher than F owing to the constructional lay-out of German instruments.

A method of writing for the horn that is somewhat akin to that in Lewy's Study XI is to be found in the horn parts of *Lohengrin*, the Introduction to Act III offering some good examples. Since Wagner composed this work while he was *Hofcapellmeister* at Dresden, where Lewy was principal horn at the Opera, it would not be surprising if he took counsel with so fine an artist as to how to get the best out of an instrument that, from the composer's angle, was as yet in the experimental stage. There is little doubt that in spite of the already widespread use of the valve horn in Germany, the instrument was still suffering from defects in its mechanism and—possibly to an even greater extent— from inferior playing. That Wagner was fully alive to this as well as to the differences of tone colour between one crook and another is clear from his introductory note to the score of *Tristan und Isolde* which, in W. F. H. Blandford's translation, reads as follows:[34]

> The composer desires to draw special attention to the treatment of the horns. This instrument has undoubtedly gained so greatly by the introduction of valves as to render it difficult to disregard this extension of its scope, although the horn has thereby indisputably lost some of its beauty of tone and power of producing a smooth *legato*. On account of these grave defects, the composer (who

attaches importance to the retention of the horn's true characteristics) would have felt himself compelled to renounce the use of the
valve-horn, if experience had not taught him that capable artists
can, by specially careful management, render them almost un-
noticeable, so that little difference can be detected either in tone or
smoothness.

Pending the inevitable improvement in the valve-horn that is to
be desired, the horn-players are strongly recommended most carefully to study their respective parts in this score, in order to ascertain
the crooks and valves appropriate to all the requirements of its
execution. The composer relies implicitly on the use of the E (as
well as the F) crook; whether the other changes which frequently
occur in the score, for the easier notation of low notes, or obtaining
the requisite tone of high notes, are effected by means of the
appropriate crooks or not, is left to the decision of the players
themselves; the composer accepts the principle that the low notes,
at all events, will usually be obtained by transposition.

Single notes marked + indicate stopped sounds; if they have to
be produced in a key in which they are naturally open, the pitch of
the horn must be altered by the valves, so that the sound may be
heard as a stopped note.

It is unlikely that anyone still living can have heard the hand horn
at its best, since the valve horn has, for nearly a century, so completely
supplanted the older instrument that comparisons are no longer possible.
Moreover, not only has the mechanism of the valve become as near
perfect as it is ever likely to be, but ample time has elapsed for valve-
horn technique to have become stabilized along strictly chromatic lines.
It would be useless to ask any present-day player to conform to Wagner's
desiderata, which imply the use of a technique long since abandoned.
Even if a revival of interest in hand technique should come about—and
this is not impossible—what Wagner asks for would still be out of the
question since orchestral players all rely so much nowadays on the B-flat
horn in works as physically exacting as those of Wagner.

P.-J. Meifred was the first Frenchman to turn his attention seriously
to the valve horn. As was said in Chapter 3, the first German valve horns
to reach France had valve loops that were unprovided with slides and
were built in the fixed tonality of F. Meifred remedied these defects,
and played a solo of his own composition on his improved valve horn at
the first concert ever given by the Société des Concerts du Conservatoire
in 1828. In 1833 a valve-horn class was instituted at the Paris Conserva-

toire with Meifred as its professor, while so successful was his instrument (see above, p. 32–5) that it became currently known in France as *le cor Meifred.*

Meifred makes it quite clear that his *Méthode pour le Cor Chromatique ou à Pistons* is only complementary to Dauprat's great tutor which, he insists, should be on every horn player's bookshelf. He tells us that when he first set out to improve the German instrument he had in view five objects:

1. To restore to the horn the notes it lacks;
2. To improve the intonation of some of its notes;
3. To make the muffled notes sonorous, while retaining those that need only slight stopping, the tone of which is so agreeable;
4. To give all leading notes, whatever the key or mode, the character they have in the natural scale;
5. Lastly, not to deprive composers of crooks, each of which has its own particular tone colour.[35]

To sum up, his horn was to give a chromatic scale of open notes with good intonation throughout, endowing with adequate power such notes as ♩ which hitherto had needed very heavy stopping, and making it possible to play all leading notes by reading a semitone higher and half stopping; finally it was to be provided with the means to use loose crooks, the slides of the valve loops making it possible to tune the valves correctly for the crook in use.

The *Méthode pour le Cor Chromatique* is written for the two-valve horn, and the fingering chart contains some interesting, and to modern eyes curious, features. Below are a few of the fingerings that differ from present-day practice:

(*a*) C-sharp is treated as a leading note, the E above it being lowered by stopping; the amount of latitude allowed to the lip with these very low notes makes it possible to produce it with no more than half stopping. The D-flat is raised from C by increased lip tension and by opening the hand very wide.

(*b*)   G-sharp and A-flat are treated in the same manner as the C-sharp and D-flat above, G-sharp being lowered a semitone from A-sharp.

(*c*)   A-sharp is treated as a leading note.

(*d*)   C-sharp is treated as a leading note. The fingering for D-flat (1 + 2) is what we should use nowadays for both notes.

(*e*)   G-sharp is treated as a leading note. In the absence of a third valve the A-flat has perforce to be taken as a seventh harmonic.

(*f*)   A-flat is treated as a leading note and is a hand-flattened seventh harmonic.

(*g*)   F-sharp is here presumably considered as a leading note. Otherwise it seems certain that it must have been fingered like the G-flat as, for instance, when playing a part for horn in E on the F crook.

(*h*)   These fingerings are quite unorthodox. Both notes would surely be better in tune and safer with 1 + 2, which would give a fifteenth harmonic, a good note. Alternatively, slight stopping of the thirteenth harmonic gives an excellent A-flat, and this method is often employed for the well-known passage for horn in F in the *Eroica* Symphony:

Until about 1847 Meifred was a firm partisan of the two-valve horn, on the ground that a third valve, in the then existing state of development, was not only unnecessary but actually prejudicial to the tone. He contended that the two-valve instrument, aided by the hand in the bell and the use of suitable crooks, was able to do all that could be asked of the chromatic horn, while the tone was adversely affected by the repercussion of air due to the abrupt angles in the windways of the Stölzel valve, then in universal use in France, which was increased by the addition of a third valve. The Meifred-Deshays *valvules*, described in Chapter 3, got over the repercussion difficulty, but proved too costly to be put on the market. Meifred was always hoping that some practical solution to the problem would sooner or later be found, as in fact it was (about 1847) by the ascending third-valve system. This ingenious device was due to one of Meifred's best pupils, Jules Halary, who won a *premier prix* for valve horn in 1845. The son of Antoine Halary (who had, from the very first, taken great interest in Meifred's ideas for improving the original German model), Jules Halary constructed a horn the third valve loop of which formed part of the main windway of the instrument. Played with a G crook the horn stood in F, while depression of the third valve put it into G.

This system offered a number of advantages. It restored to full volume the notes that were still feeble on the two-valve horn though it was impossible to produce or anything below as valve notes pure and simple, as could be done on the ordinary three-valve descending horn. Other advantages of the ascending system were alternative fingerings for one or other of which was always liable to be treacherous with the orthodox fingerings, and diffi-cult and uncertain with the descending system, which now became excellent notes as the twelfth harmonics respectively of the F-sharp and G horns. In Meifred's fingering table for the ascending horn there is no longer any indication of half-stopped leading notes, except in the case of the missing low D-sharp/E-flat, which he shows thus: ; all the rest are fingered as in Appendix 1. This probably means that he now recognized the three-valve horn as a completely chromatic instrument that could be played, with practically no aid from the hand, throughout its entire compass; the use of the hand in the future would be a matter of artistic refinement instead of one of necessity. The problem of the still missing could be, and generally was, solved by regular second- and fourth-horn players by the use of a crook with a thumb valve or by a fourth valve on the instrument itself.

Thus two of the leading protagonists of the valve horn in its early days. Of the third, Joseph Kail, we know nothing beyond the fact that he was a player of distinction, and that he interested himself right from the start in the mechanical improvement of valves and in their application to various brass instruments which he taught at the Prague Conservatory. Lewy favoured the three-valve horn, and no doubt adopted the double-piston (Vienna) or the rotary valve as soon as they became available; both were much superior to the Stölzel valve to which France remained faithful until about 1850. To what extent he actually made use of hand technique in his day-to-day orchestral work we have no means of knowing, but it does seem certain that he held no brief for loose crooks although, on the evidence of the note in the score of *Tristan*, Wagner does not appear wholly to have shared this view. The German instrument, however, still had room for considerable improvement at the time of the completion of the score of *Tristan*, and Halary's system, in all essentials the same today as when it first appeared, was unknown in Germany then as now. Meifred, on the other hand, had always preferred the two-valve horn with loose crooks and a good deal of hand technique—until the advent of Halary's ascending horn, which he presumably adopted then and there for his own use. One cannot help speculating as to which of these two very distinguished artists produced the more beautiful sound.

In spite of the practical efforts of Meifred and the writings of Kastner, Escudier, and other influential people in Paris musical circles, prejudice against the valve horn was for long an obstacle to its general adoption in France. Although the Opéra had its valve horns since the early 1830s, no other Paris theatre—not even the Opéra-Comique—had them in 1843. By that time it had become quite impossible to play second-horn parts effectively.

As a curiosity we give on page 114 a fingering table for Adolphe Sax's horn with six independent ascending valves, compiled by a former professor of the horn at the Brussels Conservatoire, H.-L. Merck. There is a specimen of this instrument in the Brussels Conservatoire museum (No. 3176).

By 1850 or thereabouts all the hand-horn soloists of international repute still living were well past their prime, while the valve horn had not as yet quite emerged from the experimental stage. Its technique had not so far been stabilized, and undoubtedly there was a great deal of inferior playing as well as a lot of bad teaching. It is evident, too, that there was much muddy thinking as to what was now the function, if any, of the hand in the bell. In his excellent and comprehensive *Horn-Schule*, first published in 1865, H. Kling deals with this point. The following extract is taken from an undated edition of this work which has English as well as German text:

> The position of the right hand in the bell of the instrument should be regulated strictly in accordance with the instructions contained in this 'School', albeit by the great majority of hornists in the present day this important particular is entirely ignored—one

of the reasons, indeed, for the increasing scarcity of competent horn-players. Some time since, I happened upon the following passage in a 'Method for the Horn':—'In the case of the Ventil Horn, the right hand performs another function; the three middle fingers being employed in manipulating the valves, while the hand is only placed in the bell of the instrument when a tone requires to be stopped'.

Such a procedure must indeed be productive of some rather singular 'virtuosity' in horn-playing. It may be asserted with some confidence that the author of this 'Method' [!] has in all probability never held a horn in his hand, or been within measurable distance of playing it. The accuracy of tone-production, as well as the proper holding of the hand in the bell of the instrument, impart to the horn its distinctive charm, which consists in a truly melodious and sympathetic tone.[36]

Another instance occurs in a Viennese *Vollständige Horn-Schule*, which has an illustration showing a gentleman who holds his hand in the bell with his thumb upright and supporting the instrument: of all hand positions this is about the worst. It is therefore hardly to be wondered at if the new, but still largely unmastered, valve horn made no headway as a solo instrument and failed to regain the popularity once accorded to the hand horn. Not only was there a widespread lack of skill, but composers were discovering new ways of writing for the horn which added considerably to the worries of even the very best players. Before the end of the century the horn player found himself faced with the formidable technical problems that abound in the works of Richard Strauss, which not only demand complete mastery of the entire compass of the instrument but very great physical endurance as well. This new and complex writing, if it was to be played successfully by any but a very small élite, called for radical revision of horn technique on the part of player and manufacturer alike. How well the challenge has been met during the last forty-five years or so is manifest in the ability of the average student of today in any of the major music schools to take in his stride not only the horn parts that seemed so formidable at the turn of the century, but also the even more difficult parts with which present-day music is so plentifully larded. This is all the more remarkable when even so distinguished a hornist as Fr. Gumbert said, shortly after his retirement: 'Composers like Wagner, and those of today like Strauss and Mahler, really require a little motor in the horn to play the parts; therefore I retired'.[37]

'SYNONYMIC TABLE SHOWING THE SEVEN POSITIONS OF THE HORN
WITH SIX INDEPENDENT PISTONS by H. L. MERCK'

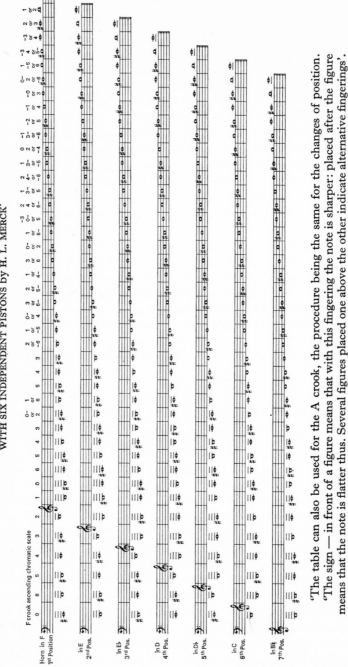

'The table can also be used for the A crook, the procedure being the same for the changes of position.
'The sign — in front of a figure means that with this fingering the note is sharper: placed after the figure means that the note is flatter thus. Several figures placed one above the other indicate alternative fingerings'.

One solution was for first- and third-chair men to exchange the F horn for one in B-flat alto. This was ideal for sureness of attack and ease of execution, but these advantages were, in the majority of cases, more than counteracted by poor tone quality and doubtful intonation. Many of the old conductors—among them Reinecke (1824–1910), of the Gewand-haus, and von Bülow (1830–94), of Hamburg, Berlin, etc.—would not countenance in orchestras they conducted the use of the B-flat horn, with its comparatively thin, harsh tone, unless the composer demanded it. It was only after such excellent specialists as Preuss in Frankfurt had demonstrated its advantages that it began to win general acceptance. The alternative solution, and the one that has now gained universal accept-ance, was the F/B-flat double horn, the genesis of which has been des-cribed in detail in Chapter 3. It is given to few players to be able to pro-duce a consistently fine tone from the single B-flat instrument, and with the small-bore French horn crooked in B-flat a fine tone is virtually impossible under any circumstances. The double horn has proved an immense boon to the average performer of good symphony-orchestra standing, for it has put him more or less on a par technically with the exceptional player of an earlier generation.

As some indication of what had to be faced with the old French horn

crooked in F let us take the twelfth harmonic, sounding c″ 🎼.

This twelfth harmonic is most uncomfortably sandwiched in between two others, both of which are out of tune with the tempered scale (see Appendix 1) whose proximity makes it imperative, metaphorically speaking, to score a perfect 'bull's eye'. It must be hit plumb in the middle, too, for a 'nicked' bull inevitably meant a cracked note.[38] The

same difficulty arises with the 🎼 , which have to be taken as

twelfth harmonics of the E-flat (1st Valve) and E (2nd Valve) horns respectively. The fragility of the twelfth harmonic is of course due in the main to close crowding by its neighbours on either side, for with the lower and more widely spaced harmonics there is not the same danger if the note is not hit right in the middle, though it is still real enough when blowing through twelve feet of narrow-bore tubing, with one's ear and one's instinct as the only guidance. So it is hardly surprising if only the gifted few were really 'safe' players on the old French horn. The German horn with its larger bore which, to continue the metaphor, seems to offer a bigger target, was never so distinguished—or so temperamental—as its slenderer and more elegant French counterpart.[39] Assuredly there have always been exceptionally gifted players able to overcome every technical difficulty with that seeming ease that is the hallmark of the potentially great artist, but they have been very few, and fewer still those who, like the late Aubrey Brain, superimposed on their technical mastery the musicianship and artistry without which mere virtuosity is like some monstrous, artificially grown vegetable—superb to look upon, but to the gastronome completely tasteless. However, modern demands on the horn player are such as to be hopelessly incompatible with adequate performance on the old French horn in F, and even so great an artist as Dennis Brain was obliged to give up his French horn and take to the German B-flat instrument.

Technique has advanced tremendously within living memory, and the horn is now expected not only to be immune from cracked notes but as agile as the bassoon as well. Big skips were generally avoided by the classical composers, though there is an instance of a two-octave jump in Mozart's Quintet in E-flat for horn, violin, two violas[40], and 'cello (K407). Such skips were, of course, always practised, but the writers on instrumentation discouraged their use by composers as too uncertain. This is now *vieux jeu*, and skips of two octaves or more are almost a commonplace for the soloist of today.[41] In an article that appeared in the May 1958 issue of an American musical paper, *Woodwind World*, the well-known American hornist Joseph Eger aptly compares horn playing today with the four-minute mile. The barrier having once been breached a number of athletes followed suit. With the horn it was Dennis Brain who first showed what could be accomplished in the way of technical mastery, and there are now many players who can perform with equal virtuosity if not always with the same artistry.

Where shall we go from here? It would seem that all the possibilities of the horn as we now know it have been explored and mastered. In all likelihood the trend will be for the student to become more and more proficient technically, so that with increasing numbers of first-rate executants the horn will once more emerge from the relative anonymity of the orchestra, to which it retired more than a hundred years ago, and regain its erstwhile wide popularity as a major solo instrument.

NOTES

1 Marc-Antoine marquis de Dampierre (1676–1756). He became Master of the Hunt to the duc du Maine in 1709, transferring to the service of Louis XV as Master of the King's Harriers in 1727 and Master of the Royal Buckhounds in 1738: he composed his first fanfares for Louis XV

in 1723. Dampierre, who may justly be called 'the father of the trompe de chasse', was an exceptional performer on the instrument. At a concert given in the Louvre on the occasion of a royal state banquet the orchestra performed a *symphonie guerrière* by 'Philidor le père'—no doubt André, more usually called Philidor *l'aîné*—with a solo horn part played by 'M. Dampierre, lieutenant des chasses de M. le duc du Maine' ('La situation des musiciens en 1700 et après' by L.-A. de Pontécoulant in *L'Art Musical*, Vol. 2, No. 7, 16 January 1862).

² Keyed horn. Valve horn is meant, this instrument often being miscalled keyed horn in its early days when its mechanism was still a mystery to the layman.

³ This is, of course, Punto, whose name was frequently misspelt in England, even by Dr Burney.

⁴ *Musical World*, Vol. 18, No. 31, 3 May 1843.
'Mr. Editor—Having read in the different newspaper criticisms extraordinary accounts of the celebrated horn player Mr. Puzzi (who is generally termed unrivalled) may I ask what are his principal qualities? The last time he visited us, I really could not find out anything but a continued jumble of noise, as I thought, quite unconnected with music. I have never heard any other performer (but the above gentleman) play on the French horn, and indeed if that is a specimen of the capabilities of what I have always heard called that fine instrument, I hope never to be in the way of such a "treat" again. If it would not be trespassing on your valuable time, I should feel obliged if you would give some account of the peculiar excellence on which Mr. Puzzi's ability is founded. Yr. obedient servant, sd. "A Constant Reader"'. To which the Editor gives the withering reply 'We know nothing of the French horn, and less than nothing about Signor Puzzi'.

⁵ *Revista Musicale Italiana*, Vol. XVIII, anno 1911.

⁶ '*Tantivy*: an exposition of the "Antient Hunting Notes"', *Proc. R. Mus. Assn.*, 80th Session, 1953/54.

⁷ From the 'Sculpture of Notes for blowing on the Horn', reproduced as a frontispiece to the reprint of Nicolas Cox's *The Gentleman's Recreation* (4th edition, 1697, with a preface by E. D. Cuming). London, 1928.

⁸ J. P. Hore, *History of the Royal Buckhounds*. London, 1893.

⁹ Mr Winch was Handel's principal horn player, and a noted soloist of his day.

¹⁰ Presumably Michael Christian Festing, who was appointed director of music and leader of the band at Ranelagh when the pleasure gardens opened in 1742. Festing was also one of the founders of the Society of Musicians, serving that institution for many years as honorary secretary. He died in 1752.

¹¹ *Forhuer*. A hunting term meaning to sound *le forhu*, a horn call to call in the hounds.

¹² op. cit.

¹³ Lyciscas having, with the greatest possible difficulty, got on his feet began to yell at the top of his voice, whereupon several horns were heard and, in concert with the violins, played the opening bars of an entry danced by six hunt servants who, at certain cadences, took up their horns

again. The performers were Messrs Paysant, Chicanneau, Noblet, Bonard, and La Pierre'. In the original production Molière himself played the part of Lyciscas.

[14] J.-B. Morin (1679–1745) is said to have been the first to compose fanfares for recreational purposes as opposed to those by Dampierre and others which were part of the recognized code of signals used in the hunting field. Two of Morin's fanfares are reproduced in Appendix 3(g), as well as a *Relancé* by M. de Dampierre and *La Louise Royale* composed by Louis XV.

[15] J. E. Altenburg, *Versuch einer Anleitung zur heroisch-musikalischen Trompeter- und Pauker-Kunst*. Halle, 1795.

[16] A. Hyatt King suggests that this work was probably written for the Eisenstadt virtuoso Thaddäus Steinmüller. *Musical Times*, December 1945.

[17] M. Ernst, Allemand, a exécuté seul un concerto à deux cors de chasse. Cette nouveauté a paru plus singulière qu'agréable'. *Mercure de France*, April 1751.

[18] 'Denn, des edlen Waldhorns zu geschweigen, darauf sich vor einiger Zeit ein Blindgeborner in Hamburg hören liess der mehr Klänge hervolbrachte, als eine Orgel hat, wienwohl ohne Schwert und Wage der Mathematic. . ' .' J. Mattheson, *Der volkommene Capellmeister*. Hamburg, 1739.

[19] The Rev. Daniel Lysons, *History of the origin and progress of the meeting of the Three Choirs of Gloucester, Worcester and Hereford*. Gloucester, 1812.

[20] This must have been one of the very first orchestras to have resident horn players, for according to Furstenau (*Zur Geschichte der Musik und des Theaters zu Dresden*, Vol. 2: Dresden, 1861–62) two Bohemian horn players, Johann Adalbert Fischer and Franz Adam Samm, joined the court orchestra in 1711.

[21] H. L. Eichborn, *Das alte Clarinbläsen auf Trompeten*. Leipzig, 1894.

[22] Mersennus, *Harmonicorum Libri XII*, Propositio XX. Paris, 1635.

[23] 'A la même époque, le Hautbois, bien éloigné du point de perfection ou il est parvenu de nos jours, était un instrument aigre, criard et peu propre à l'accompagnement d'un chant gracieux ou d'un morceau d'expression. Quand on l'employait à cet usage, on avait coutume, pour l'adoucir, d'introduire du coton dans la concavité du pavillon. Hampl, un des plus célebres cors du tems [here a footnote says, "il vivait à la cour de Dresde, il y a environ soixante ans"] conçut l'idée de substituer cette méthode à celle des sourdines. Il fit un tampon de coton disposé de manière à remplir l'objet qu'il avait en vue. Sa surprise fut extrême, la première fois qu'il s'en servit, d'entendre que son instrument était haussé d'un demi-ton. Ce fut pour lui un trait de lumière, et son génie étendant rapidement une découverte due au hazard, il vit le moyen, en présentant et retirant alternativement son tampon, de parcourir sans interruption l'échelle diatonique et chromatique de toutes les gammes. Alors il composa pour le Cor une musique nouvelle, où il fit entrer des notes qui jusques-là lui étaient étrangères. Quelque tems après, ayant remarqué que le tampon pouvait être avantageusement remplacé par la main, il cessa de se servir du tampon'.

[24] *Bulletin Français de la S.I.M.*, 1908 (pp. 1066–82).

[25] Constant Pierre, *B. Sarrette et les Origines du Conservatoire National de Musique et de Déclamation.* Paris, 1895.

[26] The sense of these rather obscurely worded instructions is as under:

1. The word DAON must be pronounced when making a strongly tongued attack, the sound being allowed to die away after the manner of a struck bell.
2. The word TA should be pronounced when tongueing a staccato attack.
3. The word DA is to be pronounced for soft attacks in adagios.

[27] Here is a free translation of the instructions as to how these exercises are to be studied:

> Particular attention must be paid to all the attacks and slurs marked in these exercises if the student aspires to be able to play without hesitation any quick passage he may encounter.
>
> In every case the attack is to be made exactly as indicated over the first dotted minim, which must be tongued on the word DAON. This produces a sound like that of a bell when struck by its clapper, and gives a rich quality of tone. All other attacks and slurs, down to the last demi-semiquaver, are to be played exactly in accordance with the signs.
>
> The student is enjoined not to allow himself to be discouraged by so tedious a labour in the knowledge that with perseverance he will soon be able to deal successfully with every kind of difficulty that may present itself.

[28] Birchard Coar, *A Critical Study of the Nineteenth-century Horn Virtuosi in France.* DeKalb, Ill., 1952.

[29] A. Elwart, *Histoire de la Société des Concerts.* Paris, 1860.

[30] This poster is reproduced in Th. de Lajarte, *Les Curiosités de l'Opéra.* Paris, 1883.

[31] There is no reason to suppose that the 'Vienna chromatic horn' was necessarily of the double-piston type, although it is possible that this action, in its earlier form, may have been in existence in 1827. The improved action was only patented by Uhlmann of Vienna in 1830, and it is unlikely that the term *Wiener-Ventil* came into use before then. The Lewy brothers were both living in Vienna in 1827. It is not known who made the original double-piston action, the reputed resemblance of which to Shaw's *Transverse Spring Slides* is so superficial that there can scarcely be any connection between them.

[32] See *Musical Times*, Jan., Feb., Mar., 1925.

[33] J. Meifred, *Méthode pour le Cor Chromatique ou à Pistons.* More than one edition of this work appeared, and when Halary's ascending third-valve system came on the market, a supplement was added about 1849 giving a fingering chart for it.

[34] W. F. H. Blandford, 'Wagner and the horn parts of Lohengrin'. *Musical Times*, Sept. and Oct. 1922.

[35] 1. De restituer au *Cor* les sons qui lui manquent;

2. De rétablir la justesse de quelques uns;

3. De rendre sonores les Notes qui sont sourdes, tout en conservant celles qui sont légèrement bouchées, et dont le timbre est si agréable;

4. De donner à la note sensible, quel que soit le Ton et le Mode, la physionomie qu'elle a dans la gamme naturelle;

5. Enfin, de ne pas priver les compositeurs des corps-de-rechange qui ont, chacun, une couleur spéciale.

[36] H. Kling, *Horn-Schule*, Leipzig, 1865. A later edition has German and English text.

[37] A remark made, two years after his retirement, by Fr. Gumbert to his former pupil Anton Horner. This, and the information about the reluctance of German conductors to accept the B-flat horn as an all-purpose instrument, is contained in a letter from Horner to the writer's friend, Osbourne McConathy, of the Boston Symphony Orchestra.

[38] These four notes are notoriously treacherous on the French horn crooked in F.

(a) 12th harmonic of E-flat horn;

(b) 12th harmonic of E horn;   sounding

(c) 16th harmonic of D-flat horn;

(d) 16th harmonic of D horn.

Played on a B-flat instrument they become much safer and have alternative fingerings:

(a) 8th harmonic of B-flat horn (open); 9th harmonic of A-flat horn (1st valve); 10th harmonic of G-flat horn (valves 2+3);

(b) 9th harmonic of A horn (2nd valve); 10th harmonic of G horn (valves 1+2 or 3);

(c) 10th harmonic of A horn; 12th harmonic of G-flat horn;

(d) 10th harmonic of B horn; 12th harmonic of G horn.

[39] Aubrey Brain, one of the greatest players of his day, wrote as follows in the *Monthly Musical Record* of 31 July 1931: 'The most casual of listeners, hearing a performance by a German orchestra, cannot but be struck by the peculiar, euphonium-like quality of the horn tone'.

[40]   Andante

[41] Instances of a skip of more than two octaves occur in the cadenza of Ethel Smyth's Concerto for violin, horn, and orchestra. The solo horn has the following passage:

This cadenza has also a series of three-note chords for the horn.

CHAPTER 6

Metals and Manufacture

A MALLEABLE ALLOY composed of approximately 70 per cent copper and 30 per cent zinc is the metal generally used for the manufacture of French horns. This is the yellow brass of which probably 90 per cent or more of all horns are made, although until the 19th century, when satisfactory processes for the extraction of pure zinc from the various ores that contain it became available, the brass was composed of copper and calamine. In the 18th and early 19th centuries it was not uncommon for brass instruments of all kinds to be made of pure copper, usually with yellow brass embellishments, a case in point being the Bull horn shown on Plate II, 2. Another type of brass has come into use more recently, especially in Germany, known as *Goldmessing* or gold-brass—called copper-brass in America—in which the proportion of copper to zinc is in the region of 80 per cent: 20 per cent. Naturally rather more expensive—and rather heavier—than the ordinary yellow brass, it certainly looks very handsome when nicely polished, though whether it offers any other appreciable advantage is open to question.

Considerable use is also made of a white metal alloy composed of nickel, copper, and zinc, which, according to the proportions of the constituents, is variously known as German silver, nickel silver, *Neusilber*, and *maillechort*—sometimes erroneously called *melchior*.[1] These white metals, being more difficult to work, are not very often used for an entire instrument, though Kruspe, the famous horn maker of Erfurt, has produced some fine *Neusilber* instruments. German silver garnishings are, however, extensively used, and most of the better-class German model horns have white metal valve casings, valve-slide sleeves, and mouthpipe casings. Sterling silver, too, has been used to make horns, though very exceptionally. During the second half of the 18th century Raoux of Paris made at least one *Waldhorn*[2] and three *cors-solo*,[3] these last for prominent virtuosi of the day. They were expensive luxuries costing 100 *louis d'or* (about £100 in English money of the time), but they seem to have had quite a considerable publicity value for their owners. Two of these virtuosi, the famous duettists Palsa and Türrschmidt, performed at a Salomon concert in London on 2 March 1786, and that garrulous gossip and captious critic W. T. Parke[4] has this to say about it:

Two new French horn players, Messrs. Palsa and Thurshmit, who had only played previously at the Anacreontic Society,[5] made their first appearance in public in a concertante for that instrument. The most striking part of their exhibition was their horns, which were made of silver.

Although horns made throughout of sterling silver were understandably very exceptional, silver bell-rims, stays, mouthpipes, and garnishings in general were the rule rather than the exception for instruments of the highest quality at the outset of the 19th century: mouthpieces were commonly made of silver before the outbreak of World War I.

As far as the playing qualities of the different metals are concerned, experts have occupied themselves with these matters for a very long time. In the Talbot manuscript (see above, p. 17), there is a note under the heading *Trumpet* which reads: 'Best mettal Bastard-Brass mixed with solid Brass: Worse Silver and worst copper springy'. This is far from clear, but it is enough to show that as long ago as the 17th century makers and others were preoccupied with the problem of finding the most suitable alloys. From the foregoing it would appear that some type of yellow brass was even then considered to be the best musically. Much thought has been devoted not only to the problem of finding the most suitable alloy, but also to the best thickness of the metal. According to Pontécoulant[6] the horn player Lebrun 'succeeded in improving the instrument by altering the thickness of the brass of which it was made, thereby facilitating the emission of semitones'. Pontécoulant is presumed to mean that the quality of the stopped notes was improved. That Raoux in Paris had also been working on these problems is evident from the fact that during the 19th century the so-called 'Raoux French horn metal' was very highly thought of by English makers.

Silver is now, of course, quite out of the question on the ground of cost alone, but cost apart, it does not appear to have suited everybody. Here are the views of two outstanding players and teachers of their respective generations, separated in time by almost exactly a century: Louis-François Dauprat, who won his *premier prix* at the Paris Conservatoire in 1798 and retired in 1842; and Anton Horner, already mentioned in connection with the introduction to America of the F/B-flat double horn, who left the Leipzig Conservatory about 1894, retiring about 1940 after a distinguished career as a player and teacher in the United States.

Dauprat expresses his preference for yellow brass (*laiton*) not only on account of its relative light weight but also because it will give a very powerful tone without prejudice to quality 'which', he says, 'players are unable to achieve with instruments made of silver or copper'.[7] Horner, at least for his own personal use, found German silver the best. Many years ago, when the double horn was in its infancy, Horner ordered two instruments from Kruspe, one of gold-brass and the other of German silver. The first he found lacking in brilliance for himself, though excellent for a harder embouchure: the second he used throughout his career until his last day in the orchestra. This would appear to be one more nail in the coffin of the theory that, given identical proportions, instruments will sound the same no matter what they are made of. Individual preferences are bound to intrude, but there seems little doubt that for the general run of players the 70 : 30 per cent alloy is still the best, while it has the further advantage of being less costly than gold-brass or German silver.

All tubing was formerly made from sheet brass bent round a shaped mandrel, the edges being then brazed together. Except for the bell section which, at least for horns of the best quality, is still shaped by hand, drawn tubing has superseded the older kind, while mass-production has become practicable thanks to the greater speed and accuracy that have been made possible by modern mechanization.

The frontispiece shows the interior of an 18th-century horn- and trumpet-maker's workshop, and some of the processes involved in the manufacture of a horn. It is unnecessary to add anything to the descriptions that accompany the drawing, except perhaps to say that the bell section of the three-coil horn shown on Plate II, 6, which is contemporary with the drawing, measures 4 ft. 6 in. (approximately 1.35 m.); this would be about the same length as the portion of horn being bent (Fig. 4 of frontispiece).

For the bell section the procedure in use today is briefly as follows. A master pattern is laid on a sheet of brass—the bell section of an orchestral horn is very much shorter and wider than that of the crookless horn—on which its outline is traced. The traced figure is then cut out, bent round a steel mandrel, and hammered roughly into shape with a wooden mallet. Since the brass cannot be splayed out sufficiently for the edges to meet on the everted portion of the bell, a triangular gusset is inserted and brazed into position. This gusset, for the widely flared French horn bell, will, at its base, measure about half the circumference of the bell mouth. In some cases a multiple gusset is used, a case in point being the horn by Courtois *neveu aîné* shown in Plate III, 6: this instrument has a triple gusset composed of a large central portion with two small 'wings' on either edge of the base.

After more shaping with the pickaxe-like 'pegging hammer' on a wooden block, and further hammering on the steel mandrel, the bell is annealed, a process which is carried out by means of a powerful blow-lamp and which calls for considerable skill on the part of the operator. The bell is then replaced on the mandrel for further hammering, the hammering and annealing processes being carried out alternately until the proper shape is attained. It is then put on the mandrel again and the edges are brought together and 'dovetailed'. This dovetailing is done by making shallow cuts along one of the edges, turning up alternate pieces between the cuts, and pushing the uncut edge hard up against the bent-up pieces and hammering these pieces down again. The whole seam is then brazed with a mixture of spelter—a brass alloy having a slightly lower melting-point than the brass of which the bell is being made—and borax all along the seam, so as to ensure a perfect and in-separable join. When sufficiently cool the bell is put into a sulphuric acid pickle to clean up the metal and remove any remaining traces of borax. Further hammering then takes place to flatten the seam, followed by further annealing. The part is now replaced on the mandrel and drawn backwards under enormous pressure through a lead drawplate to within a foot or so of the bell-rim, so that it now fits the mandrel with absolute precision and all irregularities are smoothed out. The part, still on the mandrel, is now put on a lathe and rotated, the bell itself being finally shaped and burnished by hand with a burnishing tool. The edge of the bell is now trimmed and turned back over a strengthening wire which is soft-soldered into place.

In the United States horn bells are often made by 'spinning', a method which does away with the necessity of a gusset. For instruments of high grade bells are made from a disk of sheet brass spun on to a shaped form to a depth of flare of eight inches. Five spinnings are neces-sary, the bell being annealed after each spinning. It is then brazed to a stem made from sheet brass formed on a mandrel in the manner already described, all seams being then hammered and the whole assembly spun to shape as a complete bell. Similar methods are employed for instru-ments of cheaper grade, but in this case the original disk is spun only to a depth of flare about five inches, this process requiring only two opera-tions instead of five. Subsequent treatment is the same for all grades.[8]

To curve the tube, the tube is filled with molten lead, or other filler having a low-temperature melting-point, and after cooling is bent round a shaped pattern until it attains the desired arc: it is then reheated and the filler emptied out.

The modern highly mechanized horn carries a large proportion of cylindrical tubing, whereas the old hand horns were made as nearly conical throughout as was possible, the only cylindrical tubing being just the length of the sliding portion of the tuning slide or body-crook. One leg of the slide was made a trifle larger than the other, the connecting tubing being conical whatever its length. A conical bore of even gradation throughout is, of course, impossible on any type of horn except one built to a fixed pitch, like the *trompe de chasse*.

Within comparatively recent times some instrument makers in a very large way of business have been using what is known as the hydraulic expansion process for making bends of all kinds (bows, Fr. *potences*; knuckles, Fr. *coudes*, etc.) to a mathematically accurate taper. This process has, moreover, the advantage of eliminating all tendency to wrinkle on the inside, which is liable to occur when a tube is bent by the old molten-lead method. The tooling necessary is, however, too costly for any but firms with a vast output of standardized instruments to be able to avail themselves of it. Very briefly, for it does not at present appear to be used for the manufacture of horns beyond bows and the knuckles used for the valve slides, the hydraulic forming process is as follows. A tube of the desired gauge, bent to an approximate curve, is placed in an accurate white-brass die, the two halves of which are then locked together in a hydraulic press. The smaller end of the tube is securely stoppered, and specially treated water is forced through the larger end at a pressure of from 3,000 to 5,000 lb. per square inch. This expands the tube to fit exactly against the walls of the die, while at the same time it smooths out any kinks due to the preliminary bending, which could only otherwise be done by hand. Uniform thickness and perfect standardization are thus assured.[9]

From what has already been said in Chapter 3, it will rightly be inferred that the manufacture of valves is not without its problems. The assembly of piston valves especially calls for the most meticulous workmanship, for not only must the piston itself be able to move up and down with perfect accuracy and at lightning speed, but the whole assembly must be absolutely air-tight. In spite of its more complex finger action and plethora of small screws, the rotary valve is actually far simpler to make; Figs. 21 and 22 overleaf will help to explain why.

When the pump is depressed, port *c* takes the place previously occupied by port *a*, so that the wind-stream passes from the main windway into *c* and thence, via *y*, to port *d*, round the valve loop (not shown), back into port *e*, through *z* to port *f*, and so once again into the main windway: the necessity for precision workmanship is evident. The rotor is just a solid brass cylinder through which two, or in the case of the

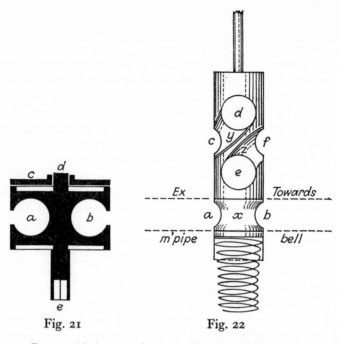

Fig. 21   Fig. 22

Fig. 21   Rotor with its two channels. For the double horn the rotor is
          deeper and the channels are duplicated
          a & *b* parallel channels
          c loose cover-plate
          d spindle over which the cover-plate fits
          e end of spindle to which the driving mechanism is connected
Fig. 22   Pump, or moving part of the piston valve
          a & *b* main windway entry and exit ports
          c & *f* valve-loop entry and exit ports from and to main wind-
          way
          d & *e* entry and exit ports of actual valve loop
          x, y, z cockades (Fr. *coquilles*) connecting respectively ports *a*
          and *b*, *c* and *d*, *e* and *f*

double horn four, parallel channels are bored, and to which is added a
cover-plate to make the assembly air-tight. The extent to which the
rotor turns when the finger lever is depressed is nowadays controlled
by two cork buffers placed on the underside of the valve casing (see
above, p. 42, Fig. 11d). Other methods have been used in the past, but
have now been abandoned. Although, unlike the piston, the rotary valve

is not self-contained but is composed of two separate units, the valve proper and the actuating mechanism, it is really the simpler of the two systems. It has remained in all essentials the same as when it was first invented, whereas it took about forty years before a really efficient piston valve found its way on to the market.

The manufacture of the piston valve, with its six holes and three channels—twice that number for French double-horn piston valves—is a very delicate affair. To make the pump, or inner reciprocating part of the valve, a tube of thin brass or nickel-silver is prepared and holes of the same diameter as the bore of the valve loops are cut in the appropriate places. These holes are then connected in pairs by straight or curved sections of extremely thin brass tubing known as 'cockades'—no doubt a corruption of the French *coquilles*—which are forced into position and brazed, thus forming three channels. The pump is then cleaned up and fitted to the outer casing, which is usually lined with phosphor-bronze and is bored with four holes. Two of these holes fall opposite ports *a* and *b* (Fig. 22) when the piston is in the 'up' position carrying the wind-stream direct from mouthpipe to bell, while the other two, connected by the valve loop, are so placed that when the piston is depressed, they are opposite ports *d* and *e*. Needless to say, the adjustment of the pump and its casing must be carried out with micrometric precision, so that the cost of production when every operation is carried out by hand is of necessity very high; prohibitive nowadays for any but instruments of the very best quality.

Machine tools and presses have come to the aid of the manufacturer, reducing hand work to a minimum and making it possible to produce efficient standardized brass-instrument components on a mass-production basis at a very much reduced cost. But in spite of the marvellous advances of recent years in the mechanical processes of instrument manufacture, it is not without a twinge of regret that some of us regard its almost complete transformation from an art to a science, from a craft to an industry. The factory-made instrument which, as a tool in the hands of the performer, may be as good as or even better than anything made in the old days by hand, still lacks an indefinable something that can be put there only by the craftsman, in all probability himself a performer of high standing, who has nursed the instrument with loving care from the sheet metal to the finished product. The feeling is akin to that of seeing a beautiful house or garden taken over by the state: the house or garden is still beautiful, but without its individual owner some virtue has gone out of it. The love that once cared for it is no longer there.

NOTES

[1] *Maillechort.* So called after the two Lyons metallurgists who invented it *c.* 1820, Maillot and Chorier.

[2] The *Waldhorn* is that described under No. 105 of Bierdimpfl's catalogue of the musical instruments in the Bavarian National Museum. The hall-marks indicate its date as between 1774 and 1780.

[3] Raoux is known to have made silver horns for Punto, Palsa, and Türrschmidt about 1780.

[4] W. T. Parke, *Musical Memoirs.* London, 1830.

[5] An aristocratic club of musical amateurs at whose fortnightly concerts the leading professionals used to perform. The Anacreontic Society was founded in 1766 and continued until 1794.

[6] L.-A. de Pontécoulant, *Organographie,* tome II, p. 110. Paris, 1861.

[7] op. cit., Part I, p. 20, footnote: *'Ce dernier métal* [laiton] *a été préféré comme plus léger et plus sonore; la 1ère qualité est incontestable; la 2e est encore réelle, en ce que le son peut acquérir une résonnance très grande, sans que sa qualité en soit altérée ce que les exécutans n'obtiennent pas avec les instrumens d'argent, ou de cuivre rouge'.*

[8] For this information and that concerning modern hydraulic forming techniques the writer is indebted to the late Eric McGavin of Boosey & Hawkes Ltd.

[9] For fuller information see *Machinery,* 12 and 26 June 1953—'Hydraulic Forming Techniques applied to the manufacture of Musical Instruments'.

CHAPTER 7

Miscellanea

ON TONE: ITS PRODUCTION AND QUALITY

NO ATTEMPT WILL be made to discuss the acoustics of the horn. The science of acoustics is so abstruse that, without scientific training and familiarity with up-to-date experimental apparatus, it would be most imprudent to venture into its labyrinths: to do so would, in modern jargon, simply be 'sticking one's neck out'. But for all their laboratory paraphernalia none of the acousticians has offered, as far as we know, a convincing explanation of the rise of pitch—real or apparent—that occurs when we 'stop' a note. This problem will be considered at greater length under 'Stopping on the B-flat horn' later in this chapter. Another question as yet unanswered is why such differences can exist in the tone quality produced by different players using similar instruments and mouthpieces. So we are driven meanwhile to formulate our own empirical theories.

Like all brass instruments, the horn is sounded by the vibration of the lips within the cup of the mouthpiece. This causes the air-column in the instrument to vibrate in its turn, the pitch of the sounds thus engendered depending on the length of the tube and the rate of vibration. The vibration speed can be altered, within practical limits, by varying the tension of the lip muscles, so that any one of the harmonics available with a given tube length may be sounded at will. The number of harmonics obtainable from such a tube by the agency of the human lips will depend on the length: bore ratio of the tube and on the physical endowments of the player. Thus, the sixteenth harmonic of the F horn is within the competence of every player, but few indeed can be sure of the sixteenth harmonic of the B-flat instrument. At the other extreme, the fundamental of this last can be sounded with ease by all and sundry while that of the F horn, and lower, is available only to an exceptional lip. The standard range, which has increased considerably of late years chiefly owing to the general adoption of the double horn, may now be said to extend from the fundamental of the B-flat horn to the sixteenth harmonic of the F instrument, or three octaves and a perfect fifth. The old, well-defined classification of players into 'first' and 'second' horns according to their respective ranges is a thing of the past. All can now

cover the very considerable standard range, some exceptional performers being able to add a few notes at one end or the other, and
whether one is a 'first' or 'second' today is, granted the requisite skill,
just a matter of temperament.

Opinions as to what constitutes ideal horn tone differ no less from
one country to another than from one individual to another. In Germany
a rather dark tone having affinities with the euphonium is favoured,
while the French like a much brighter sound: the English seem to prefer
something in between the two. Austrian horn tone is again something
quite different from all others. Nevertheless, all these varieties of tone
colour remain unquestionably genuine horn tone, unmistakable for
anything else and, as far as the quartets of the major European and
American orchestras are concerned, of first-rate quality after its kind.
No doubt some of the tonal difference between the quartets of, say, the
Vienna Philharmonic, the Berlin Philharmonic, the New York Philharmonic, the *Société des Concerts*, and the B.B.C. Symphony Orchestra
arises out of the demands of their resident conductors. In two cases,
the Vienna Philharmonic and the *Société des Concerts*, the instruments
used differ considerably from the German single B-flat and double horns
in universal use elsewhere; this would naturally account to a large extent
for tonal differences. National preferences have doubtless grown out of
long familiarity with the tone most readily produced from the type of
instrument used in different countries. Thus, for more than a century
the Germans have used large-bore horns and the Austrians their special
Vienna model. The French have never strayed far from the bore established in the late 18th century by the famous Paris maker Raoux, such
small modifications as have been made in their present-day double horn
having become necessary owing to the demands of modern orchestral
music. In England the French model was favoured prior to World War
II, and, therefore, although the German instrument has been adopted,
German tone has not. Is it perhaps because for so many years the two
leading players in Britain, Franz Paersch and Adolf Borsdorf, were
Germans who used French instruments that English taste now seems to
prefer a tone quality that lies somewhere between the French and
German extremes? Is it yet another manifestation of the reputed British
genius for compromise?

The tonal differences that can exist between two first-rate artists
using similar instruments and mouthpieces offer a far more delicate
problem. Obviously it cannot be the instrument—unless there be some
subtle difference in that most sensitive part of the horn, the mouthpipe—
for any change would equally affect both. Small differences in the inner

profile of the mouthpiece would, as such, be more or less negligible. The effective position in the bell of the hand, on whose size and shape this must depend, can have a very marked influence, but there is pretty general agreement as to what is the best effective position, so that two experts are unlikely to differ to any great extent about this. The only plausible explanation seems to lie in the physical conformation of the oral cavity and sinuses, and of the buccinator and oral sphincter muscles; perhaps, too, the disposition of the teeth. It is these factors combined with the inside profile of the mouthpiece, and of course correct use of the abdominal muscles and diaphragm in breathing, that seem to be responsible for the *quality* of the tone. Variations, within limits, of any or all of these factors may affect the shade of *colour*, but the quality will be there. It is very important that the mouthpiece should be as nearly as possible a perfect match with the physical endowments.

A factor that has a considerable influence on tone quality is the position in which the instrument is held. Nowadays many players rest the bell of the instrument on the knee, which tends to darken the tone. This position was unknown in the days of the true French horn, and its adoption was no doubt originally due to the excessive weight of the double horn. Others again, especially in Italy, turn the bells of their horns into stomach shields, to the grievous detriment of the tone. The position in which the instrument is held, no less than the type of instrument; method of using the hand in the bell; and so on, are of course, chiefly a matter of outstanding teachers in the major conservatories and music schools who have remained long enough in office to have trained so many excellent pupils that their methods have survived them and become standard.

It is taken for granted that the tone produced by every horn player approaches as nearly as may be to his own ideal. Although quite a lot is known about visual aberrations, it is by no means so well established to what extent aural aberration may be present in the individual. If such aberrations do in fact exist, they might have a very definite bearing on the differences in tone colour between one player and another.

ON 'STOPPED' NOTES IN GENERAL, AND THEIR
PRODUCTION ON THE B-FLAT HORN
Sons bouchés—gestopft—chiuso— +

It is commonly believed that in order to get this effect the player closes the bell of his instrument as tightly as possible with the hand, and transposes his part down half a tone. This is true enough as far as it goes, but it applies only to the F horn, in length midway between those in B-flat alto and C basso and from which 'stopped' sounds emerge just a semitone higher than the open notes. With longer or shorter horns the rule of the semitone is no longer valid, but becomes 'the shorter the horn the greater the rise, and *vice versa*'. Thus the rise in pitch will be rather less than a semitone in the case of a horn crooked in C basso, but considerably more than a semitone for one in B-flat alto: a horn in F alto was found to rise by as much as a whole tone. The deviations from the semitone rule appear less pronounced on small-bore French horns than on their larger-bore German counterparts.[1]

Acousticians have so far been chary of putting anything about this rise, or apparent rise, of pitch in writing. Three, however, have touched on the subject at greater or less length, Mahillon of Brussels, Blaikley of London, and the French physicist Bouasse. The first says that 'stopping' shortens the air-column, the second that the rise in pitch is apparent only, and the third takes a rather similar line to Blaikley, but appears to base his view on Mahillon's early work, *Eléments d'Acoustique*, published in 1874. None offers any scientific explanation of the phenomenon in support of his belief, and so it really amounts to no more than an opinion, with which one may, or may not, agree.

According to Mahillon,[2] partial closing of the bell with the hand lowers the pitch a semitone or more, according to the degree of occlusion, but such *sons bouchés* are not to be confused with what he calls *sons en sourdine*, obtained by a greater degree of occlusion 'which occasions a kind of shortening of the air-column, causing a semitone rise in pitch of every harmonic'. He makes no mention at all here of the curious method of stopping described in *Eléments d'Acoustique*, but which is resuscitated by Bouasse.

Blaikley[3] holds the rise in pitch to be apparent only, due to the formation of an 'inharmonic, or disturbed, harmonic series of tones', and that the apparent sharpening of, say, two Cs (the fourth and eighth harmonics) is 'really the production of the 5th and 9th proper tones of a new inharmonic, or distorted, scale'. Even so he does not seem to have been wholly convinced of the correctness of his theory since, in his Proceedings of the Musical Association paper, he says: 'It must be admitted, however, that under certain conditions an obstruction or apparent obstruction to free vibration at the open end of the tube may exist without flattening the pitch, and indeed may raise it'. He gives the impression of having founded his theory on the belief that, since gradual closure of the bell flattens the pitch, it is not logical to suppose that maximum occlusion could possibly have the opposite effect. What the eminent acoustician has overlooked here is that the apparent rise of pitch occurs only when 'stopping' is accompanied by a special, rather astringent, mode of attack—unless, of course, this is what is meant by 'under certain conditions'. Without a slight tensing of the lip muscles in attacking the note, closure of the bell merely flattens the pitch until, with maximum occlusion, we get a heavily blanketed, dull note half a tone to a tone lower than the open note; of the characteristic tone colour associated with 'stopped' notes which, sharp and pungent, differs entirely from the veiled quality of hand-horn *sons bouchés*, there is not a trace. Nor is it clear why, if the ninth harmonic only comes down a semitone, the fifth should come down a tone and a half. As it stands, this theory is anything but convincing.

Bouasse,[4] the latest writer of the three—his work appeared in 1929—devotes considerably more space than the other two to the *sons bouchés* question, but his argument contains much to which the experienced horn player will demur. Such statements, for instance, as that 'partial closure of the tube lowers the pitch by an interval exceeding the semitone', and that 'the artist can obtain this flattening of half a tone with his lips',[5] are half-truths only. How much given harmonics can be lowered by lip alone or with the aid of the hand depends upon their position in the harmonic series. Up to and including the sixth they can be lowered a semitone without any help from the hand, or with the hand a whole tone. Higher than this all notes require a considerable degree of stopping to flatten them a semitone, while a whole tone is out of the question. Bouasse then goes on to say:

> Beware of what musicians tell you! Widor adds a note to his *Traité d'Orchestration*[6] to say that in the upper register stopped notes are always higher than the equivalent open harmonic, but that (oddly enough!) in the lower register they are lower. Need I add that they are *always* lower?

Bouasse was no doubt unaware of the great difficulty of producing an efficient 'stopped' tone by raising the pitch of any note below the fourth harmonic of the F horn, which leads the vast majority of players, when they have low notes to stop, to fall back on the technique of lowering the pitch (reading a semitone above the written note instead of a semitone below it) and making the best noise they can.[7]

As every horn player knows, the pitch will not rise unless the note is attacked with a certain amount of 'bite', and it seems odd that even so important a tutor as that of Oscar Franz should ignore this point and merely say that stopping will 'raise the pitch a half tone, consequently the notes about to be played must be transposed a half tone lower than written'.[8] Philip Farkas, on the other hand, in his excellent treatise on horn playing deals in great detail with the technique of stopping, though the present writer cannot agree with him that it is impossible to stop in tune on the B-flat horn without the aid of a muting valve; it is hoped, in what follows, to show the fallacy of this widespread belief. Farkas's book, an American publication, is now obtainable in England, and it should be on every horn player's bookshelf.[9]

At the risk of being one of those fools who rush in where angels fear to tread, the present writer advances his conviction, admittedly based on empirical grounds alone, that maximum occlusion of the bell with the hand shortens the air-column of any horn, *irrespective of its basic length*, by an amount equal to the length of a semitone valve loop *tuned as for horn in F*, that is about $8\frac{1}{2}$ inches, or 21·6 cm. To lower the B-flat horn by a semitone needs only $6\frac{1}{2}$ inches (16·5 cm.), but valve loops are provided with slides and can be adjusted to suit either contingency. Not so the hand, whose stopping position is invariable whatever the basic length of the horn. The result is that just as the addition of $8\frac{1}{2}$ inches to the B-flat horn would lower its pitch well over half a tone, so stopping shortens its air-column by 2 inches too much, and the pitch rises more than a semitone in consequence. The *muting valve*, when one is available, must therefore increase the overall length of the instrument by $8\frac{1}{2}$ inches.

How then, without the aid of a muting valve, can we counteract this excessive rise in pitch? Given certain postulates it is not difficult, once the underlying principles and the *modus operandi* are grasped. In all the following examples the notes are written as for horn in F, while the fingerings are those for horn in B-flat.

In the first place a very accurate sense of pitch and perfect co-ordination of ear and lip are absolutely essential, for stopped notes need a good deal more humouring with the B-flat horn than they do with the F. Fortunately the horn is a very flexible instrument up to and including the sixth harmonic, though above this point there is little latitude. Advantage will be taken of the tendency of fifth harmonics to be rather flat—more pronounced on the B-flat than on the F horn—and the third

valve will be tuned on the low side so that played with this valve

or open (rather flat fifth harmonic) will agree, and seventh harmonics will be used whenever available. Incidentally, the little extra length on the third valve slide will help to improve the intonation of notes obtained with this valve in combination with others. Given the accuracy of ear required to ensure perfect intonation of the notes up to and including the sixth harmonic, and using the fingerings shown below, every one of these notes can be played stopped perfectly in tune. Hand-stopped notes below the fourth harmonic are almost always unsatisfactory, and for them one of the special pitch-raising mutes specially made for the purpose is strongly recommended.

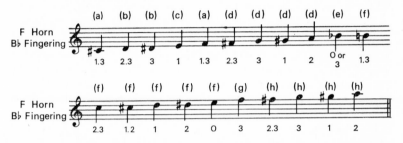

(a)   1 + 3 to put the horn in F, which gives an exact semitone rise.

(b)   Take advantage here of the slightly flat tuning of the 3rd valve.

(c)   No help here from the 3rd valve, and the note must be humoured accordingly. It is quite possible to get it in tune with a little practice.

(d)   Use here the 5th harmonics of the G-flat, G, A-flat, and A horns.

(e)   We can either use the 5th harmonic of the B-flat horn, or the 6th harmonic of the G horn taken with the 3rd valve.

(f)   The written notes are the 8th harmonics of the F, G-flat, G, A-flat, and A horns. Finger as for a semitone *higher*, but play the 7th harmonic of the new series. The inherent flatness of 7th harmonics exactly cancels out the sharpness due to stopping.

written note   read (for fingering)   blow   *this last*

note being the 7th harmonic of the A-flat horn.

(g)   Use the 9th harmonic of the G horn.

(h)   Use respectively the 10th harmonics of the G-flat, G, A-flat, and A horns.

Note   The alternative fingering of 1 + 3 (F horn) could be used for the notes given below. It is not, however, recommended since the indicated fingerings will provide equally good intonation, and will at the same time be much safer.

To the non-player all this may appear well-nigh incomprehensible, but the practitioner will find that it works. For the single B-flat horn a muting valve certainly offers an easy way out of 'stopping' problems, although it means extra weight and cost: but it is not indispensable.

MUTES

Mutes were known and used—for the trumpet—at least as far back as the early years of the 17th century, and Mersenne gives a drawing of one. No record of their earliest use with the horn has come to light, but it may be safely assumed that it was well before 1750. One imagines their primary purpose in those days to have been the preservation of friendly relations with neighbours when a player practised his instrument. They were no doubt also used at an early date—and later—by soloists and duettists to produce meretricious echo effects, to the probable wonder and certain delight of the less cultured among their audiences. Once again, as so often with the musical evolution of the horn, we are reduced to speculation. The earliest mute seems to have been a solid wooden cone with a hole through its centre, and it was no doubt the unsatisfactory nature of these primitive dampers that led Hampel to embark on the experiments that culminated in his hand-stopping technique. According to Frölich,[10] Hampel made a wooden 'stopper' (Ger. *Schedel*—presumably the same word as *Schädel*, a skull) that closely filled up the bell, and which not only muted the sound but lowered the pitch a semitone as well. Domnich[11] says that the first horn mutes were made of wood in the form of a truncated cone with a hole in the base through which the sound issued, but that as the contact between wood and brass gave rise to an unpleasant buzzing (*frémissement désagréable*), cardboard mutes were made and used for a long time, although the tone quality was not as pure as could be wished.

Several varieties of mute appeared in the latter part of the 18th century, including at least one with which chromatic intervals could be played as though the hand were free to manoeuvre in the bell. Satisfactory details of this mute, which was invented by Carl Türrschmidt or possibly by the brothers Boeck, are not available. Frölich,[12] in very cryptic language, describes a mute of this kind that consisted of a

> hollow papier mâché ball, about six inches across, with an open neck
> to be inserted into the bell of the horn. Inside this ball was another
> covered with leather and with a cord attached to it which hung

down from the bell. With this the neck could be more or less fully occluded at will, in the same way as by hand stopping.

Beethoven and Weber must have had some such contrivance in mind when they wrote the passages for muted horns given below:

Beethoven. *Rondino for Wind Instruments*

Weber. *Concerto for Clarinet*

It was Wagner, and even more Debussy, who first showed how effective muted horns could be as an orchestral colour when skilfully used, both of them clearly distinguishing between those passages they wanted hand stopped (*gestopft, bouché,* +) and those for which a mute was to be used (*gedämpft, avec la sourdine*).

Present-day mutes are made in widely varying shapes and of many different materials, including cardboard, papier mâché, wood, wood-fibre, brass, aluminium, and even suitably shaped gourds: there is therefore no uniformity of tone colour. It can be safely said that all commercial mutes are efficient in the high and medium registers, but this is by no means always the case in the low register. Intonation offers its problems as well, for a mute that is perfect with one instrument may be unsatisfactory with another whose bell section is of slightly different proportions; 'fine adjustment' here must be dealt with by the player himself. This may be done by inserting a thin metal or cardboard tube through the open end, and fixing it in place when the desired effect is achieved. If there is already a tube fixed inside the mute, a paper tube inserted into this will give some idea of what is required; the permanent tube can then be taken out and shortened if necessary, or replaced by a longer one. Many mutes are provided with strips of cork—usually three—and on the thickness of these will depend the more or less 'open' quality of the tone. Horns are apt to vary so much that hard and fast rules cannot be laid down, and a new mute will nearly always require some adjustment by the player before it is completely satisfactory. It is, therefore, not surprising that a player, when he has found a mute that fulfils all his desiderata, looks upon it as a most valuable possession.

The commonest type of mute is probably the hollow truncated cone closed at its base and open at the apex, made of rexine-covered cardboard; it is usually ribbed and without cork strips (Fig. 23) or, alternatively, without ribs but with cork strips. Inside this cone is an open tube about an inch in diameter which projects inwards to within about a couple of inches of the base. The French mute shown at Fig. 24 follows approximately the shape of the French—not German—horn bell. It has no interior tube, but there are two small holes in the base at the points marked × in the sketch. This mute, intended for use with French instruments, requires not only readjustment of the cork strips but also the insertion of an inner tube to correct the intonation when it is to be used with a large-bore German horn. Fig. 25 shows an American aluminium mute that is tunable from the outside, a portion of the inner tube being provided with a screw thread (Sansone's patent). Another American mute, made of wood-fibre and similar in its characteristics to the German model (Fig. 23), is shown at Fig. 26. Fig. 27 is a modified form of the original Zephyr mute introduced by the London makers Henry Keat & Sons about eighty or ninety years ago. It is made of brass and is very heavy, and in consequence liable to severe damage if accidentally dropped. The inner tube is conical and is fixed to the shell at the neck by three small stays, its top being soldered to the dome in which a hole is

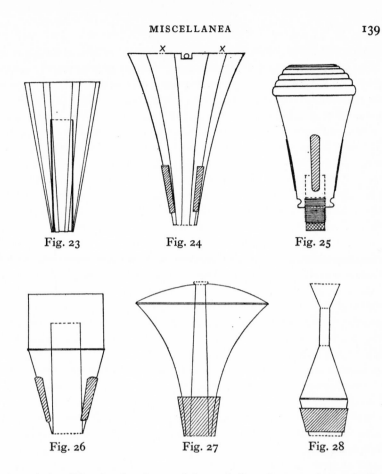

Fig. 23   Fig. 24   Fig. 25

Fig. 26   Fig. 27   Fig. 28

pierced. A solid strip of cork round the neck fixes the mute hermetically into the instrument. Intonation is consistently good, and it is equally efficient in every register. Its tone, however, resembles rather too closely that produced by hand stopping, but as such it is almost, if not quite, as efficient for producing brassy stopped notes in the low register as the pitch-raising mute specially made for this purpose.

None of the foregoing calls for any transposition on the part of the player, but Fig. 28 shows a German type of mute that acts in the same way as the hand in the case of stopped notes and raises the pitch a semi-tone. To get a 'brassy' quality into low stopped notes with the hand is exceedingly difficult, and needless to say this special mute is much more effective.

Modern composers call for muted horn effects so frequently that the mute has now become an essential part of the horn player's equipment.

There is, however, no standard type of mute—at any rate in England—and every player of experience has tried out many different kinds. Not surprisingly he will have selected the one that seems to suit his instrument the best, although it may be totally unlike that of his colleague at the next desk. This results in a lack of uniformity in the muted tone colour of the horn quartet. The fact that muted horns are now so often required in the orchestra makes it desirable that there should be a standard type of mute to be used by all players and on all occasions, unless there is a special indication in the score. For sooner or later the horn player, like the jazz trumpeter, will have to carry round several mutes for different effects, including perhaps—who knows?—a 'wah-wah'. . . .

BACH'S NOMENCLATURE

Another of those mysteries that cloud the early years of the horn's orchestral odyssey is the curious and varied nomenclature found in the scores of J. S. Bach. *Corno, cornu, corno da caccia, corne de chasse, corne par force,* and *lituus,* as well as the enigmatical *corno da tirarsi* that occurs in Cantatas 46, 67, and 162, all are used. Do these names indicate different instruments, or do they only imply some variance in the playing technique? Until fresh evidence is available we can only hazard a guess.

The horn as an orchestral instrument was almost a complete novelty when Bach made his first use of it in his *Jagdkantate* (BWV 205), composed in 1716, the score of which calls for two *corni* in F. These would no doubt have been what Kinsky[13] calls *grosse Jagdhörner in Waldhornform,* for although crooks had been applied to the horn earlier than the date of the composition, there is no reason to suppose that crooked horns immediately supplanted existing types. Indeed, the whole history of the development of wind instruments clearly shows that any revolutionary invention, however desirable or advantageous, always took many years before it was adopted by the general run of professional players, cases in point, among others, being the valve, the Boehm system, and the double horn.

Charles Sanford Terry grouped this nomenclature under two heads, *Waldhorn* and *Jagdhorn,* basing his classification on the nature of the work and deeming the *Waldhorn* to be the more intimate and the *Jagdhorn* the more ceremonial instrument.[14]

The table below, compiled from Terry's book and Kurt Janetzky's (of Leipzig) complete collection of Bach's horn parts, shows the name used by Bach (BWV), Terry's grouping, and the date of the composition.

Date	Terry	Janetzsky	Pitch	BWV No.
1716	Waldhorn	Corno da caccia 1.2.	F	208
1721	Jagdhorn	2 corni da caccia	F	1046
		(Brandenburg Concerto No. 1)		
1723	Waldhorn	Corno 1,2,	F	40
1724	Jagdhorn	Corno da caccia	C	16
1724	Jagdhorn	2 cornes de chasse	C	65
1724	Waldhorn	Corno 1.2.	F	83
1725	Waldhorn	Corno 1.2.	D	205
		(Aeolus)		
c. 1725	Zugtrompete	Corne	C-alt	73
c. 1725	Zugtrompete	Corno (?Zink)	C-alt	105
c. 1725	Waldhorn	Corno	A	136
c. 1726	Waldhorn	Corno 1.2.	G	195
1729	Jagdhorn	2 corni da caccia	G	174
c. 1730	Waldhorn	Corne 1.2.	F	52
c. 1730	Zugtrompete	Corne de chasse	C-alt	89
1731	Waldhorn	Corno 1.2.	G	112
c. 1731	Zugtrompete	Corne de chasse	C-alt	109
1732	Waldhorn	Corno 1.2.	G	88
1733	Jagdhorn	{ 2 corni da caccia { Cornu 1.2.	F } F }	213
		(Hercules)		
1733	Jagdhorn	Corno da caccia	D	232
		(B mi. Mass)		
1734	Waldhorn	2 corni da caccia	F	248
		(Christmas Oratorio)		
1735	Waldhorn	Corne par force	F and B-flat alt	14
1735	Zugtrompete	Corne	C-alt	68
1735	Waldhorn	Corne 1.2.	G	79
1735	Jagdhorn	2 corni da caccia	G	128
1735	Jagdhorn	Corni da caccia 1.2.3.	B-flat	143
c. 1735	Waldhorn	2 corni da caccia	G	100
c. 1736	Waldhorn	Corno 1.2.	F	233
		(Mass in F)		
c. 1737	Waldhorn	Lituus 1.2.	B-flat alt	118
c. 1740	Waldhorn	Corno 1.2.	F	1
c. 1740	Zugtrompete	Corno	C-alt	78
c. 1740	Waldhorn	Corno 1.2.	G	91

				BWV
Date	*Terry*	*Janetzsky*	*Pitch*	*No.*
1742	Waldhorn	Corne de chasse	G and D	212
?1749	Waldhorn	Corno 1.2.	G	250
				251, 252

(Three Wedding Chorales)

An inventory of instruments belonging to the Cöthen (Anhalt) Capelle, where Bach was Capellmeister between 1717 and 1723, includes the following items:[15]

An Parforce Hörnern

Ein Paar C Hörner mit seidnen Pantroullen hat Matthieson.
Ein Paar F Hörner mit seidnen Pantroullen sind im Hirsch.[16]
Ein Paar DIS Hörner sind im Hirsch.
Ein Paar G Hörner sind im Hirsch.
Krummbogen, Setz Stück sind im Hirsch.
Ein Paar Hüthe worinen A Hörner.

'Parforce' horns were made specifically for mounted sportsmen and would normally be of the open-hoop pattern—French horns, in fact. The two pairs provided with *Pantroullen*—presumably baldrics—may well have been small helical horns, with the first mentioned pair in C-alt, while the E-flat (DIS) and G instruments would have been ordinary French horns. The two A horns 'contained in hats' were no doubt of the model supplied by Gleichmann, of Ilmenau,[17] and not unlike that shown on Plate II, 3. The mention of crooks and tuning bits arouses curiosity, since Parforce horns properly so-called, though they might conceivably have had tuning bits, could not possibly have had crooks. These last, if they were horn crooks, must have belonged to orchestral horns not included in the inventory at all: otherwise they might have been trumpet or even trombone crooks. Alternatively the heading 'Parforce Hörnern' may simply have been used as a generic term, much as *cor de chasse* was in France during the 18th century: as late as 1785 the *Almanach Dauphin* (*Tablettes de Renommée des Musiciens*) shows all horn players—among them such notabilities as Rodolphe, Punto, Palsa, and Türrschmidt, as well as Siéber and Mozer, of the Opéra and Concert Spirituel orchestras —under the heading *Cors de Chasse*. By that time the horn with crooks had completely superseded the ordinary hunting horn for orchestral purposes. Be that as it may, this inventory was only compiled in 1768, forty-five years after Bach had left Cöthen for Leipzig and eighteen years after his death. It is most improbable that Bach had anything like this number of horns at his disposal in Cöthen, for he makes scarcely any use of the instrument before his move to Leipzig. There, no doubt, he did, sooner or later, have a similar or even more varied collection of them, with the probable addition of a couple of crooked orchestral horns.

On the face of it, it looks as though Bach, when he wanted a particularly brilliant effect, used an Italian, French, or German term meaning specifically a crookless hunting horn, and that when he wished for a more intimate and subdued effect, he simply wrote 'corno', with the idea that the part should be played on the less strident orchestral horn.

There is, however, a great deal to be said for the theory put to the present writer by Janetzsky that Bach's indications did not imply the use of different types of instrument, but simply different ways of holding them, bells pointing skywards for all hunting horns, and downwards—or perhaps more likely at shoulder level—for plain *corni*. Such a hypothesis is at least logical even if, pending fresh evidence, it is no more than conjectural.

While *lituus* (Cantata No. 118) was an unknown quantity until the publication in 1921[18] of a catalogue of musical instruments at Osseg (Bohemia) compiled in 1706, which mentions two *litui* 'vulgo Waldhörner', the *corno da tirarsi* still remains a complete mystery. Terry classifies all the *corno da tirarsi* parts (Cantata Nos. 46, 67, and 162) under the heading *Zugtrompete*, and expresses the view that the instrument may have been just a slide trumpet played with a deep cone mouthpiece instead of the usual shallow-cup trumpet mouthpiece. This theory is unsatisfactory, if only because the French use cone mouthpieces with the cornet and the trombone, yet neither on that account sounds in the least like a horn. Furthermore, the famous Berlin trumpeter Julius Kosleck, who was the first modern performer successfully to play Bach's clarino parts, used a mouthpiece made of sheet metal, just like the old horn mouthpieces: yet he was judged to have the ideal clarino tone. No doubt the structure of Kosleck's oral cavity and sinuses was very exceptional and combined in an extraordinary manner with the inner profile of his mouthpiece, which certainly would not suit the very great majority of good trumpet players.

The *corno da tirarsi* must be ruled out as a genuine horn, for it would have been impossible to apply slide mechanism to an instrument that was then perfectly conical from mouthpipe to bell. So, in the absence of an actual specimen, or even of any contemporary description, we are driven to surmise that the parts must have been played on some species of trombone, possibly muted in some way.

HORN CHORDS

The trick of producing two, three, and four notes simultaneously was no novelty when, something over a hundred years ago, that master mountebank Eugène Vivier burst upon the Parisian scene, and so mystified the French musical pundits of the day that they thought he had discovered something on a par with the squaring of the circle.[19] The trick must, however, have been known during the first half of the preceding century, for how else could those early virtuosi Creta and Ernst—perhaps also Mattheson's blind horn player—whose exploits are noted in Chapter 5, have accomplished the feats attributed to them? From contemporary sources we know that the great Punto himself was an adept at chord production;[20] Weber's Concertino, with chords in the cadenza, had been written nearly thirty years before Vivier's appearance in Paris; and Dauprat's horn tutor,[21] the standard work used at the Conservatoire since about 1825, explains, though very superficially, how what he calls 'les doubles sons' are produced. The fact that Dauprat condemns them as worthy only of charlatans, and that his predecessor Frédéric Duvernoy dismissed them as 'futilities', in no way excuses the ignorance and exaggerated astonishment of such academic musicians as Auber, Directeur of the Conservatoire, Adam and Halévy, both professors at that institution, and Castil-Blaze, the foremost musical writer and critic of his day.

Apart from two studies by J.-R. Lewy,[22] No. 2 and No. 4, the only works containing chords with which the present writer is acquainted are the Concertino in E by Weber[23] and the Concerto for violin, horn, and orchestra by Dame Ethel Smyth.[24]

As is now pretty widely known, chords are produced by playing one note and humming another at a suitable interval either above or below the horn note. The phenomenon of the three- or four-note chord arises from a reinforcement of certain combination tones which, though always present when two notes are sounded together, are normally too weak to be audible. How this reinforcement is brought about has never been satisfactorily explained, but given acoustic conditions that are not unfavourable, first-order differential and summational tones do, in fact, become powerful enough to sound like three or four horns playing very softly.[25]

In order to produce effective chords three conditions—outstanding skill as a horn player is not one of them—are essential: a singing voice that matches up well with the timbre of the horn; an unimpeachable ear, for the intervals must be absolutely true in just temperament; and the ability to keep both horn and voice notes absolutely steady and dynamically balanced.

The problem being essentially one of acoustics, it is hardly surprising if the authors of practical horn tutors offer little in the way of explanation, the one exception being H. Kling.[26] Still more valuable are the writings of Professor Kirby,[27] W. F. H. Blandford,[28] and Birchard Coar[29] who analyses all the chords resulting from the more important intervals. It must, however, be admitted that the chief interest in chords is scientific rather than artistic, for musically they can never be much more than an eyebrow-raiser for the uninitiated.

NOTES

[1] A French horn was used to test the C crook, the result being checked against a German instrument in F with valves $1+3$ so tuned as to give a C horn perfectly in tune. The B-flat section was tested on both types of horn, the rise being noticeably greater on the German than on the French model.

[2] V.-C. Mahillon, *Le Cor*. Bruxelles, 1907. *Eléments d'Acoustique*. Bruxelles, 1874.

[3] D. J. Blaikley, 'Horn'. *Grove's Dict. of Music and Musicians*. 3rd edition. London, 1927. 'The French Horn'. *Proc. Mus. Assn*. 15 June 1909.

[4] H. Bouasse, en collaboration avec M. Fouché, *Instruments à vent*. 2 vols. Paris, 1929.

[5] He appears to base this assumption on the fact that Fouché was able to lower the 4th harmonic of the cornet in C to B-natural without touching the valves. No difficult feat, this; had he tried to do the same with the 8th harmonic he might have found it less easy.

[6] The note in question appears as an appendix on p. 275: 'Note sur les sons bouchés et les trilles du cor'.

[7] Aug. Pree, in his *Waldhorn-Schule* (Dresden, 1911), deals with this point as follows: 'Many horn players think that certain notes, especially in the lower register, are lowered a semitone by stopping, and must be transposed accordingly: this view is erroneous. When the bell is completely stopped every note, even the lowest, can be produced when transposed a semitone lower. This, however, is difficult to do, and needs a lot of practice'. This statement is entirely confirmed by the present writer's own experience.

[8] Oscar Franz, *Waldhorn-Schule*. n.d., but *c*. 1880. English edition, *School for the Horn*. Edited by Thomas R. Busby. London, 1902.

[9] Philip Farkas, *The Art of French Horn Playing*. Chicago, 1956.

[10] Ersch u. Gruber, *Encyclopædia*.

[11] H. Domnich, op. cit.

[12] *Zeitschrift für Instrumentenbau*. Vol. VI, p. 325 (footnote).

[13] Georg Kinsky, *Kleiner Katalog der Sammlung alter Musikinstrumente*. Cöln, 1913.

[14] Charles Sanford Terry, *Bach's Orchestra*. London, 1932.

[15] *Bach-Jahrbuch*, 1905.

[16] This was a hostelry called 'Zum Goldene Hirsch' (The Golden Hart), with an assembly room in which concerts were given.

[17] See above, Chapter 2.

[18] *Bach-Jahrbuch*, 1921.

[19] In particular Auber, Halévy, Adolphe Adam, and Castil-Blaze. Adam, indeed, made rather an ass of himself in *Le Charivari* of 29 May 1843, where he wrote a long article entitled 'La Chose Impossible', which he begins thus:

> Posez-vous un problème insoluble et figurez-vous qu'il est résolu: la quadrature du cercle, la navigation aérienne, la paix universelle, toutes les utopies réalisées ne nous étonneraient pas davantage que ce que nous avons entendu hier . . .
>
> Il s'agit d'un jeune artiste. . . . M. Vivier, qui fait entendre sur le cor (un cor ordinaire sans aucune espèce de mécanisme) des passages à deux, trois et même à quatre parties. Quel moyen M. Vivier emploie-t-il pour produire cet étrange phénomène qui renverse toutes les lois de l'acoustique et de la physique? C'est là son secret que nul ne saurait deviner . . .

> Think of an insoluble problem and imagine it solved: squaring the circle, aerial navigation, universal peace, the realization of any utopia could not surprise us more than what we heard yesterday . . .
>
> This was a young artist. . . . M. Vivier, who plays on the horn (an ordinary hand horn without any mechanism whatsoever) passages in two, three, and even four parts. How does M. Vivier accomplish this extraordinary feat which upsets every law of acoustics and physics? That is his unfathomable secret . . .

The following month, in a letter to *La France Musicale* (18 June 1843), Alexis Martin explained how the trick was accomplished, adding that Duvernoy, under whom he studied, had advised him not to waste his time on such futilities, which might prejudice his intonation.

[20] (*a*) *Prager neue Zeitung*, 1801, No. 39, p. 473.

    (*b*) Frölich's article on the horn in Ersch u. Gruber, *Encyclopædia*.

[21] Dauprat, op. cit., 2e partie, p. 152.

> Punto qui les faisait [*les doubles sons*] beaucoup mieux que tous ceux qui s'en sont mêlés depuis, en avouait lui-même la facilité et le ridicule.
>
> Laissez donc aux charlatans les moyens extraordinaires qui ne conviennent qu'à la médiocrité, qui n'étonnent que les ignorans et que repoussent également les connaisseurs et les vrais Artistes'.

> Punto, who produced them [*chords*] far better than any who have since attempted them, himself admitted how easy and how silly they were.
>
> So leave it to charlatans to perform these extravagant feats, which surprise only the ignorant and which connoisseurs and true Artists alike reject.

[22] J.-R. Lewy, *Douze études pour le cor chromatique et le cor simple, avec accompagnement de piano*. Leipzig. Undated, but presumably written about 1850.

[23] This concertino was originally written in 1806 for the Carlsruhe player Dautrevaux, but revised in 1815 for Rauch, of Munich. The earlier version has been lost, so it is not known whether it contained the chords.

[24] The Ethel Smyth Concerto for violin, horn, and orchestra was first performed at a Henry Wood Symphony Concert on 5 March 1927. The soloists were Mme Jelly d'Aranyi and the late Aubrey Brain. The present writer has heard this work broadcast, with that distinguished artist Barry Tuckwell as horn soloist. Tuckwell not only gave an impeccable performance of the concerto and its exceedingly difficult cadenza but also succeeded in making the chords sound really resonant.

[25] The frequencies of the differential and summational tones are respectively equal to the difference between and the sum of the frequencies of the generators.

[26] H. Kling, *Horn-Schule* and *Le Cor de Chasse*.

[27] Percival R. Kirby, 'Horn Chords: an acoustical problem.' *Musical Times*. Sept. 1925, p. 811.

[28] W. F. H. Blandford, 'Some observations on "horn chords: an acoustical problem" '. *Musical Times*. Feb. 1926, p. 92.

[29] Birchard Coar, *The French Horn*, pp. 92 et seq.

CHAPTER 8

Biographical Notes on a few Distinguished Players and Teachers of the Past

DURING THE LAST quarter of the 18th century and the first third or so of the 19th a galaxy of virtuoso horn soloists bestrode the musical firmament, their names as familiar to the contemporary concertgoer as those of the leading keyboard and string instrumentalists. Thereafter solo horn playing suffered an eclipse that was to last about a hundred years.

The eclipse was not, as may appear at first sight, due to any decline in the quality of the best players, nor even—though a contributory factor—the gradual supersession of the natural horn by the mechanized instrument; the real reason was that by then the hand horn had given everything of which it was artistically and technically capable, and any further advance was impossible. The valve horn to which composers were more and more turning their attention was a new instrument which, for a considerable time, was inferior to the simple horn in beauty of tone. A long period of trial and error was needed to determine a technique that could master the increasingly complex music that, from Wagner on, was being written for it. The horn concerto therefore ceased to be a welcome addition to a symphony programme, and the players, fully occupied in battling with the difficulties of the new orchestral writing, had neither time nor incentive to take up serious solo work.

It is rare indeed for an orchestral player *as such* to acquire more than a local reputation, so except for two of the earliest, Meifred and Lewy, we know little about the valve-horn pioneers beyond what may be gleaned from such tutors and/or studies as they may have left behind them, for their names are seldom to be found in musical dictionaries. No foreign horn soloist seems to have visited England since Vivier—and he was a hand-horn player—until, a few years ago, an American and an Italian gave horn recitals in London.[1]

Probably the first major work for solo horn in the modern idiom—the Strauss No. 1 Concerto is an early effort not technically in advance of Schumann—was the Ethel Smyth Double Concerto of 1927, the solo horn part being written for Aubrey Brain, then first horn of the B.B.C. Symphony Orchestra, who went to Berlin to play it with the Berlin

Philharmonic Orchestra. This, however, did no more than crack the ice, and for a genuine renaissance of solo horn playing we had to wait for the arrival, in the immediate post-war years, of Aubrey Brain's remarkable son, Dennis. An American writer[2] has aptly compared Dennis Brain's accomplishment of what had hitherto been thought impossible to Roger Bannister's four-minute mile. In both cases, the impossible having been proved possible, others have followed their lead, and just as there are now several who can run a mile inside four minutes, so there are now young horn players on both sides of the Atlantic who are successfully pursuing the road opened up by Dennis Brain.

SWEDA, Wenzel (*c.* 1638–*c.*1710) and RÖLLIG, Peter (*c.* 1650–1723). The two bandsmen of Franz Anton, count von Sporck originally taught to play the horn at Versailles in 1680 or '81. Sweda appears to have been the founder of the famous Bohemian School of horn playing.

ZEDDELMAYER, Johann (*c.* 1675–post-1736). The engagement of Zeddelmayer at Weissenfels in 1706 is the first known engagement of a horn player.

MATIEGKA, Joseph (1728–1804). A famous teacher and virtuoso in Prague. He trained upwards of fifty players, among whom were Hampel, the introducer of hand stopping, and the celebrated Punto.

HAMPEL (or HAMPL), Anton Joseph (*c.* 1710–71). Very little is known about the life of Hampel beyond the fact that he entered the Dresden Court Orchestra in 1737 as second horn and retained this position until his retirement or death. In 1747 he was joined by Haudek, and the pair, with Haudek as first horn, soon made a great reputation both as duettists and as teachers, their star pupil being Stich, better known as Punto. Hampel's chief claim to celebrity is, of course, his initiation of hand-stopping technique, which has already been dealt with in Chapter 5 (phase 2). Whether the priority really rests with Hampel or with Rodolphe and whether Rodolphe carried it further than Hampel (for it was Punto who really developed the Hampel technique and he can hardly have become Hampel's pupil before the early 1760s) is a question that cannot at the moment be answered. Hampel's methods were certainly given wide publicity by the many pupils he and Haudek trained, and by Punto most of all, whereas Rodolphe neither taught the horn nor travelled widely, apart from his early sojourns in Italy and Stuttgart. Then Domnich, himself a German and perhaps a thought jealous of Rodolphe, has given us the most detailed account we have of the beginnings of hand stopping and in it gives all the credit for the discovery to Hampel, and for its extension to Punto: of Rodolphe, Domnich says only that he was the first to promulgate the result of this discovery in France. Hampel is certainly entitled to the credit of designing the *Inventionshorn*, a great improvement on the terminally crooked horns in use at that time. It is a great pity that not more is known about his life and teaching methods, and that it is impossible to pinpoint with any accuracy the date when he first brought his new technique to the notice of musicians generally. According to Profeta, Hampel died in Dresden on 30 March 1771. Hampel's compositions amount to very little: a few exercises, some trios, and the tutor, revised and published shortly before the turn of the century by Punto. All remained in manuscript except, of course, Punto's version of the tutor.

SCHINDELÁRŽ, Johann (*c.* 1715–?). Principal horn in the Mannheim orchestra under J. Stamitz; chiefly notable as one of the teachers of Haudek and Punto.

HAUDEK, Karl (1721–18?). Haudek was born at Dobrzisch (Bohemia) and, when seventeen, went to study under Schindelárž with whom he remained for six years. After two years in the service of Count Kinsky he was appointed *Konzertmeister* to Prince Johann Adam von Auersberg, whom he left in 1747 to become Court Virtuoso at Dresden. Here he met Hampel, and together they played the most difficult duets before the Court, Haudek playing first horn. He and Hampel quickly acquired a widespread reputation not only as virtuoso duettists but also as teachers.

According to contemporary orchestra lists Haudek was still playing with the Dresden orchestra in 1783, and Dlabácž says he was still living in Dresden in 1800. He was succeeded in the orchestra by his son, Joseph (1762–1832).

STEINMÜLLER, Thaddäus (*c.* 1725–90). For many years principal horn in the Esterhazy orchestra. Noted for his command of the very high register. The Haydn Divertimento for violin, horn, and cello, said by Hyatt King to have been written for Steinmüller, shows his astonishing all-over technique.

RODOLPHE, Jean-Joseph (1730–1812). Born in Strasbourg, Rodolphe was taught the horn and violin from the age of seven by his father. When he was sixteen he went to Paris to study the violin under Jean-Marie Leclair, one of the foremost violinists of his time. After fulfilling engagements as a violinist in Bordeaux, Montpellier, and other towns in the south of France, he entered the service of the duke of Parma in 1754, devoting himself especially to the horn. His achievements on this instrument have already been told in some detail (see Chapter 5, phase 2) and need not be repeated here. In 1760 he left the duke of Parma's band to enter that of Duke Karl von Württemburg at Stuttgart, where he studied composition with Jommelli: it was here that he composed his first ballets. Three years later he returned to Paris and joined the band of Louis François de Bourbon, prince de Conti. He played concertos of his own composition on several occasions at the Concert Spirituel in 1764, earning the praise of the critics.[3] In 1765 Rodolphe apparently became a member of the Opéra orchestra as a violinist, probably with a note after his name *et pour le cor de chasse*, for although in that year he gave the opera audience its first taste of the hand horn in the obbligato to Boyer's air 'L'amour dans ce riant bocage', and played other obbligatos when they occurred, he was never a member of the regular horn desk. He was appointed to the *Musique des Petits Appartements du Roi* in 1770, and four years later to the Royal Chapel. He had much to do with the formation, in 1784, of the *Ecole Royale de Chant*, of which he was professor of composition until 1788 when he was succeeded by Gossec. He became professor of *solfège* at the newly formed Conservatoire in 1798, but had to retire in 1802 on the grounds of ill-health (he was then seventy-two); he was granted a pension of 1,200 francs a year. He died in Paris on 18 August 1812.

Rodolphe must have been an exceptionally fine performer on the horn, as witness not only the many laudatory notices of his playing in the *Mercure de France*,[3] but also the flattering terms in which La Borde speaks of him in his *Essai sur la musique*.[4] He evidently commanded a very large compass, and Dauprat tells us that his efforts to cover both extremes of the range cost him an incurable hernia.[5] One wonders what Dauprat would say if he could hear some of our present-day hornists!

Rodolphe composed a number of works for the theatre, the most important being *La Mariage par Capitulation* (1764), *L'Aveugle de Palmyre* (1767), and *Ismenor* (1773), composed for the wedding of the comte d'Artois. His instrumental works include two concertos for horn; *Fanfares faciles pour deux Cors*; twenty-four fanfares for three horns; as well as duets and studies for the violin. His best-known work was, of course, the famous *Solfèges de Rodolphe*. This was said to have been written originally in 1772 for the girl pupils of the Paris opera school who were then known as *les filles du Magasin*:[6] it was first published in 1786 and, in spite of Fétis's severe condemnation of it, had run into thirty editions in Fétis's day and was still in use in primary schools in France at least up to the outbreak of World War I.

Confusion, due originally to Gerber, sometimes arises between Jean-Joseph Rodolphe and Johann Anton Rudolf, another famous horn player in the band of prince von Thurn und Taxis in Regensburg. There is no connection whatever between the two. Rudolf was born in Vienna in 1770[7] and became director of the theatre orchestra in Regensburg.

STICH, Jan Václav: better known as Giovanni PUNTO (1748–1803). A serf of Count Joseph Johann von Thun, Stich was born at Žehužice, near Czaslau in Bohemia. He showed such early musical promise that his master sent him, together with Franz Weisbach, to study first under Matiegka in Prague, then to Schindelárž in Mannheim, and finally to Hampel and Haudek in Dresden. During his stay in Dresden he lodged in the house of Haudek. While still quite young he created astonishment by often playing, one after the other, two or three difficult *Sekond-conzerte*—presumably concertos written within the range of a second horn—although his physique was by no means robust. His studies completed, he returned to serve his master, but after three years he found his service irksome and decided to become a travelling virtuoso. According to Gerber, he and four of his colleagues ran away; count von Thun, furious, sent in pursuit of them, having given orders that if Stich could not be captured, at least his front teeth were to be knocked out. Stich, however, evaded the count's bum-bailiffs and reached the territory of the Holy Roman Empire in safety, and after Italianizing his name into Punto set out on his European travels. Between 1768 and 1781 he appears to have visited Germany, Hungary, Italy, England, and France. He must have been in England in the early part of 1772, for Burney, who later that year heard him in Coblenz where Punto was then a member of the elector's band, refers to his performance in London.[8] During 1776–78 he appeared on several occasions at the Concert Spirituel, earning enthusiastic praise from the critics on each occasion. During the latter year he met Mozart, who was so impressed by his playing that he wrote to his father 'Punto bläst magnifique', and composed a *symphonie concertante* to be played by Wendling (flute), Ramm (oboe), Punto (horn), and Ritter (bassoon) (Einstein K 297b). In 1781 Punto entered the service of the bishop of Würzburg, but in the following year an attractive proposal from the comte d'Artois, who later became Charles X and whose favourite instrument was the horn,[9] brought him back to Paris: he was given a life pension for what was virtually a sinecure. At some time when he was in Paris, probably during the 1770s, Raoux made him a horn of silver which, unlike Dauprat, he preferred to any other metal. Obtaining leave of absence in 1787 he visited the Rhineland towns, and in the following year was engaged by Madame Mara for her concerts at the Pantheon in London.

The French Revolution in 1789 forced d'Artois to flee the country, and for a time Punto conducted the orchestra of the Théâtre des Variétés Amusantes. After a visit to Munich, where he gave a concert in December 1799, he went on to Vienna. Here he met Beethoven, who wrote for him the well-known Sonata in F (op. 17), of which they gave the first performance together in April 1800. The following year Punto returned to his native Bohemia for the first time in thirty-three years and gave a grand concert in Prague, at which his performance elicited the highest praise from the critic of the *Prager neue Zeitung*.[10] In 1802 he joined forces with the pianist Dussek and together they visited his home district, giving a concert at Czaslau on 16 September, at which they played the Beethoven Sonata. Punto then appears to have made a short visit to Paris, and on his return to Prague was overtaken by a fatal illness—some form of chest dropsy or hydrothorax—to which he succumbed on 16 February 1803, in his fifty-sixth year. He was given a magnificent funeral, Mozart's Requiem being performed at the graveside. The following Latin couplet is inscribed on his tomb:

> Omne tulit punctum Punto, qui Musa Bohema
> Ut plausit vivo, sic moriente gemit.

Punto had, unquestionably, an enormous influence on the development of horn technique, an influence comparable with that, in modern times, of Dennis Brain. Both had a technical mastery far in advance of their contemporaries, and both had a personality that acted as a stimulus alike on the young generation of players to emulate their achievements and on the public to accept the horn as a major solo instrument.

LEITGEB (or LEUTGEB), Ignaz. Although we do not know the actual date of Leitgeb's birth, it can, with reasonable certainty, be placed about 1745 and probably at Salzburg. He was first horn in the band of the prince archbishop of Salzburg when he toured various European cities, among them Paris where he appeared on several occasions as a soloist with the orchestra of the Concert Spirituel in April and May 1770. He got excellent notices from the critics,[11] winning, on his first appearance, applause that was 'well merited by the superior talent he showed in the performance of a concerto of his own composition'. After his performance in May it was said of him that he

played two concertos with the utmost artistry. The tones he elicits from his instrument are a continual source of wonder to his hearers.

His outstanding quality is to 'sing' adagios as perfectly as the most mellow, the most interesting and the most accurately pitched voice.

Though he was already on friendly terms with the Mozart family, it was not until ten or eleven years later, when they were both settled in Vienna, that Mozart began composing horn music specially for Leitgeb. In fact the Concert-Rondo, the four concertos, the wind and piano quintet, and the so-called *Leitgebischer* quintet for horn, violin, two violas, and cello, this last extremely difficult for the horn. In 1777 Leitgeb settled in Vienna, and added to his horn-playing activities a cheesemonger's business for which Leopold Mozart put up the capital. Leitgeb, for his part, made himself useful in a number of practical ways to the Mozarts. Perhaps because of this and because nothing is known about his education, musical or otherwise, as well as the fact that his intimate friend, Mozart, was sometimes inclined to indulge in horse-play at Leitgeb's expense, it has been generally assumed that he was lacking in culture. But surely if he had really been the insignificant personality that some writers would have us believe, he would hardly have satisfied, as he did, the Paris critics who were apt to be very severe with any who did not come up to the approved standard of artistry. As for the notion that Mozart 'wrote down' to his interpreter, as one writer has suggested, it is laughable: artists of the calibre of Mozart do not do such things. It is not unlikely that Leitgeb avoided the cultural gatherings of the rich from a natural distaste for such functions, and so got an undeserved reputation of being a bumpkin. One cannot help feeling, however, that whatever his shortcomings in the matter of drawing-room manners and culture, he was at heart one of Nature's gentlemen and an extremely sensitive artist. He died, in prosperous circumstances, in Vienna on 27 February 1811.

TÜRRSCHMIDT, Carl (1753–97). Studied the horn with his father, Johann Türrschmidt, who was first horn in the band of Prince Kraft Ernst von Oettingen-Wallerstein. In his eighteenth year he joined forces with Johann PALSA (1752–92), his senior by eight months, who played first horn. In 1770 they visited Paris together and attracted the notice of the prodigal Henri-Louis-Marie de Rohan, prince de Guémenée, who took them into his service. The two, who always seem to have played together as duettists until Palsa's death, performed on many occasions at the Concert Spirituel, always to the satisfaction of the critics. After the resounding bankruptcy in 1783 of prince de Guémenée they were engaged by the Landgrave of Hesse-Cassel, and in 1786 visited London where they performed first at the Anacreontic Society and then at a

Salomon Subscription Concert.[12] They returned to Cassel, and on the death of the Landgrave went to the Prussian Court Orchestra in Berlin. Here, in 1792, Palsa died of a chest dropsy, like Punto a few years later, his place being taken by the French virtuoso Jean Lebrun. Palsa was noted for the beauty and purity of his *cantabile*, while Türrschmidt was renowned for his facility of execution and the skilful use he made of his hand in the bell. Although these two artists are known to have been in Berlin from 1786 onwards, Framery, in his *Calendrier Universal Musical* for 1788 and 1789, shows them both as freelances in Paris. Palsa and Türrschmidt jointly published three sets of duos for horn, while Anton Rosetti wrote a *Concerto für Waldhorn mit Orchester* (in E-flat) which is inscribed 'Pour Monsieur Dürrschmied'.

Like Hampel, Türrschmidt was of a mechanical turn of mind. While in Paris about 1780 he redesigned, in collaboration with Joseph Raoux, the *Inventionshorn* as it was then made in Germany (see Plate IV, 1), and together they evolved the model that came to be known as the *cor-solo* (Plate IV, 2). It was this model that Raoux made in silver for Türrschmidt, Palsa, and Punto, and which became the instrument *par excellence* of the concert soloist everywhere. Türrschmidt is also credited with the invention of a mute with which it was possible to play a chromatic scale. A close friend of Gerber, Türrschmidt supplied most of the information about the horn in Gerber's *Lexikon*. He died in Berlin on 1 November 1797.

DUVERNOY, Frédéric-Nicolas (1765–1838). Born on 16 October 1765, at Montbéliard in the east of France, he was, according to Fétis, a self-taught musician. We find him in Paris in the orchestra of the Comédie Italienne in 1788 and as a soloist at the Concert Spirituel. Two years later he joined the band of the Garde Nationale and in the same year became second horn at the Opéra-Comique, with Vandenbroek as first. In 1795 he was appointed senior professor of the horn at the Conservatoire, the other three being Buch (first horns), with Kenn and Domnich (second horns). He entered the orchestra of the Opéra in 1796, becoming solo horn three years later, with Buch, Kenn, Vandenbroek, and Paillard as the regular supporting quartet. On the re-establishment by Napoléon Bonaparte of the *Chapelle Musique*, Duvernoy, whom Napoléon is said greatly to have admired, was appointed first horn, a position he held until 1830. He retired from the Opéra in 1816 and from the Conservatoire in 1817, and was succeeded in both posts by Dauprat. His artistic success as a *cor-mixte* has already been spoken of in Chapter 5 (phase 2). In 1803 Duvernoy published his *Méthode pour le Cor*, which broke new ground and was far in advance of anything of the kind published previously: it is by no means the *méthode de cor-mixte* that Fétis labels it, for, although the exercises it contains are in the main restricted to the *cor-mixte* register, he insists on the student adopting either the 'first horn' or 'second horn' category at the outset. Duvernoy was a *Chevalier de la Légion d'Honneur*: he died in Paris on 19 July 1838.

DOMNICH, Heinrich (1767–1844?). Domnich's place in the gallery of famous horn players is as a teacher rather than as a virtuoso. Born in Würzburg, his father was a horn player in the service of the elector of Bavaria. In or about 1783 he went to Paris and studied under Punto, for whom he had the greatest admiration. In December 1785 he made his first appearance at the Concert Spirituel, playing second to Lebrun in a *symphonie concertante*, and earning the critic's praise for the neatness and rapidity of his execution and for the way he backed up Lebrun. Apart from one occasion in 1788, when he played a concerto by Devienne, he seems always to have played in duos or trios. He joined the Opéra orchestra in 1787 as second to Lebrun, the band of the Garde Nationale in 1793, and in 1795 was appointed a professor of the horn at the Conservatoire, resigning this last position in 1817 when his class was merged in that of Dauprat. Domnich was also a member of the *Chapelle Musique* of Napoléon Bonaparte from 1806 to 1816.

Of his admirable *Méthode de Premier et de Second Cor* enough has already been said in Chapter 5 (phase 2), but Domnich also composed three concertos for horn and orchestra, a *Symphonie Concertante* for two horns and orchestra, and two collections of ballads; some of these last, so Fétis tells us, were quite charming and had considerable success.

Domnich trained a number of outstanding pupils, among them E.-C. Lewy and J.-B. Mengal.

What happened to Domnich after his retirement from the Conservatoire is uncertain. There is no further mention of him in the archives of the Conservatoire, but Mendel (*Musikalisches Conversations-Lexikon*) says that he retired after the abdication of Charles X in 1830 and died in Paris on 19 July 1844. He was not, however, a member of the *Chapelle Musique* of Charles X and on the whole it seems probable that when he gave up his Paris appointments he returned to his native land and passed the remainder of his days in retirement.

He had two brothers who were also distinguished horn players. The elder, Jacob (1758–?), went to America and was last heard of in Philadelphia in 1806. The younger, Arnold (1771–1834), was first horn in the Meiningen Kapelle.

STÖLZEL, Heinrich (1777–1844), was born in Scheibenberg (Saxony). The importance of Stölzel lies rather in his connection with valves than his prowess as a performer on the horn, in which role he appears to have been no more than adequate. His part in the invention and dissemination of the valve has been fully dealt with in Chapter 3, so it is only necessary here to mention such few facts as are otherwise known about him. In 1817 he became a member of the Royal Opera orchestra in Berlin, from which he retired in 1829 with a pension. That he also became a maker is evident from the catalogue quoted below, taken from the last page of Sundelin's *Die Instrumentirung für das Orchester*, but whether or not any of his instruments still survive, the present writer does not know.

PRICE LIST OF CHROMATIC BRASS INSTRUMENTS INVENTED BY ME

A chromatic French horn	40 Rsf.
A chromatic Bass Horn or Bass Trumpet in F or E-flat	45 Rsf.
A chromatic Tenor Horn or Tenor Trumpet in B-flat	40 Rsf.
A chromatic Trumpet in F or E-flat	25 Rsf.
A chromatic Trumpet in B-flat alto	21 Rsf.
A chromatic Bugle [*Signalhorn*]	16 Rsf.

In order to allay false rumours and abuses lately current, H. Stölzel begs to make the following announcement:

All chromatic brass instruments manufactured by me will in future carry my registered trade-mark as a guarantee of their authenticity. Every purchaser of one of these instruments will be given free of charge a leaflet of instructions which will enable the player to maintain his instrument in perfect working order. Composers who may be desirous of receiving detailed information on the subject will find what they require in A. Sundelin's *Instrumentirung für Militär-Musik*, price 25 sgr.[13] (Wagenführ's Buch- und Musik-Handlung in Berlin, Leipziger Strasse No. 50.)

All other instruments required for brass bands [*Horn- und Trompeten-Musik*] may be had from me of the best quality and at the most reasonable prices.

Berlin, March 1828.

Stölzel,

Königl. Kammermusikus und Mechanikus.

(Address, Lindenstrasse No. 28)

Stölzel died in Berlin in 1844, apparently leaving a widow and children in very poor circumstances.[14]

DAUPRAT, Louis-François (1781–1868). Although Dauprat was a virtuoso of the first rank, he lacked the self-confidence necessary to pursue the career of a concert soloist and preferred to devote his great gifts to teaching, orchestral playing, and composition for his instrument. His *Méthode de Cor Alto et Cor Basse* is incomparably the greatest didactic work ever published on the horn, and it is much to be regretted that it is not readily available to present-day horn students. Although, of course, a purely hand-horn tutor, it is full of the soundest possible advice both as regards instrumental technique and musical interpretation. With this, and Farkas's excellent *The Art of French Horn Playing* for the special technique of the double horn, the student has all he needs until he reaches the point where he is ready to work on his own, without a preceptor. It appears that Dauprat also wrote a valve-horn tutor—or rather a supplement to his *Méthode*—but which, unfortunately, was never published. All that ever appeared in print was a single sheet with a few exercises on it and a text that is no more than a publisher's blurb and an advertisement for Meifred's improved horn as manufactured by Halary-Antoine. It was published by Zetter & Cie., Paris, and is undated.[15] No doubt the appearance of Meifred's *Méthode pour le Cor Chromatique ou à Pistons*, published by Richault in 1841, was the main reason why Dauprat's work remained in manuscript. There would have been no call for two valve-horn tutors at that time, and it would be quite in keeping with Dauprat's generous nature to withdraw his own work in favour of that of his pupil, Meifred, the acknowledged valve-horn expert of his day.

Dauprat was born in Paris on 24 May 1781, and as a boy was a chorister at the Cathedral of Notre Dame. In 1794 he entered the Institut National de Musique as a pupil of J.-J. Kenn, principal *cor basse* at the Opéra. He was put in the band first of *Les Elèves de Mars* and then in that of the camp of twenty thousand men set up at the *Trou d'Enfer*, near Marly. He won a *premier prix* at the first public examinations ever held by the Conservatoire in 1798, and the silver-mounted horn presented to him by L.-J. Raoux on that occasion is illustrated in Plate IV, 2.

In 1799 he joined the band of the Gardes des Consuls, accompanying the regiment throughout the Italian campaign of 1800. On his return to Paris he obtained his discharge from the army and got a position at the Théâtre Montansier, at the same time rejoining the Conservatoire to study harmony with Catel and composition with Gossec. Later, between 1817 and 1820, he also studied under Reicha, for whose wind-instrument works he had the greatest admiration. When Kenn retired from the Opéra in 1808, Dauprat took his place, succeeding to the position of solo horn when Duvernoy gave it up in 1817, relinquishing it in his turn in 1831 owing to a disagreement with the management. He was appointed an honorary member of the imperial *Chapelle Musique* in 1811, and taking over from Domnich in 1816, was a member of the royal band under Louis XVIII and Charles X until 1830. From 1832 to 1842 he was *cor basse* in Louis-Philippe's *chapelle*, retiring altogether from public musical life in 1842.

Dauprat was honorary assistant professor of the horn at the Conservatoire from 1802 until, in 1816, he was appointed professor in the place of Duvernoy, and when in the following year Domnich also retired, Dauprat became sole professor, to be succeeded in 1842 by his pupil, Gallay. Dauprat trained a number of distinguished players, among them Meifred, Gallay, J.-F. Rousselot, Urbin, and Paquis.

After his retirement Dauprat lived mostly with a married daughter in Egypt, but made occasional visits to Paris, where he died on 17 July 1868.

Modest by nature and abhorring publicity, Dauprat preferred the comparative anonymity of the orchestra to the life of the concert virtuoso, in spite of the success he had when a young man as a soloist at the Odéon and Rue de Grenelle concerts.

In addition to his monumental *Méthode* Dauprat left a number of studies for horn, with detailed instructions as to how they are to be played, five concertos, various solos, duos, trios, etc., for horn, as well as sundry unpublished works. His attempt to have 'first' and 'second' horns renamed 'cor-alto' and 'cor-basse' was unsuccessful.

Dauprat was one of the founders, in 1828, of the *Société des Concerts du Conservatoire*, of which he was first horn until 1841. The present writer's teacher, François Brémond, had, as a young man, met Dauprat in Paris and never tired of singing his praises.

MEIFRED, Pierre-Joseph-Emile (1791–1867), is especially important for his pioneer work in improving the original German valve horn, as we have already seen, and in getting it generally accepted.

He was born at Colmar, learned the rudiments of music as a child, and appears to have been educated first at the *Prytanée Militaire* at La Flèche and then at the *Ecole des Arts et Métiers* at Châlons. Through the influence of the duc de La Rochefoucauld he obtained a post on the secretarial staff of Empress Joséphine, and after her death was for a very short time private secretary to La Rochefoucauld. In 1815 he entered Dauprat's horn class at the Conservatoire, winning a *premier prix* in 1818: he also studied composition with Reicha. Then, after three years at the Théâtre Royal Italien, a vacancy occurred in the Opéra orchestra owing to the premature death of P.-L. Colin; Meifred obtained the position and remained at the Opéra until 1850. Meifred was a co-founder of the *Société des Concerts du Conservatoire*, and for twenty years its secretary: at the Society's first concert in 1828 he played a valve-horn solo of his own composition, introducing the new instrument to the Paris public.

A valve-horn class was instituted at the Conservatoire in 1833, with Meifred as professor, but was suppressed on his retirement in 1864. Meifred was also the prime mover in the creation of the *Gymnase Musical Militaire* in 1836, but Berr, the clarinettist, was appointed its director, and when Berr died two years later, Meifred's claims were again passed over in favour of Carafa, who had recently been elected *Membre de l'Institut*.

Meifred wrote a most excellent *Méthode pour le Cor Chromatique ou à Pistons*, the first important valve-horn tutor. It was first published in 1841 (two-valve horn), and the appendix to Part 2, dealing with the three-valve instrument with Halary's ascending third valve, in 1849. This tutor is dealt with above in Chapter 5, phase 3. Other technical works of his include *De l'étendue, de l'emploi et des ressources du cor en général et de ses corps de rechange en particulier* (1829), for the guidance of young composers, and 'Notice sur la fabrication des instruments de musique en cuivre en général et sur celle du cor en particulier' (1851), this last being an essay on the evolution of the valve. Meifred, a reputed wit, published some amusing light verse, and was for a time on the editorial staff of two periodicals, *Mélomanie* and *La Critique Musicale*. He was made *Chevalier de la Légion d'Honneur* in 1848, and died in Paris on 28 August 1867.

PUZZI, Giovanni (1792–1876), was perhaps the greatest horn virtuoso of the first half of last century. He was born in Parma and was probably a pupil of the famous Italian horn player Luigi Belloli. Little seems to be known of his life before 1817, except that he is said to have been in Paris some time before then. Certainly the name 'Buzzi' as one of the five horns at the Odéon Opéra Bouffon Italien in 1815 (*Almanach des Spectacles de Paris* for that year) looks like a garbled version of Puzzi. He came to England, where he remained for the rest of his long life, in 1817, under the patronage, it is said, of the duke of Wellington. He made his first appearance as a soloist with the Philharmonic Society on 28 April 1817, and his last on 15 May 1837, having, in the course of those twenty years, performed on eight occasions as a soloist and on nine in small combinations of wind and string virtuosi.

During his first ten years or so in England he was principal horn of various London orchestras and the more important provincial festivals. In 1826, however, the director of the King's Theatre, where Puzzi was solo horn, sent him abroad talent-scouting for singers. One of those whom he engaged was Signorina Giacinta Toso, who became his wife and was, as Mme Puzzi, one of the most admired and successful concert singers in London. About this time Puzzi appears to have given up orchestral work altogether and confined himself to solo playing and his increasing activities as an impresario. After about 1840 he was seldom heard in public, though he evidently retained all his powers, for in September of that year at a Cheltenham concert he not only accompanied Mme Persiani in a song, 'La Potenza d'Amore', 'in fine style'— the song elicited 'unanimous encores'—but he, and the pianist Cianchettini, played a Scottish rondo composed by Moscheles. The critic of the *Musical World* says: 'As for Puzzi—he still continues *il maestro* on the horn'. At another concert in 1847 the critic says: 'The horn performance of Sig. Puzzi which exhibited all the usual excellencies and peculiarities of that artist's very individual talent was foremost among the morning's attractions'. Once more, in 1850, he again drew praise from the critic of the *Musical World*. He was a great personality in London musical circles, even if perhaps a little overshadowed by his wife, who, as a singer, was more widely known to the public at large, and he set a standard of horn playing hitherto unknown in England.

As far as is known he did no teaching, though Pougin, in the supplement of Fétis's *Biographie universelle*, credits him with an unpublished *Nouvelle Méthode pour apprendre le Cor*. Two of his compositions for horn and piano, one of them variations and the other a fantasia, are said by Schilling[16] to have been published, and other works of a similar character in manuscript are preserved in the British Museum.

Two, if not three, instruments that belonged to Puzzi are still in existence. One, a very fine silver-mounted *cor-solo*, by M.-A. Raoux, is said to have been given to Puzzi by Louis XVIII. The appearance and workmanship of the instrument, however, lead the present writer to believe that the giver is more likely to have been Charles X, the erstwhile patron of Punto, whose passion for the horn was notorious, and that it was made about 1826 or 1827. The mouthpiece with this instrument is practically identical in measurements with Domnich's model for second horn (see above, p. 102, Fig. 20, 3b). A second instrument is an orchestral horn by L.-J. Raoux, dated 1821. It was used for many years by the late Adolf Borsdorf and is now in the possession of his son, Francis Bradley. The third is also a silver-mounted *cor-solo*, but by

L.-J. Raoux and dated 1814. It has been cut to take a set of two early Périnet-type valves and has the initials G.P. engraved on the bell, from which it is assumed that it originally belonged to Puzzi. The horn first mentioned is now in the Victoria and Albert Museum, and the last is in the Horniman Museum (No. 166 in the Carse Collection).

GALLAY, Jacques-François (1795–1864), is chiefly interesting for his excellent studies that are still in use today, but he was also a remarkable virtuoso. He was born in Perpignan (Pyrénées-Orientales) and received his first lessons from his father, who was a good amateur horn player. At the age of fourteen he deputized for the first horn of the Perpignan theatre and had a resounding success with his playing of the solo in Devienne's opera *Les Visitandines*. It was not until 1820—Gallay was then twenty-five—that he was able to go to Paris, but in spite of being over-age he was admitted into Dauprat's class, and at the end of his first year was awarded a *premier prix*. After a spell at the Odéon he entered the orchestra of the Théâtre Italien in 1825, and about the same time was admitted to the orchestra of the royal *chapelle*. In 1832 he became first horn in the private band of Louis-Philippe and ten years later succeeded Dauprat as professor at the Conservatoire.

As a virtuoso Gallay was a natural first horn, though in practice he appears to have restricted his range as a soloist to that of a *cor mixte*. His *Méthode pour le Cor*, published about 1845, has already come under review (see Chapter 5, phase 2): it is now, of course, completely out of date, and for those who care today to acquire some knowledge of the hand horn Dauprat's tutor is greatly to be preferred. Gallay's chief legacy to horn players is his studies, of which perhaps the best are the *Trente Etudes* and the *Préludes mesurés et non-mesurés*, which are still used today. A list of his more important concertos, solos, and duos for horn will be found in Fétis's *Biographie universelle*. A *Chevalier de la Légion d'Honneur*, Gallay died while he was still professor at the Conservatoire on 18 October 1864.

MENGAL, Jean-Baptiste (1796–1878), was one of Domnich's most distinguished pupils. In 1820 he became solo horn at the Paris Opéra-Comique, and it was no doubt he who drew from the Paris correspondent of the *Harmonicon* (November 1830) the following laudatory remarks: 'It would be invidious to distinguish one performer more than another, yet I cannot help remarking that the first horn-player has an exquisite tone, and as much command of his instrument as Puzzi himself: can praise go higher?' In 1831 he succeeded Dauprat as principal horn at the Opéra. He was a member of the *Chapelle Musique* of

Charles X in 1830 according to Castil-Blaze's list, and it may well be that he took the place of P.-L. Colin, who died in 1822. Mengal was a founder-member of the *Société des Concerts du Conservatoire*; third horn until 1841 when he became first, on Dauprat's retirement, to be succeeded in his turn by Mohr some time before 1859. He published a *Méthode de Cor* and a certain amount of music for the horn.

LEWY, Eduard-Constantin (1796–1846) and Joseph-Rudolph (1804–1881). Two brothers who made a great name as virtuosi of the valve horn in its very early days. The elder brother, who was born at Saint-Avold (Moselle), joined a military band when he was sixteen and appears to have been in Paris at the time of Waterloo. Before this he had apparently studied the horn (under Domnich) as well as the violin and cello at the Paris Conservatoire, through the influence, it is said, of a French general. After 1815 he toured France and Switzerland, settling in Basel in 1817. Here he made the acquaintance of Konradin Kreutzer who, in 1822, invited him to Vienna where he became principal horn in the Imperial Opera Orchestra. A criticism of the concert he gave in Strasbourg in 1827, when he played a 'keyed' horn, has already been quoted (see Chapter 5, p. 71). In 1834 he was appointed professor at the Vienna Conservatory, and in the following year became first horn in the Court Orchestra. He died in Vienna on 3 June 1846.

The younger, Joseph-Rudolph, was born in Nancy and was taught the horn by his brother. He was attached to the royal *Kapelle* at Stuttgart from 1819 to 1822, when he left to join Eduard-Constantin at the Imperial Opera in Vienna. The brothers occasionally gave concerts together, appearing as duettists, one such, in Vienna in 1827, being very favourably spoken of in the *Harmonicon* (Vol. 5, 1827, p. 118). In 1834–35 J.-R. Lewy visited Russia, Sweden, Germany, England, and Switzerland. He gave several successful concerts in London, at one of which he is described on the programme as 'First Professor of the newly-constructed French horn and Director of the Chapel Royal of Sweden'. In 1837 he became first horn of the royal *Kapelle* in Dresden and was there when Wagner was appointed *Hofkapellmeister*. Some account of his conception of valve-horn technique and of how this may have influenced Wagner has already been given in Chapter 5 (phase 3). In Dannreuter's translation of Wagner's *Ueber das Dirigen* we read in connection with a performance in *Der Freischütz*: 'Discreetly led by R. Lewy, the cornists entirely changed the tone of the soft wood notes in the introduction which they had been accustomed to play as a pompous show piece'. It was for J.-R. Lewy that Schubert wrote the horn obbligato in 'Auf dem

Strom'. Lewy retired with a pension in 1851 and died at his home in Oberlossnitz, near Dresden, on 9 February 1881.

GUMBERT, Friedrich Adolf (1841–1906). Gumbert, the distinguished first horn of the Leipzig Theatre and the Gewandhaus concerts, was born at Lichtenau (Thuringia); he studied under Hammann at Jena, and when his military service was accomplished, he played for two years at Halle. In 1864 Reinecke, then conductor of the Gewandhaus concerts, engaged Gumbert as principal horn, a position he held until, in 1898, he began to find the performance of latter-day horn parts too much of a strain and retired.

He was professor of the horn at Leipzig Conservatory and published a *Praktische Horn-Schule*. He was the first to publish collections of difficult passages from symphonic and operatic works, of which there are some twelve books. Others, with extracts from more modern works, have since appeared. Such collections are as invaluable to the neophyte as yet unfamiliar with the classical repertoire as to the seasoned performer who can refresh his memory of some tricky passage. It is regrettable that owing, it seems, to copyright difficulties, there is no available collection of extracts from the works of Mahler or of Stravinsky, which simply bristle with difficulties for the horn. Gumbert numbered among his pupils the distinguished German-American horn player and teacher of Philadelphia Anton Horner and Franz Paersch, the greatly admired principal horn of the Hallé concerts (Manchester) and the Royal Italian Opera (Covent Garden).

Gumbert died in Leipzig on the last day of the year 1906.

KLING, Henri-Adrien-Louis (1842–1918), the son of a German father and a French mother, was born in Paris. The family returned to Carlsruhe, his father's native town, when he was two years old and very soon afterwards his mother died. His father married again, but domestic difficulties arose that clouded his childhood. He was, however, allowed to study the horn, for which he had a special predilection, and was fortunate enough to have as his teacher the virtuoso Jacob Dorn. In 1861 he broke away from home and went to Geneva where he became solo horn at the Grand Théâtre and the *Concerts Classiques*. Four years later he was appointed professor of the horn and *solfège* at the Geneva Conservatoire where he continued to teach until his death. A man of wide and varied musical interests, he was for many years organist of Cologny church, conductor of the casino orchestras at Geneva and Evian-les-Bains, bandmaster of the *Landwehr* military band; taught singing at the Geneva High School for girls, and in addition was a much sought-after adjudicator at Swiss and French brass band and *trompe-de-chasse* contests. In spite of all this activity Kling was a prolific composer and writer, his musical works including four operas, a symphony, a number of overtures and light pieces; solos for wind instruments; piano accompaniments for the four concertos and the Concert-Rondo for horn of Mozart; an important treatise on instrumentation for orchestra and military band; an exhaustive *Horn-Schule* (German and English text); small tutors for other wind instruments and for the double-bass; and two excellent and well-documented essays, one on the virtuoso Punto and the other on the horn itself (see below, pp. 184–8). Kling died in Geneva on 2 May 1918. His son, Otto Kling, was well known in London musical circles, first as manager of Breitkopf & Härtel's London branch and then, from 1915 until his death in 1924, as proprietor of J. & W. Chester.

BRÉMOND, François (1844–1925), who was born at Nîmes in the south of France, went when quite young to live with his uncle and guardian, Joseph Rousselot, in Paris. Rousselot was then sharing the duties of first horn at the Opéra with J.-B. Mohr. Brémond was a pupil of Mohr's at the Conservatoire, winning his *premier prix* at the end of his first year.

Besides being a very fine horn player Brémond was the possessor of a pleasant light tenor voice, and as a young man sang leading *opéra-comique* roles at many of the larger provincial theatres. He it was who, when a suitable décor offered, would have a horn hung up and when he came on stage would affect surprise and delight at seeing it, and say 'Ha! a horn . . . but I play the horn' and would thereupon toss off a solo, to the great delight of the audience.

The present writer studied with him for a couple of years just before World War I, and a more delightful personality than Brémond would be difficult to find. At heart he was a true hand-horn player, and his principles regarding the valve horn—which he looked upon as a necessary evil—were those of Meifred. It was at his insistence that Massenet wrote the obbligato to 'Comme l'oiseau qui chante' (*Manon*) for horn in F-sharp, as with this crook it lies so well for the hand horn. In 1891 he succeeded Mohr as professor at the Conservatoire, holding this post for thirty-one years, and it is because of his continued backing of the Halary ascending third valve that this system is now in universal use in France.

Brémond was renowned for his full and beautiful tone, and for the perfection of his trills which, he used to say, took him ten years to master. He was left-handed and it was his left hand that he used in the bell, and he always tried to make his pupils, whether left- or right-handed, do the same, but, of course, without success. Other foibles of his were that horn players should always wear moustaches and that little tuft of hair beneath the lower lip, known as an 'imperial'; should not smoke; nor ever eat fried potatoes or salad on account of the oil. These precautions did not noticeably prolong his career as a player, since he had to give up when he was about fifty-five. One has known moustache-less horn players who smoked and drank in moderation, denying them-selves neither salads nor fried potatoes, who nevertheless lasted longer, with far harder work than Brémond ever knew. So much, then, for fads, the effect of which in most cases is purely psychological.

After a year in the orchestra of the Théâtre des Bouffes Brémond be-came professor at the Lyons School of Music in 1872, and it was during the next year or two that he appeared on the operatic stage. In 1875 he returned to Paris as first horn of the *Opéra Populaire* and the *Concerts du Châtelet* (the origin of the *Concerts Colonne*) until, in 1878, he was appointed first horn of the *Société des Concerts* and of the Opéra-Comique, giving up these posts when his lip began to fail him in 1898. He stayed on for a few more years at the Opéra-Comique as second horn, but when the writer knew him, he had not played for ten years or more.

He used a *cor-solo* by L.-J. Raoux, dated 1823, for which Besson had made him a set of valves with extra slides so that he could, if he wanted to, use the valves with the lowest crooks.

Brémond relinquished his professorship at the Conservatoire in 1922; he had stayed on well beyond the normal retiring age owing to the war. He died three years later, at his house in Houilles (near Paris), on 15 July 1925.

The only compositions he left were a few solos for use as examination test pieces, but his *Exercices Journaliers* is a most excellent work. He also revised a number of studies by Dauprat and Mohr, adapting them for use with the valve horn.

BORSDORF, Friedrich Adolf (1854–1923), was not only a very fine orchestral and chamber music player, but he revolutionized horn teaching in England where it had been in a bad way for a very long time. He was born in Dittmansdorf (Saxony), entered the Dresden Conser-vatory in 1869, and studied the horn for five years with Lorenz and Oscar Franz. After serving his time in a military band he obtained a contract to play with the stage band at Covent Garden Opera, and arrived in England in the spring of 1879. In addition to a number of provincial engagements he went for ten weeks every year with August Manns to the Scottish Orchestra in Glasgow. He also played the viola for a time at the London Gaiety Theatre.

His horn playing attracted the attention of Hans Richter, himself an erstwhile horn player, for whom he played third to begin with, then alternating with Paersch as first, and finally as first altogether. Thereafter he became the leading London horn player and was a member of King Edward VII's private band. Borsdorf was principal horn of the original Queen's Hall Orchestra until 1904 when some forty members resigned on the introduction of a 'no deputies' rule and, headed by Borsdorf, Busby, Van der Meerschen—all horn players—and the trumpeter John Solomon, founded the London Symphony Orchestra. The horn section of this orchestra, Borsdorf, Van der Meerschen, T. R. Busby, and A. E. Brain, senior (the grandfather of Dennis Brain), attained such a perfect ensemble that they became known to musicians as 'God's own Quartet'.

Throughout the greater part of his career Borsdorf played on the horn by L.-J. Raoux already mentioned above (p. 161). As a performer he was renowned for his breath-control, dynamic command, phrasing, and breadth of interpretation. Meticulous to a fault, he left nothing to chance: the conscientious artist *par excellence*.

As a teacher Borsdorf trained some sixty or seventy pupils, among the more distinguished of whom were his sons Oskar, Francis—who adopted the surname of Bradley—and Emil and, of course, the brothers Alfred and Aubrey Brain. Another of his pupils, Frank Probyn, succeeded him at the Royal College of Music. Borsdorf was professor at the Royal College from its reorganization in 1882 and at the Royal Academy of Music from 1897, retaining both posts until his death in London on 15 April 1923. The present writer played next to him at the last concert in which he took part—a concert at Harrow School—when he complained of feeling unwell: a few days later he was dead.

PAERSCH, Franz Friedrich (1857–1921), was the contemporary of Adolf Borsdorf, and these two young Germans quickly became the leading horn players in England, with Paersch usually principal when they played together. Paersch, the son of a farmer who also kept the village inn, was born in Thalheim, near Halle—by a curious coincidence he made his career chiefly with the Hallé Orchestra (Manchester)—and, like so many other distinguished horn players, began his musical life in the village church, becoming in due course principal tenor. From 1872 until he was called up for military service he studied under Gumbert at the Leipzig Conservatory. He came to England in 1882, his first engagement being a summer season at Buxton Gardens. When that orchestra visited Manchester Sir (then Mr) Charles Hallé heard him and invited him to join the Hallé Orchestra: he did so and, making his home in Manchester, remained their principal horn from 1883 until his retirement in 1915. This did not prevent him from being for a time first horn at the Richter Concerts or from being principal horn of the Royal Italian Opera (Covent Garden) for the Grand Opera Season, a post he held from 1883 to 1914.

Paersch was renowned for his superb tone, effortless emission, and absolutely safe attack. The late H. F. Thornton, former professor at the Royal Military School of Music, Kneller Hall, who at one time played *ripieno* first to Paersch at the Opera, used to say of him that he never deviated from the composer's nuances or altered the phrasing to suit himself; nor was he ever known to crack a note. At one time he used an old Raoux horn and when that wore out, he played on an instrument made by W. Brown & Sons, of London. He was professor at the Manchester Royal College of Music, but his influence on horn playing in England was one of example rather than the formation of pupils. He died at his home in Manchester on 30 March 1921. One son, Otto Paersch, was third horn in the B.B.C. Northern Orchestra until his retirement in 1953.

In an obituary in the *Manchester Guardian* the paper's music critic, Samuel Langford, recalled that '*The Spectator*, at the close of a memorable festival at Leeds, spoke of one phrase played by Mr. Paersch upon the horn as the most memorable experience of the Festival'. Seldom has such a compliment been paid to a horn player. As a chamber music player, too, he was unsurpassed, and he played with many world-famous pianists, violinists, and other instrumentalists.

BRAIN, Aubrey Harold (1893–1955), was the son of A. E. Brain, the distinguished fourth horn of the famous London Symphony Orchestra quartet. Aubrey Brain and his elder brother, Alfred, set a standard never before attained by English players. Brain early showed exceptional aptitude for the horn, winning a scholarship at the Royal College of Music, where he studied under Borsdorf for two years.

In 1911 he was appointed principal horn in the New Symphony Orchestra, and in the following year went with the London Symphony Orchestra on its American tour. He was first horn with the Beecham Opera Company which toured England in 1913 with a repertoire that included *The Ring*, *Salomé*, *Elektra*, and *Rosenkavalier*. He married in

1914, and had two sons, Leonard, an excellent oboist, and Dennis, the phenomenal horn virtuoso who lost his life so tragically in 1957.

Aubrey Brain became principal horn in the B.B.C. Symphony Orchestra in 1928, remaining with them until an accident, from which he never really recovered, brought about his premature retirement in 1945: he was, in fact, a war casualty. He appeared as a soloist on many occasions with the B.B.C., and it was for him that Dame Ethel Smyth wrote her concerto for horn and violin. After its first performance in London Brain went to Berlin to play it with the Berlin Philharmonic Orchestra, with Marjorie Hayward as the solo violinist. This was probably the first time that any English horn player had appeared as a soloist in a foreign country.

On the death of Borsdorf in 1923 Brain was appointed to succeed him as professor at the Royal Academy of Music, a post he retained until his death on 20 September 1955. He trained a number of excellent performers, of whom the most outstanding apart from his son, Dennis, are Douglas Moore, late principal horn of the B.B.C. Symphony Orchestra and professor at the Royal College of Music, John Burden, and the distinguished present-day soloist Alan Civil.

Brain would have no truck with the German double horn and insisted always that the B.B.C. quartet should use only instruments of the French model. He himself played on a horn by Labbaye, the successor of Raoux. His tone was exceptionally pure and classical, albeit somewhat lacking in warmth: his execution was phenomenal, and he seldom, if ever, cracked a note. He made some first-class recordings, of which perhaps the most notable is that of the Mozart Concerto No. 3 (K 447).

Aubrey Brain's elder brother, Alfred, also an exceptionally fine horn player, was for some years principal horn in Sir Henry Wood's Queen's Hall Orchestra. The writer well remembers his magnificent playing before World War I. He went to New York in 1923 to join the Damrosch orchestra, remained in the United States, and adopted American nationality.

BRAIN, Dennis (1921–1957), the first horn player of genius since Punto, who did for the hand horn very much what Dennis Brain has done for the valve horn. Dennis was the second son of Aubrey Brain. He was born in London and educated at St Paul's School and the Royal Academy of Music, where he studied the horn under his father and the organ under G. D. Cunningham. He made his first public appearance at the Queen's Hall, London, in a Bach series with his father and the

Busch Chamber Players. He subsequently played with many well-known quartets, including the Lenar, Griller, and Busch. He made a number of superlative recordings, which included the four Mozart Concertos, the two Strauss Concertos, the Benjamin Britten Serenade for tenor voice, horn, and strings (with Peter Pears and the Jacques Orchestra), the very difficult horn part of which was specially written for him. He also introduced to English audiences the Hindemith Concerto and Sonata for four horns (with Neill Sanders, Aubrey Thonger, and Alfred Cursue); Nocturne by Matyas Seiber; Rhapsody and Rondo by Ernest Tomlinson; Gordon Jacob's Concerto; and a host of other works. He played at the Lucerne Festival in 1948, the Aix-en-Provence Festival in 1949, the International Contemporary Festival of Music in Holland, and gave the second performance of the No. 2 Strauss Concerto with Krips in Vienna.

Until the early 1950s he used a French Raoux-Millereau horn to which, shortly before he discarded it in favour of a German instrument, he had an ascending thumb valve added which put the horn, now with a fixed mouthpiece and permanently in B flat, into C alto. He later used a specially-built Alexander B-flat horn, of which the thumb valve had a long slide to enable him to play the lowest notes and a rotary tap that turned it into a muting valve when required.

In the writer's view his tone lost something of its superlative quality when he changed to a German instrument, but it was the only answer to the ever-increasing difficulties of the music that was being composed for him. Indeed one may say without fear of contradiction that it is as impossible for the horn player to cope adequately with present-day demands on the old French horn as it is to play modern trumpet parts on the long F trumpet.

That Dennis Brain had genius cannot be denied. Before he was thirty, and in spite of the interruption caused by the war, he had got the horn out of the cold-storage in which, as a major solo instrument, it had lain for a century, and blazed a trail that is now being followed far and wide. Brain was also a superb organist and when he decided to make his career with the horn, his teacher said that it would be a great loss to English organ playing.

He was the ideal virtuoso, whose sunny temperament had already won over his audience before he put the mouthpiece to his lips. A man of great personal charm, he was that all-too-rare phenomenon in the musical—or for that matter in any other—profession, one who was always ready quietly to help a lame dog over a stile. Horn players recognized his superiority to the point that he aroused no jealousy among his colleagues: the best of them were always only too happy to play beside him.

It was a great tragedy for the musical world when he was killed in a motor-car accident on his way home from the Edinburgh Festival on 1 September 1957. On the night following his death Tchaikowsky's Sixth Symphony was on the programme of a Henry Wood Promenade Concert at which the writer was present. This was the last work in which Dennis Brain had taken part two evenings before, and as a token of the esteem in which he was held by musicians the audience were asked not to applaud. The work was received in absolute silence. He founded the wind quintet that bears his name, and which still carries on with Neill Sanders, Brain's erstwhile colleague in the Philharmonia Orchestra, as the horn player.

A few more distinguished horn players, whose names have been recorded but whose influence on horn playing in general seems to be less than that of those given longer notices above, are mentioned below. Doubtless many others ought to be included, did one but know even their names, such as the outstanding orchestral players and teachers from 1850 onwards. Since then musical dictionaries, while including countless obscure singers and composers, have been singularly chary of admitting orchestral players and teachers of orchestral instruments. And so, for lack of any information, they must perforce continue to go unsung.

Spandau (*c.* 1750?–?). Famous virtuoso in the band of the Stadtholder of the United Provinces at The Hague. He visited London as a soloist in 1773. One of the pioneers of hand stopping.

Boeck, Ignaz (1754–?) and Anton (1757–?). Famous duettists. One of them is said to have invented a mute with which chromatic passages could be played.

Petrides, Joseph (1755–?) and Peter (1766–?). Two Bohemian horn players who settled in London and were the leading horn players in England from 1802 until 1824, when they retired and returned to their native land.

Kenn, Jean-Joseph (1757–?). Noted *cor basse*, professor at the Paris Conservatoire and the teacher of Dauprat.

Lebrun, Jean (1759–1809). Famous French virtuoso (*cor alto*) who played first with Türrschmidt after Palsa's death. He is said by Fétis to have committed suicide, but there are some doubts about this, as about the year of his death.

Pokorny, Beate (*c.* 1760–?). The first outstanding woman horn player and forerunner of the distinguished British phalanx headed by Livia Gollancz, Muriel Roberts, Shirley Hopkins, and Valerie Smith. Pokorny, who hailed from Regensburg, played a concerto by Punto on 24 December 1779 at a Paris Concert Spirituel, to the entire satisfaction of critics and audience.

Dornaus, Philipp (1769–?) and Peter (1770–?). Famous duettists, first as infant prodigies and then as mature virtuosi.

Belloli, Luigi (1770–1817). Remarkable Italian virtuoso and professor at the Milan Conservatory (1812). One of the earliest to adopt the genre *cor-mixte*. Almost certainly the teacher of Puzzi.

Gugel, Joseph (1770–?) and Heinrich (1780–?). Two brothers who from about 1802 to 1816 were considered the finest duettists in Germany. The younger brother spent much time in St Petersburg, and it is of him that Pearsall tells the almost incredible story of how, finding his lips grew thicker, pared them down with a razor, having been unable to get a surgeon to do it for him. Pearsall says he met him in Paris in 1830 in a state of great destitution, but Mendel says he was in St Petersburg with his son in 1837. He published some good studies.

Schuncke, Gottfried (1777–1860), Andreas (1778–1849), Michael (1780–1821), Christoph (1796–?), and Gotthilf (1799–?). Five brothers, all front-rank horn players. Gottfried and Michael visited England in 1814 as soloists. Another brother, probably Gotthilf, played twice at Philharmonic Concerts in 1825, and shared the duties of first horn with Puzzi at the Birmingham Musical Festival of 1826.

Jarrett, Henry (?–1886). Probably the best native English player until the advent of the Brains, and the leading soloist in London after Puzzi retired. He became first horn and orchestral manager for Jullien's Promenade Concerts. Later he became an impresario in America and amassed a considerable fortune. He died in Buenos Aires in 1886.

Vivier, Eugène-Léon (1817–1900), was chiefly remarkable for his success in producing chords on the horn, which he appears to have done with quite extraordinary skill. He was also a consummate practical joker. He must, however, have been a good horn player, though he does not seem ever to have done any orchestral playing. He was a favourite of Napoléon III, and was extremely popular with royalty and the aristocracy of most European countries. He visited England with great success on more than one occasion. His popularity in aristocratic circles undoubtedly aroused the jealousy of professional horn players who thought little of his powers, and Brémond once stigmatized him to the writer as 'le roi des bouffons'. Perhaps, but a cleverer man for all that than many of his detractors. He died in Nice.

Chaussier, Henri (1854–?). Probably the last real hand-horn virtuoso. In this role he was very successful: less so as an orchestra performer. He invented a system with every instrument in C, but it came to nothing. For a description of his horn on this principle see above, pp. 63–6.

Stiegler, Karl (1876–1932). Famous Viennese horn player and teacher. Appointed solo horn at the Vienna State Opera in 1899, and professor at the Vienna Conservatory in 1917. He died in Vienna.

NOTES

[1] Joseph Eger and D. Ceccarossi.

[2] Joseph Eger, 'Breaking the Endurance Barrier'. *Woodwind World*, May 1958 (Mount Kisco, N.Y.).

[3] Notices of his playing will be found in the *Mercure de France*, avril et juin 1764, avril 1765, octobre 1768, and avril 1769. One at least of these is worth quoting to show how much Rodolphe's playing was esteemed by the critics: '*On ne craint pas de dire que jusqu'à ce qu'on l'eût entendu, on ne croyait pas possible de rendre sur cet instrument, comme le fait M. Rodolphe, toutes les difficultés d'une musique savante, les intonations les plus difficiles avec le son le plus flatteur et les cadences de la plus belle voix*'.

'It can be truthfully said that until one had heard him one would not have believed it possible for the horn to overcome, as it does in M. Rodolphe's hands, all the difficulties of advanced music and the most awkward intonations with, at the same time, a very pleasing tone and trills like those of the most beautiful voice'.

[4] J.-B. de La Borde, op. cit., Tome III: '*Quoique second, il monte aussi haut que premier cor ait monté, et donne toujours les sons les plus beaux, ainsi que les plus agréables. Son exécution est incroyable, et il a trouvé moyen de faire entendre sur cet instrument ce qu'on n'avait jamais entendu avant lui*'.

'Although a "second" horn, he can reach notes as high as any "first" ever could, whilst his tone is always of the finest and most pleasing. His execution is unbelievable, and he has found a way of producing on his instrument sounds that before him had never been heard'.

[5] L.-F. Dauprat, op. cit., 1ère partie, p. 9, footnote.

[6] M. Lassabathie, *Histoire du Conservatoire Impérial de Musique et de Déclamation*. Paris, 1860.

[7] According to Fitzpatrick, op. cit., he was born at Bürschau in Bohemia in 1742. His birthdate and place (1740, Vienna) are those given by Mendel (*Musikalisches Conversations-Lexikon*).

[8] C. Burney, *The Present State of Music in Germany, the Netherlands and United Provinces*. London, 1773. 'The elector has a good band, in which M. Ponta, the celebrated horn from Bohemia, whose taste and astonishing execution were lately so much applauded in London'. Burney would have visited Coblenz in early August 1772.

[9] *Tablettes de Renommée des Musiciens (Almanach Dauphin,* 1785): Punto. 'Célèbre cc. [i.e., cor-de-chasse], ordinaire de la musique de M. le comte d'Artois. Ce virtuose a trouvé l'art de vaincre toutes les difficultés de cet instrument et d'en adoucir les sons. Plusieurs Quatuors, Trios et Concertos de sa composition, qu'il a exécutés au Concert Spirituel, lui ont mérité du public, à juste titre, des témoignages flatteurs de sa satisfaction'.

Punto. 'Renowned horn player and member of the comte d'Artois's private band. This virtuoso has succeeded in vanquishing every difficulty of the horn and in rendering its tone more mellow. The several quartets, trios, and concertos which he has composed and performed at the Concert Spirituel, have deservedly earned flattering tokens of the public's satisfaction'.

[10] *Prager neue Zeitung.* 1801, No. 39, p. 473.

[11] *Mercure de France.* avril et mai 1770.

[12] W. T. Parke, op. cit., Vol. I, p. 63.

[13] The writer has been unable to trace a copy of this work.

[14] Kastner, *Manuel général de musique militaire*. Paris, 1848. p. 192, footnote.

[15] *Du Cor à Pistons. Extrait d'un Traité théorique et pratique de cet Instrument. Composé par Dauprat.* Paris, n.d.

[16] G. Schilling, *Encyclopädie oder Universal-Lexikon der Tonkunst.* Stuttgart, 1837.

CHAPTER 9

A List of Makers

THERE HAVE BEEN, and in Central Europe still are, so many small makers—mostly family concerns on a workshop basis—that it is quite impossible to compile anything like a complete list. Indeed one is constantly hearing hitherto unknown names of all periods to add to one's files. There are certainly a great many 18th- and early 19th-century makers none of whose instruments has so far come to light. Working periods can, in the majority of cases, only be estimated from the workmanship of such of their instruments as have survived. Dated instruments, which are very few and far between, rate-books, and directories all help, but most of the date-fixing is necessarily to a very large extent guesswork based on familiarity with instruments of different periods and provenance.

For much of what follows the writer is greatly indebted to Lyndesay G. Langwill.

Name	Town	Working Period	Notes*
Alexander, Gebr.	Mainz	1782–modern	
Alexandre	Paris	c. 1850	Suspected fictitious name during the Ad. Sax controversy
Amboulevart	Paris	1777–91	*Tr.de chasse*
Apostol, A.	Helsinki	early 20th c.	
Bacher, I. F. de	Gand	first half 19th c.	
Bartsch	Paris	1835–c. 1855	
Bauer, E.	Prague	1830–54	
Bechert, Nicodemus	(see under Pechert)		
Benith, John	London	first half 18th c.	1738
Bennett, Wm.	Dublin	1795–1819	
Besson, G.-A.	Paris	1838–58	
	London	1858–62	
Besson, F.	Paris	1864–modern	
	London	1862–modern	
Bohland & Fuchs	Graslitz	c. 1873–modern	
Boosey & Sons	London	1861–1930	

Name	Town	Working Period	Notes*
Boosey & Hawkes	London	modern	
Brown, W.	London	1851–82	
Brown, W., & Sons	London	1882–1952	
Brunel	Paris	late 18th c.	*Tr. de chasse*
Buchschwinder, A.	Ellwangen	first half 18th c.	1738: 1742
Bull, Wm.	London	*c.* 1660–170?	1699
Butler, G.	London and Dublin	second half 19th c.	
Callcott, J.	London	1851	'Radius' Fr. horn
Canapel, M.	Bruxelles	first half 18th c.	1728
Carlin	Paris	mid-18th c.	
Cazzani	Milan	modern	
Červeny & Söhne, V. F.	Königgrätz	1853–modern	
Clagget, Ch.	London	1788	Patent double horn
Clarke, Esau	Dublin	mid-18th c.	
Clementi & Co.	London	*c.* 1800–*c.* 1816	Probably not an actual maker
Coecklenberg, H., & Fils	Bruxelles	modern	
Coin, Andrea	Venice	18th c.	1710:1770
Conn, G. C.	Elkhart, Ind.	modern	
Cormeri	Paris	1776–*c.*1805	
Couesnon & Cie.	Paris	modern	Successors of Gautrot
Courtois	Paris	? *c.* 1782–*c.* 1805?	
Courtois neveu	Paris	pre-1800–1857	1802. Probably the same person
Courtois neveu aîné	Paris		
Courtois frère	Paris	1813–44	1816
Courtois, Antoine	Paris	1844–modern	
Crétien or Crestien	Paris	pre-1700–post 1730	*Cors* and *trompes de chasse*
Deflas	Bruxelles	19th c.	
Deschamps	Paris	1856–64	*Tr. de chasse*
Devaster fils, C.	Bruxelles	first half 19th c.	
Distin, Hy.	London	1846–76	
Dubois & Couturier	Lyon	1834–40	
Duirschmitt, C. F.	Neukirchen	*c.* 1800	
Dujariez, E.-J.-M.	Paris	1829–55	Apprentice of L.-J. Raoux
Dupont, J.-B.	Paris	*c.* 1815	Inventor of omni-tonic horn
Ehe, F.	Nürnberg	first half 18th c.	1747:1748
Ehe, H. L.	Nürnberg	second half 17th c.	1682:1688:1694
Eichentopf, J. H.	Leipzig	first half 18th c.	1735:1738
Ellard, A.	Dublin	1818–38	

Name	Town	Working Period	Notes*
Embach, L., & Co.	Amsterdam	first half 19th c.	
Eschenbach	Markneu-kirchen	late 18th c. and modern	1818
Ferber, A.	Wien	mid-18th c.	1748
Fink, J.	Strasbourg	1835–70	
Flemming, C. B.	Breslau	late 18th and early 19th c.	
Gautrot aîné & Cie.	Paris	1845–84	The first firm to make instruments on a large-scale mass-production basis. Trade mark an anchor in an oval frame. Succeeded by Couesnon & Cie.
Gabler, J. C.	Berlin	first half 19th c.	
Gambaro	Paris	1833–54	
Geyer, C.	Chicago	modern	
Glier, W.	Warsaw	first half 19th c.	1835
Gleitzman, I. Q.	Frankenburg	mid-18th c.	1754
Goodison, J.	London	1830–63	
Goudot jne.	Paris	c. 1845	
Griessling & Schlott	Berlin	c. 1806–36	Made Stölzel's earliest valves c. 1815
Guichard aîné	Paris	1827–45	Predecessor of Gautrot. Began mass-production in a small way
Haas, J. W.	Nürnberg	early 17th c.–?	1682: 1688: 1694 Trade mark, a hare
Halary-Antoine	Paris	1825–59	Instruments usually marked: HALARI
Halary-Antoine, J.-L.	Paris	1859–75	Inventor of ascending 3rd valve
Haltenhof, J. G.	Hanau-am-Mayn	second half 18th c.	1776
Hawkes & Co.	London	1860–89	
Hawkes & Son	London	1889–1930	Amalgamated with Boosey & Co.
Herwig, W.	Markneu-kirchen	second half 19th c.	
Higham, J.	Manchester	1842–post 1928	Succeeded by Meyers & Harrison

Name	Town	Working Period	Notes*
Hofmaster, John Christopher	London	*c.* 1725–64	Succeeded by Rodenbostel
Hoyer, F.	Schönbach	18th c.	
Hoyer, J.	Nürnberg	19th c.	
Jacquot fils, P.-C.	Nancy	mid-19th c.	*Tr. de chasse*
Jahn, D.	Paris	*c.* 1819–56	
Keat, G.	London	1831–64	
Kerner, A.	Wien	*c.* 1763–*c.* 1823	1765: 1788: 1799: 1823
Kerner, I.	Wien	*c.* 1750–*c.* 1807	1798. Some instruments marked I. & A. Kerner
Kersten, J. G.	Dresden	late 18th/early 19th c.	1775
Key, T.	London	pre-1805–1853	
Key, F.	London	1853–56	Amalgamated with Rudall, Rose, Carte & Co.
Kley, A.	Berlin	modern	
Knopf, A.	Markneu-kirchen	modern	Makers of the Prager system horns
Knopf, H. F.	Markneu-kirchen	modern	
Köhler and Percival	London	1810–34	
Köhler, J.	London	1834–63	
Köhler & Son	London	1863–1904	
Korn, F.	Mainz	late 18th/early 19th c.	
Krause, A. F.	Berlin	second half 19th c.	1797
Kretzschmann, C.	Strasbourg	first half 19th c.	
Kruspe, E.	Erfurt	1834–modern	Produced the first double horn in F/B-flat
Labbaye, J.-Charles	Paris	*c.* 1815–48	
Labbaye, J.-Christophe	Paris	*c.* 1848–78	Bought up the Raoux business in 1857
Lausmann, J. A.	Graslitz	second half 18th c.	1791
Le Brun	Paris	first half 18th c.	1729. *Trompe Dauphine*
Lecomte & Cie.	Paris	1859–*c.* 1900	
Lehmann, C.	Hamburg	modern–194?	Does not appear to have carried on after the war

Name	Town	Working Period	Notes*
Leichnamb-schneider, F.	Wien	mid-18th c.	
Leichnamb-schneider, J.	Wien	first half 18th c.	1710: 1725
Leichnamb-schneider, M.	Wien	first half 18th c.	Possibly the first to make horns with crooks, 1709:1713: 1718:1719
Leydholdt, J. G.	Dresden-Neustadt	c. 1780	
Liebel, M. I. G.	Neukirchen Wien	late 18th/early 19th c.	1777 1791
Livain, C.	Mons	modern	
Lobeit, C.	?	late 18th/early 19th c.?	Horn so marked in Boston Museum of Fine Arts: No. 193
Mahillon, C., & Cie.	Bruxelles	1836–19?	
Mahillon, C., & Cie.	London	1887–1922	
Millereau, F.	Paris	1861–1931	Bought up the Labbaye-Raoux business 1878. Succeeded by H. Schoenaers c. 1898. Business acquired by Selmer in 1931
Müller, C. A.	Mainz	first half 19th c.	
Müller, J. C.	Roda	first half 18th c.	1713
Müller, W. M.	Roda	second half 18th c.	1779
Nauman	Wien	late 18th/early 19th c.	1804
Orsi, R.	Milan	modern	
Pace, C.	London	1827–49	
Pace, F.	London	1831–65	
Paxman Bros.	London	modern	Horn specialists
Pechert or Bechert, Nicodemus	Markt Gaunersdorf later Wien	late 18th/early 19th c.	
Penzel, J. C.	Leipzig	second half 19th c.	Succeeded Sattler
Percival, T.	London	c. 1800–48	
Périnet, F.	Paris	1829–c. 1847	Designed the Périnet valve. *Tr. de chasse*
Piattet & Benoît	Lyon	c. 1830–c. 1860	
Raoux	Paris	c. 1695–?	
Raoux, Joseph	Paris	c. 1750–c. 1800	b. c. 1730

Name	Town	Working Period	Notes*
Raoux, Lucien-Joseph	Paris	1776–*c*. 1825	b. 1753. Joined his father. He probably became head of the firm in the late 1790s. His horns have a small round stamp with L.J.R. monogram. This stamp, or *poinçon*, is on the horn given to Dauprat in 1798. Many of L. J. R.'s horns, between 1814 and 1824, are dated
Raoux, Marcel-Auguste	Paris	*c*. 1825–57	M. A. R. horns not dated, but carry the *poinçon* with monogram in an oval, rather larger than that of L. J. R. This *poinçon* was used by both Labbaye and Millereau
Rampone	Milan	modern	
Rampone & Cazzani	Milan and Naples	modern. Founded in 1870	
Riedlocker, F.	Paris	*c*. 1809–*c*. 1832	Apprentice and successor of Cormeri. Bought up by Halary-Antoine
Riedl, J. F.	Wien	first half 19th c.	Probable inventor of rotary valve
Ripasoli, F.	Pistoja	early 19th c.	1809.
Rivet	Lyon	mid-19th c.	
Rodenbostel, G. H.	London	second half 18th c.	
Roth, C.	Strasbourg	late 18th c.?	
Roth, C. A.	Neukirchen	first half 19th c.?	
Roth, J. G., Senr.	Adorf	early 19th c.	1810:1818
Roth, J. G., Junr.	Adorf	19th c.	
Roth, J. Christophe	Strasbourg	mid-19th c.	
Rudall, Rose, Carte & Co.	London	1854–78	
Rudall, Carte & Co.	London	1878–1955	Taken over by Boosey & Hawkes

Name	Town	Working Period	Notes*
Sandbach, W.	London	1809–31	
Sansone, L.	New York	modern	Single B-flat horns with five valves
Sattler, C. F.	Leipzig	first half 19th c.	
Sax, Adolphe	Paris	1843–1929	Bought up by Selmer
Sax, Alphonse	Paris	pre-1860–c. 1867	
Sax, Charles	Bruxelles	1815–53	Patent omnitonic horns
Schmidt, C. F.	Weimar and Berlin	modern	
Schmidt, F. A.	Köln	19th c.	
Schmidt, J.	Nürnberg	late 17th c.	
Schmidt, J. G.	Leipzig	19th c.	
Schmidt, P.	Copenhagen	late 18th c.	
Schmied, J. J.	Pfaffendorf	second half 18th c. 1771	
Schmied, M.	Pfaffendorf	first half 18th c. 1726	
Schmittschneider, A. A.	Paris	c. 1820–c. 1831	Patent horn with twenty-three crooks
Schoenaers, H.	Paris	c. 1898–1931	Took over Millereau c. 1898. Business bought up by Selmer in 1931
Schöller, P.	München	mid-18th c.	
Schott Söhne, B.	Mainz	1780–c. 1835	Probably never actual makers
Schuster, W.	Carlsruhe	pre-1818–post 1827	Original maker of the square valves, patented in 1818 by Blühmel and Stölzel
Schwabe, J. F.	Leipzig	second half 18th c. 1767	
Schwarz, R.	Hannover	modern	
Selmer, H.	Paris	modern	Bought up the businesses of Ad. Sax (1929) and Schoenaers-Millereau (1931)
Shaw, W.	London	1775–1817	
Shaw, T.	London	pre-1817–1838	
Smith, G.	Wolverhampton	c. 1818–30	
	Birmingham	1830–51	
Smith, J.	Wolverhampton	late 18th–early 19th c.	

Name	Town	Working Period	Notes*
Smith & Sons	Wolver-hampton?	late 18th–early 19th c.	
Startzer, C.	Wien	second half 18th c.	1770
Steimer, J.	Zofingen	second half 18th c.	1773
Stohr, F.	Prague	mid-19th c.	
Stölzel, H.	Berlin	first half 19th c.	Inventor of the valve
Stowasser, I.	Wien	*c.* 1839–*c.* 1892	
Sudre, F.	Paris	modern	Bought up the Halary business in 1879
Tuerlinckx	Malines	late 18th–early 19th c.	
Thibouville-Lamy, J.	Paris	1868–modern	Made the first French F/B-flat double horn as designed by L. Vuillermoz *c.* 1928
Uhlmann, L.	Wien	*c.* 1785–*c.* 1850	Inventor or im-prover of the double-piston valve
Uhlmann, L.	Wien	*c.* 1830–98	
Van Cauwelaert, F.	Bruxelles	1846–modern	
Van den Eynden	Gand	first half 19th c.	
Van der Gracht, H.	Aachen	first half 18th c.	
Van Engelen	Lierre	modern	
Vries, M. de	Lierre	modern	
Werner, J.	Dresden-Neustadt	*c.* 1733–55	Made the first *Inventionshorn* (Hampel), 1735:1740
Werner & Leydholt	Dresden-Neustadt	pre-1760–*c.* 1780	1760
White Co., The, H. N.	Cleveland, Ohio	modern	
Wiesczek	Prague	first half 18th c.	
Winkings, N.	London	18th c.	'Fr. hrn. makr. to H. M. Hunt (1763)'
Wunderlich, C. A.	Siebenbrunn, Vogtland	modern; founded in 1854	
Wunderlich, R.	Chicago	modern	Made the first five-valve B-flat horn as designed by L. Sansone in 1914

* Isolated dates in this column indicate that the whereabouts of a horn bearing this date is known.

Bibliography

THERE IS SO little specialized literature on the horn that a bibliography of the subject is necessarily comprised in the main of works of a general character—encyclopaedias, treatises on instrumentation, catalogues of old instruments, and the like. Not only is no claim made for completeness but completeness would in fact be impossible to all intents and purposes, since so much of the most informative material is in the form of articles and letters in periodicals, the discovery of which, more often than not, is just a matter of luck. Any such articles and letters that have come to the writer's notice are listed below.

Tutors and instruction books have been grouped into three sections: pre-hand-horn, hand-horn, and valve-horn. Some of the later hand-horn tutors have a brief notice about the valve horn, and some of the earlier valve-horn tutors give a scale for hand horn; such are classified according to the most important section.

The tutors are shown in chronological order, and the remainder in alphabetical order.

I. TUTORS

(a) Pre-hand horn

Eisel. *Musikus Autodidaktos* *Erfurt*, 1783.
Winch (?). *The Compleat Tutor for the French Horn.*
Simpson, London, c. 1746.
Thompson, London, c. 1756.
Instructions for the French Horn (The Muse's Delight or Apollo's Cabinet).
Liverpool, 1757.
(The text of this last is almost word for word the same as *The Compleat Tutor*.)
Anon. *New Instructions for the French Horn.*
Longman, Lukey & Co., London, 1772–79.
Reprint. *Munro & May, London*, 1820–34.

(b) Hand Horn

Hampel/Punto. *Seule et vraie Méthode pour apprendre facilement les Elémens des Premier et Second Cor aux Jeunes Elèves. Paris*, 1794–98.
Vandenbroek, Othon. *Méthode nouvelle et raisonnée pour apprendre à donner du Cor. Dédiée aux Amateurs.* *Paris*, 1797.
Also a *Méthode* in MS. (24 pp.) in the Paris Conservatoire Library (described in the catalogue as a 'suite' to the printed *Méthode*, but which looks more like a preliminary draft of it).
Duvernoy, Frédéric. *Méthode pour le Cor.* *Paris*, 1803.
Domnich, H. *Méthode de Premier et de Second Cor.* *Paris*, 1808.

183

Frölich. *Vollständige theor.-pract. Musiklehre.* 'Vom Horn'.
                                                     Bonn, 1811.
Dauprat, L.-F. *Méthode de Cor Alto et Cor Basse.* *Paris*, 1824.
Jacqumin, F. *Méthode complète de premier et second cor.* 1832.
Mengal Jne. *Méthode de Cor, suivie du Doigté du Cornet-à-pistons.*
                                                     Paris, 1835 (?).
        Méthode de Cor et Cor-à-pistons.   *Paris*, 1839–40.

These two versions are identical except that the earlier has a fingering
chart for 2-valve cornet (two pages), and the later six additional duets,
a drawing of a two-valve horn, and a fingering chart (one page).

Gallay, J.-F. *Méthode pour le Cor.*   *Paris, c.* 1845.
Mohr, J. *Méthode de Premier et de Second Cor.*   *Paris,* 1871.

(c) Valve Horn

Kastner, Georges. *Méthode élémentaire pour le Cor.* *Paris, c.* 1840 (?).
Meifred, P.-J. *Méthode pour le Cor Chromatique ou à Pistons.*
                                                     Paris, 1841.
This has a drawing of a 2-valve horn with two rotary valves of unusual
pattern. A later edition (*c.* 1849?) shows a 3-valve horn with Halary's
ascending third valve.
Urbin, D. *Méthode de Cor à trois pistons ou cylindres.* *Paris,* 1852.
Cacciamani, R. *Metodo d'Istruzione per Corno da Caccia.*
                                                     Milan, c. 1860 (?).
Fahrbach, J. *Vollständige Horn-Schule.*   *Wien, c.* 1860 (?).
Kling, H. *Horn-Schule.* (Ger. and English text.) *Leipzig,* 1879.
Gumbert, F. A. *Praktische Horn-Schule.*   *Leipzig,* 1879.
Hofmann, R. *Praktische Horn-Schule.*   *Leipzig, c.* 1880 (?).
Franz, Oscar. *Waldhorn-Schule.*   *Dresden, c.* 1880.
Garigue, H.-J. *Grande Méthode de Cor en fa à deux et trois pistons.*
                                                     Paris, 1888.
Franz/Busby. *School for the Horn.*   *London,* 1902.
Pénable, J. *Grande Méthode de Cor.*   *Paris, c.* 1905 (?).
Pree, Aug. *Theoretisch-Praktische Waldhorn-Schule.* *Dresden,* 1911.
Lambert, E. *Méthode complète et progressive de Cor Chromatique.*
                                                     Paris, 1922.
Lambert, E. *Complete and Progressive Method for French Horn.*
                                                     Paris, 1923.
Eby. *Eby's Complete Scientific Method for French Horn.*
                                                     Buffalo, N.Y., 1929.
Franz/Gebhart. *Complete Method for the French Horn,* by Oscar Franz,
    revised and augmented by Wm. Gebhart.   *Boston,* 1942.
Devémy, J. *Méthode de Cor Chromatique.*   *Paris,* 1943.
Ceccarossi, D. *Complete Course for the Horn.* (With English, French,
    Italian, and Spanish text.)   *Leduc, Paris, c.* 1950 (?).
Howe, Marvin C. *Method for French Horn.*   *New York,* 1950.
Farkas, Philip. *The Art of French Horn Playing.* *Chicago,* 1956.
    A Photographic Study of 40 Virtuoso Horn Players'
    Embouchures.   *Bloomington, Ind.,* 1970.

II. HISTORICAL, DESCRIPTIVE AND TECHNICAL

Anon.   *A Biographical Dictionary of Musicians*, 2 vols.   *London, 1827.*

Anon.   *L'Instrumental Illustré.*   *Couesnon & Cie., Paris, 1912.*

Apel, W.   *The Harvard Dictionary of Music.*   *Cambridge, Mass., 1945.*

Baines, Anthony.   *European and American Musical Instruments.*
London, 1966.

Catalogue of Musical Instruments in the Victoria and Albert Museum.
Vol. II. *Non-keyboard Instruments.*   *London, 1968.*

Berlioz, H.   *Traité d'Instrumentation et d'Orchestration modernes.*
Paris, 1844.

Bessaraboff, N.   *Ancient European Musical Instruments.* An organo-
logical study of the musical instruments in the Leslie Lindsey Mason
Collection at the Museum of Fine Arts, Boston.   *Boston, 1941.*

Blaikley, D. J.   *Acoustics in relation to wind instruments.*   (Three lectures
delivered to the students of the Royal Military School of Music,
Kneller Hall, in May 1887.)   *London, 1890.*

The French Horn.   (*Proceedings, Musical Association*, Vol. XXXV.)
London, 1909.

'Horn'.   (Grove's *Dictionary of Music and Musicians*, 3rd ed.)
London, 1927.

Blandford, W. F. H.   The following are all from the *Musical Times*:
Studies on the horn:
  1. 'The French Horn in England'.   *August, 1922.*
  2. 'Wagner and the horn parts of Lohengrin'. *September–October 1922.*
  3. 'The Fourth Horn in the Choral Symphony'.
January/February/March 1925.

'Some observations on "horn chords".'   *February 1926.*

'The intonation of brass instruments'.   *January/February 1936.*

Bouasse, H., en collaboration avec M. Fouché.   *Instruments à vent*, 2 vols.
Paris, 1929.

Brain, Aubrey.   'The German Horn: a comparison' (*Monthly Musical
Record*).   *31 July 1931.*

Brancour, René.   *Histoire des instruments de musique.*   *Paris, 1921.*

Brenet, Michel.   *Les Concerts en France sous l'ancien régime. Paris, 1900.*
La Musique militaire.   *Paris, n.d.*

Broholm, H. C., Larsen, W. P., and Skjerne, G.   *The Lures of the Bronze
Age.*   (Translation by A. Svart.)   *Copenhagen, 1949.*

Buck, Percy C.   *Acoustics for Musicians.*   *Oxford, 1918.*

Burney, Charles.   *The Present State of Music in Germany, the Netherlands
and United Provinces.*   2nd edition.   *London, 1773.*

Rees's *Cyclopædia* (the section dealing with music).   *London, 1802–19.*

Carse, Adam.   *The History of Orchestration.*   *London, 1925.*
Musical Wind Instruments.   *London, 1939.*
The Orchestra in the XVIIIth century.   *Cambridge, 1940.*
The Orchestra from Beethoven to Berlioz.   *Cambridge, 1948.*

'The French Horn in England'. (*Hallé*, No. 25, June 1950.)
Manchester.

*Illustrated Catalogue of the Adam Carse Collection of Musical Wind
Instruments* (Horniman Museum).   *London, 1951.*

Castil-Blaze. 'Actéon, Paer, E. Vivier'. (*La France Musicale*, 14 mai 1843.) *Paris.*

Chambers, James. 'Tone and Technique'. (*Woodwind World*, January 1958.) *Mount Kisco, N.Y.*

Chaussier, H. *Les Nouveaux Instruments en UT.* *Paris*, 1889.

Chouquet, G. *Le Musée du Conservatoire National de Musique.* Catalogue descriptif et raisonné. (Nouvelle édition.) *Paris*, 1884.
Also three supplements by L. Pillaut. *Paris*, 1894, 1899, 1903.
Rapport sur les instruments de musique à l'Exposition Universelle Internationale de 1878. *Paris*, 1880.

Coar, Birchard. *The French Horn.* *Ann Arbor, Michigan*, 1947.
A Critical Study of the Nineteenth-century Horn Virtuosi in France.
DeKalb, Ill., 1952.

Cousins, Farquharson. 'The degenerate horn'. (*Music and Letters*, October 1951.) *London.*

Cucuel, G. *Etudes sur un orchestre du XVIIIe siècle.* *Paris*, 1913.
La Pouplinière et la musique de chambre au XVIIIe siècle. *Paris*, 1913.

Culver, C. A. *Musical Acoustics.* *Philadelphia*, 1947.

Dalyell, J. G. *Musical Memoirs of Scotland.* *London*, 1849.

Day, C. R. *Descriptive Catalogue of the Musical Instruments in the Royal Military Exhibition of 1890.* *London*, 1891.

Daubeny, U. *Orchestral Wind Instruments.* *London*, 1920.

Diderot et d'Alembert. *Encyclopédie.* *Paris*, 1767–76.

Donington, R. *The Instruments of Music.* *London*, 1949.

Eger, Joseph. 'Breaking the Endurance Barrier'. (*Woodwind World*, May 1958.) *Mount Kisco, N.Y.*

Eichborn, H. *Die Dämpfung beim Horn.* *Leipzig*, 1897.

Ella, J. *Musical Sketches Abroad and at Home.* *London*, 1878.

Farmer, Henry George. *The Rise and Development of Military Music.*
London, 1912.
Military Music. *London*, 1950.

Fétis, F.-J. 'Cors à pistons'. (*Revue Musicale de Fétis*, tome II, 1828.)
Paris.
'Nouveau cor omnitonique (Ch. Sax)'. (*Revue Musicale de Fétis*, 1833.)
Paris.
'Cor-solo de Dujariez'. (*Gazette Musicale de Belgique*, 5 juin 1834.)
La Musique mise à la portée de tout le monde. *Bruxelles*, 1839.
Biographie universelle des Musiciens. 8 vols. and 2 supplementary vols. by A. Pougin. *Paris*, 1877–78.

Fitzpatrick, Horace. 'Some Historical Notes on the Horn in Germany and Austria'. (*Galpin Soc. Journal*, Vol. XVI, May 1963.) *London.*
'An Eighteenth-Century School of Horn-Makers in Bohemia'. (*Galpin Soc. Journal*, Vol. XVII, February 1964.) *London.*
The Horn and Horn-playing and the Austro-Bohemian Tradition: 1680–1830. *Oxford*, 1970.

Forsyth, C. *Orchestration.* *London*, 1922.

Francœur, L.-J. *Diapason général de tous les instruments à vent.*
Paris, 1772.

Francœur et Choron. *Traité général des voix et des instruments d'orchestre*

et principalement des instruments à vent. *Paris, 1812.*
Galpin, F. W. *Old English Instruments of Music.* (3rd ed.) *London, 1932.*
A Textbook of European Musical Instruments. *London, 1937.*
Galpin Society. *Musical Instruments through the Ages.* Edited by Anthony Baines. *London, 1961.*
Catalogue of European Musical Instruments at the Edinburgh International Festival 1968.
Gevaert, F.-A. *Nouveau traité d'instrumentation.* *Paris, 1885.*
Geiringer, Karl. *Alte Musik-Instrumente.* (Catalogue of the musical instruments in the Carolino Augusteum museum, Salzburg.) *Leipzig, 1932.*
Musical Instruments. (Translated by Bernard Miall.) *London, 1943.*
Gerber, E. L. *Historisch-biographisches Lexikon.* *Leipzig, 1790–92.*
Neues Historisch-biographisches Lexikon. *Leipzig, 1812–14.*
Goldschmidt, H. 'Das Orchester des Italienische Oper im 17 Jahrhundert'. (*Sammelbände der Internationalen Musik-Gesellschaft*, 2 Jahrgang, 1900–01.)
Gossec, F.-J. 'Notes concernant l'introduction des cors dans les orchestres'. (*Revue Musicale de Fétis*, tome V, 1829.) *Paris.*
Gregory, Robin. 'The horn in Beethoven's symphonies'. (*Music and Letters*, October 1952.) *London.*
The Horn. (2nd ed.) *London, 1969.*
Grove, G. *Dictionary of Music and Musicians*, 1st, 3rd, and 5th editions. *London, 1880, 1927, 1954.*
Hague, Bernard. 'The tonal spectra of wind instruments'. (*Proc. R. Mus. Assn.*, Session LXXIII.) *London, 1947.*
Halfpenny, Eric. '*Tantivy:* An exposition of the "Ancient Hunting Notes"'. (*Proc. R. Mus. Assn.* 80th session.) *London, 1954.*
Hammerich, Angul. *Les Lurs de l'Age de Bronze.* *Copenhague, 1894.*
d'Harcourt, Eugène. *La Musique actuelle en Allemagne et Autriche-Hongrie.* *Paris, 1908.*
Hind, H. C. 'The British wind band'. (*Hinrichsen's Music Book*, Vol. VII.) *London, 1952.*
Howe, W. F. *French Horns* (a lecture). *Brighton, 1886.*
Janetzsky, Kurt. *Zum erscheinen der Bach-Studien für Waldhorn.* (*Tradition und Gegenwart.* Festschrift zum 150 jährigen Besteben des Musikverlages Friedrich Hofmeister.) *Leipzig, 1957.*
'Der Korrigierte Beethoven'. (*Neue Zeitschrift für Musik*, mai 1957.) *Mainz.*
Kappey, J. A. *Military Music.* *London, n.d. (1893).*
Kastner, G. *Manuel général de musique militaire.* *Paris, 1848.*
Kingdon-Ward, M. 'Mozart and the Horn'. (*Music and Letters*, October 1950.) *London.*
Kinsky, Georg. *Kleiner Katalog.* (Musikhistorisches Museum von Wilhelm Heyer in Cöln.) *Cöln, 1913.*
Kirby, P. R. 'Horn Chords: an acoustical problem'. (*Musical Times*, September 1925.) *London.*
Kling, H. *The Art of Instrumentation.* *New York, 1902.*

'Giovanni Punto, célèbre corniste'. (*Bulletin Français de la S. I. M.*, 1908.)

Le Cor de Chasse.   *Revista Musicale Italiana*, 1911.

Koechlin, C. *Les Instruments à vent.*   *Paris*, 1948.

La Borde, J.-B. de. *Essai sur la musique.* (4 vols.)   *Paris*, 1780.

La Laurencie, L. de et Sainte-Foix, G. de. 'La symphonie française vers 1750'. (*L'Année Musicale*, première année, 1911.)   *Paris.*

Langwill, L. G. 'London wind instrument makers of the 17th and 18th centuries'. (*The Music Review*, May 1946.)   *London.*

'Two rare eighteenth century London directories'. (*Music and Letters*, January 1949.)   *London.*

An Index of musical wind instrument makers. (3rd ed.)
                                        Edinburgh, 1972.

Lavoix, fils, H. *Histoire de l'Instrumentation.*   *Paris*, 1878.

Limousin, C. *La Vie et les aventures d'un corniste.* (Eugène Vivier.)
                                        Paris, 1888.

Lloyd, Ll. S. *Music and Sound.*   *London*, 1951.

Mahillon, V.-C. *Eléments d'Acoustique.*   *Bruxelles*, 1874.

Catalogue descriptif et analytique du Musée Instrumental du Conservatoire Royal de Musique de Bruxelles. (2e éd.) (5 volumes.)
                                        Bruxelles, 1893–1922.

Le Cor. Son histoire, sa théorie, sa construction.   *Bruxelles*, 1907.

Marolles, G. de. *Essai de monographie de la trompe de chasse.*
                                        Privately printed.

Trois questions relatives à l'historique de la trompe de chasse.
                                        Privately printed.

Monographie abrégée de la Trompe de Chasse.   *Privately printed.*

Marx, Josef. Introduction to *Twelve duos for two French horns*, by W. A. Mozart.   *McGinnis & Marx, New York*, 1947.

Meek, Harold. 'On "Warming up"'. (*Symphony*, May 1949.)
                                        New York.

Meifred, P.-J. *De l'étendue, de l'emploi et des ressources du cor en général et de ses corps de rechange en particulier.*   *Paris*, 1829.

'Notice sur la fabrication des instruments de musique en cuivre en général et sur celle du cor en particulier'. (*l'Annuaire de la Société des anciens Elèves des Ecoles nationales des Arts-et-Metiers*, année 1851.)
                                        Paris.

Mendel, H. *Musikalisches Conversations-Lexikon.*   *Berlin*, 1872.

Mersenne, M. *Harmonie universelle.*   *Paris*, 1636.

Miller, D. C. *The Science of Musical Sounds.*   *New York*, 1922.

Miller, G. *The Military Band.*   *London*, 1912.

Morley-Pegge, R. 'The evolution of the modern French horn from 1750 to the present day'. (*Proceedings, Musical Association*, Vol. LXIX.)
                                        London, 1943.

'The orchestral French horn'. (*Hinrichsen's Music Book*, Vol. VII.)
                                        London, 1952.

'The degenerate horn'. (*Music and Letters*, January 1951.)

Norlind, T. *Musikinstrumentenhistorie i ord och bild.*   *Stockholm*, 1941.

Parke, W. T. *Musical Memoirs.* (2 vols.)   *London*, 1830.

Pénable, J. 'Le Cor'. (*Encyclopédie de la Musique*, de Lavignac et La Laurencie—2e partie.) *Paris*, 1927.
Piersig, F. *Die Einführung des Hornes in die Kunstmusik*. *Halle*, 1927.
Pillaut, L. *Instruments et Musiciens*. *Paris*, 1880.
Pontécoulant, L.-A. de. *Organographie*. (2 vols.) *Paris*, 1861.
Douze jours à Londres. *Paris*, 1862.
Histoires et Anécdotes. *Paris*, 1864.
Profeta, R. *Storia e letteratura degli strumenti musicali*. *Firenze*, 1942.
Redfield, J. 'Minimizing discrepancies of intonation in valve instruments'. (*Journal of the Acoustical Society of America*, October 1931.)
Richardson, E. G. *Acoustics of Orchestral Instruments*. *London*, 1929.
Rose, A. *Talks with Bandsmen*. *London*, 1895.
Sachs, Curt. *Real-Lexikon der Musikinstrumente*. *Berlin*, 1913.
Handbuch der Musikinstrumentenkunde. *Leipzig*, 1920.
Sammlung der Staatlichen Hochschule. *Beschreibender Katalog*. *Berlin*, 1922.
The History of Musical Instruments. *London*, 1942.
Sainte-Foix, G. de. 'Les Concertos pour Cor de Mozart'. (*La Revue de Musicologie*, 1929, IV.) *Paris*.
Schilling, G. *Encyclopädie oder Universal-Lexikon der Tonkunst*. *Stuttgart*, 1837.
Schlesinger, K. 'Horn'. (*Encyclopædia Brit.*, 11th edition, 1910.)
Modern Orchestral Instruments. *London*, 1910.
Schlosser, J. *Kunsthistorisches Museum in Wien, Sammlung alter Musikinstrumente*. *Beschreibendes Verzeichnis*. *Wien*, 1920.
Schneider, W. *Historische-technische Beschreibung der musikalischer Instrumente*. *Leipzig*, 1834.
Soyer, M. A. 'Des Instruments à Vent'. (*Encyclopédie de la Musique*, de Lavignac et La Laurencie—2e partie.) *Paris*, 1927.
Stone, W. H. 'Horn'. (Grove's *Dictionary of Music and Musicians*, 1st ed.) *London*, 1880.
Sundelin, A. *Die Instrumentirung für Militär-Musik*. *Berlin*, 1827 (?).
Die Instrumentirung für das Orchester. *Berlin*, 1828.
Talbot, J. 'MS. 1187 in the Christ Church, Oxford, Library'. Reproduced with comments by A. C. Baines. (*Galpin Society Journal* No. 1, *March* 1948.)
Terry, C. S. *Bach's Orchestra*. *London*, 1932.
Vandenbroek, Othon. *Traité général de tous les instrumens à vent à l'usage des compositeurs. Dédié à son ami Rodolphe*. *Paris*, 1800.

Appendices

APPENDIX 3

All the examples in Appendix 3 are taken from
The Compleat Tutor for the French Horn,
Thompson's and/or Simpson's editions.

(*a*)
Air by Mr Handel (Simpson edition)

Allegro

* The second bar of the second repeat seems doubtful. The B for
the 2nd horn would be impossible to play effectively in a quick
battement such as this.

(b)

Gigua by Mr Handel (Thompson edition)

Fine

D.C.

(*c*)
Handel's Water Piece
(Simpson and Thompson editions)

(d)

Water Piece (anon.) (Simpson edition)

(*e*)

Minuet by Mr Festin (Thompson edition)

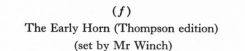

(ƒ)
The Early Horn (Thompson edition)
(set by Mr Winch)

(g)

Two fanfares by Morin believed to be among the first fanfares
ever composed for the *trompe de chasse*.

1

2

Relancé, by M. de Dampierre

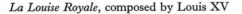

La Louise Royale, composed by Louis XV

All the above are taken from the anonymous *Manuel du Veneur*.

APPENDIX 4

(a) from Hampel's MS *Lection pro Cornui*

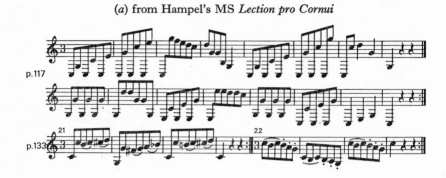

See also (b) on page 204.

(c) Two duos from the Hampel-Punto *Méthode pour apprendre* . . .

II
(p.84)

(*b*) MS trio by Hampel

No. 2 Arioso

(*d*)

Horn obbligato (extract) to an Arietta from J.-C. Trial's one-act opera *La Fête de Flore* performed at the Paris Opéra on 18 June 1771. This obbligato, written for and played by Jean-Joseph Rodolphe, was also played by Jean-Georges Siéber, one of the leading Paris horn players and a member of the Opéra orchestra. Siéber later became a well-known music publisher.

INTRODUCTION

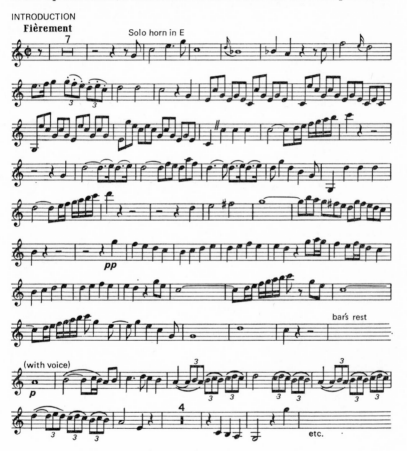

(e)

Air de Clytemnestre (*Iphigénie en Aulide* . . . Gluck)

First performance at the Opéra, Paris, 19 April 1774.
Horns: Mozer and Siéber.

Cors en Sol

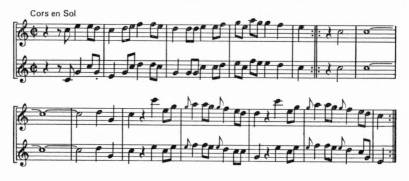

(f)

Air de Roméo (*Roméo et Juliette* . . . Steibelt)

First performance at Théâtre de la rue Feydeau, Paris, 10 September 1793.
Solo horn: Fr. Duvernoy.

Cor obligé en Mi♭

(g)

Trio 'Pietà di me' for two sopranos and tenor, with horn, cor anglais, and bassoon obbligato.

By J. Haydn

Said to have been composed for the famous 18th-century operatic and concert singer Mrs Billington. Nothing is at present known of any performance in London of this work previous to the distinguished Broadcast by the B.B.C. on 17 December 1956. The artists were: Joan Sutherland and April Cantelo, sopranos; Raymond Nilsson, tenor; Dennis Brain, horn; Peter Graeme, cor anglais; John Alexandra, bassoon; the Goldsborough Orchestra, conducted by Charles Mackerras.

The very high tessitura of the horn part, of which only a fragment is quoted below, is noteworthy: it is pure clarino writing.

Allegro moderato

(*h*)

Horn obbligato, with parts for two horns in the accompanying orchestra, from Air No. 8 (Act II, Scene 2) of Spontini's *La Vestale*. It was first performed at the Paris Opéra on 15 December 1807. (From the full score published by Erard, *c.* 1807.) The solo horn part was played by Frédéric Duvernoy.

Larghetto espressivo

APPENDIX 5

(a)

From Punto's *Exercice Journalier*

1

2

3

4

Note at the top of page 39, where this type of slur begins:
*Dans ces liaison il faut bien prononcer les mots da hi a da sur chaque nôte
comme il sont indiquer [sic]*

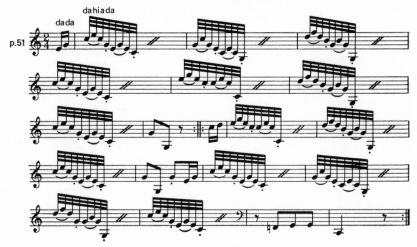

(b)   Bars from Study No. XI from J.-R. Lewy's *Douze Etudes pour le Cor chromatique et le Cor simple avec accompagnement de Piano.*

At the beginning of these studies Lewy says that, though meant to be played on the chromatic horn in F, the valves are to be used only for notes that would otherwise be too dull and indistinct. When *Cor simple* or *avec la main* is indicated valves are to be used as the equivalent of a crook change—E, 2nd valve; E-flat, 1st valve; D, 3rd valve. He ends by saying that this is the only way to preserve the beauty of tone of the natural horn while retaining the advantages of the extended capacity of the valve horn. The few bars quoted below give a good idea of the principles underlying the technique of such valve-horn pioneers as Meifred and Lewy.

Bars 1 *and* 2

Bars 19 *to* 25

Bars 34 *to* 38

Bars 47 *to* 49

Subject Index

Name Index